Counselling Children, Adolescents and Families

About the Author

Dr John Sharry is a social worker and psychotherapist at the Department of Child and Family Psychiatry, at the Mater Hospital, Dublin. He is also a Director of the Brief Therapy Group (along with Melissa Darmody and Brendan Madden) and a Consultant Research Scientist, with Media Lab Europe, a research institute based in Dublin and affiliated to the MIT in Boston. John is co-author and producer of the *Parents Plus Programmes* (video-based parenting guides), which are used as the basis of parenting groups throughout the UK and Ireland. He is also the co-author of several self-help books for parents including *Parent Power: Bringing up Responsible Children and Teenagers* (Wiley, 2002) and two previous psychotherapy books *Solution-Focused Groupwork* (Sage, 2001) and *Becoming a Solution Detective* (BT Press, 2001; Haworth, 2003). More information can be obtained on the following websites:

- Brief Therapy Group http://www.brieftherapy.ie
- Parents Plus http://www.parentsplus.ie
- Media Lab Europe http://www.mle.ie

Counselling Children, Adolescents and Families

A Strengths-based Approach

John Sharry

SAGE Publications

London • Thousand Oaks • New Delhi

SAGE Publications Ltd
1 Olivers Yard
London EC1Y 1SP

SAGE Publications Inc
2455 Teller Road
Thousand Oaks, California 91320

SAGE Publications India Pvt Ltd
B-42, Panchsheel Enclave
Post Box 4109
New Delhi 100 017

British Library Cataloguing in Publication data

A catalogue record for this book is available
from the British Library

ISBN 0 7619 4950 X
ISBN 0 7619 4951 8 (pbk)

Library of Congress Control Number: 2003109267

Typeset by C&M Digitals (P) Ltd., Chennai, India
Printed and bound in Great Britain by Athenaeum Press, Gateshead

To the families who keep hope alive.

Contents

Foreword

Every generation has its challenges. When I was growing up during the 1960s and 1970s, my parents worried about drugs and changing sexual mores. 'We just didn't do the kinds of things you kids do nowadays,' I can remember my mother saying to me on repeated occasions during my childhood and adolescence. My father would invariably add something on the order of, 'Yes, Scott, listen to your mother. It's a lot harder growing up in today's world,' and then, after a brief pause, he would continue. 'There are more temptations and the consequences more severe, less room for a miss-step. Don't make any choices that might ruin your future.' Commentators of the time described my generation as rebellious like no other in history – a label many of us at the time wore as a badge of honor. We *were* striking out against the established order. We were for peace instead of war, love instead of hate, freedom in place of rules and restrictions.

Now a parent myself, I have a much better appreciation of my parents' concerns. As Mark Twain once wryly observed, 'When I was a boy of fourteen, my parents were so ignorant I could hardly stand to have them around. But when I got to be twenty-one, I was astonished at how much they'd learned in seven years.' And while I hate to admit it, I find myself believing at some deep level that *these* are the most troubling times yet in which to raise a child. In addition to the drugs and changing social mores, we now have AIDS, violence, sexual abuse, high divorce rates, as well as a frightening number of psychiatric disorders that were either rare or non-existent during my generation.

Attention-deficit disorder, depression, anxiety, eating disorders, learning problems, Asperger's syndrome, conduct disorder, autism, anger and emotional dyscontrol, obsessive-compulsive disorder, and childhood onset schizophrenia are but a few of the maladies in recent years to provoke public anxiety about the status of children's mental health. One can rightly wonder, what is happening to our kids? Has the world grown so toxic? Is modern life merely too complex? And, perhaps most important, what should I do as a parent, educator, counselor, or social worker?

The answer to these questions have far reaching implications for how we handle the problems that invariably show up in the rearing of children. For example, a recent study found a three-fold increase in the use of psychotropic drugs in children between 1997 and the present. Never mind that most such drugs have never been approved by the FDA (Food and Drug Administration) for use with kids *under any circumstances*. In fact, seven out of ten drugs given to children have never been tested and proven safe or effective for use by them. All of this, however, begs the question: is such widespread use of medication with kids the right thing to do? Sadly, the answer, at this point in time, is unknown. We simply don't know the long-term consequences of this increasingly popular form of intervention.

When the health and well being of children is at stake, whatever we do, however much we spend, may never seem adequate. The serious nature of the problems unites with our strong desire for change, compelling us to take dramatic and immediate action. Unfortunately, history shows that *perspective* is a frequent casualty of this process. For example, many treatment approaches have, with time, later proven ineffective or actually dangerous – and not just in the past. Recently, when the public was concerned about a rise in the juvenile crime rate, many adolescents were sent to inpatient settings to be treated in groups. Only later did research find that this approach actually made the problem worse! At the same time, diagnostic labels seem to come in and out of professional and public focus with some regularity. Not long ago, for example, there seemed to be a dramatic increase in the numbers of kids with eating disorders. Anorexia and bulimia were the focus of a wide number of books, workshops, and talk shows. And then suddenly, and without fanfare, the problem simply receded into the background.

Returning to the question posed earlier, 'So what is a parent, educator, counselor, or social worker supposed to do?', I remember a quote from a textbook I read during my second year as an undergraduate student in psychology. We were studying adolescent development at the time. Specifically, we were learning about the challenges parents face raising kids during this difficult phase of life. The authors of the text cited various parents, including the following:

> The children now love luxury; they have bad manners, contempt for authority; they allow disrespect for elders and love chatter in place of exercise. Children now are tyrants, not the servants of their households. They contradict their parents, chatter before company, and tyrannize their teachers. (Patty and Johnson, 1963: 277)

The comments were hardly surprising in their own right. After all, the sentiments sounded similar to those expressed by adults about my generation and me. Imagine my surprise, however, when I learned that the quote was nearly 2500 years old! Although edited somewhat to fit modern times, Plato was the parent complaining about the problem of 'today's youth'.

From that experience, I learned a lesson about the importance of maintaining perspective that has stayed with me to this day. These are *not* the worst of times; neither are they the best. True, we don't want to look at the world through rose-colored glasses. It is equally important, however, that our lenses not be tinted in a way that always has us seeing smoke and fire. In other words, when trying to determine how best to be helpful, maintaining a balanced view is critical. It is a *simple* idea that is not always *easy* to put into practice.

In his book *Counselling Children, Adolescents and Families: A Strengths-based Approach*, Dr John Sharry accomplishes exactly that. First, he addresses the many serious issues facing children and adolescents without ever losing sight of the fact that the kids themselves are the greatest problem-solving resource available to helpers. Second, in a clear, engaging, and step-by-step fashion, he describes how therapists, social workers, and helpers of all stripes, can tap into the many assets and abilities lying in wait in today's youth. Troubled children and adolescents will most certainly benefit from the *perspective* offered to their therapists within these pages. I highly recommend it.

Scott D. Miller, PhD
Institute for the Study of Therapeutic Change
Chicago, Illinois, USA
www.talkingcure.com

Preface

It's the space between the bars that holds the tiger and it's the silence between the notes that makes the music.

Zen Proverb

The map is not the territory.

Bateson

Writing a book on how to help people therapeutically as a professional is somewhat a doomed project. At the heart of the helping process are human relationships and the experience is far too subjective and personal to be satisfactorily summed up in a theory. No therapeutic model is a complete explanation and no set of techniques will lead to perfect therapy. Therapy is more of an art than a science, and though models can sometimes illuminate the way, they can also sometimes obscure, especially when people believe the model to be truer than the unique reality of the clients in front of them and forget that the 'map is not the territory'. Solution-focused therapy, the model that underpins this book, is equally prone to these dangers. Exponents can over-rely on the techniques and miss the strengths-based thinking that underpins the model. Or they can neglect aspects of the helping relationship such as empathic listening, hearing the client's story and establishing an alliance that are not explicitly emphasised in the original model.

I'm reminded of a story told by Irvin Yalom about a young cook who wished to learn the skill of a master chef renowned for his legendary cooking. The young man obtained copies of the great chef's recipes and though he followed them to the letter, he could never arrive at the master's standards and his meals always fell a little short of excellence. Undeterred, he went to the master chef's restaurant and sneaked into the kitchen to observe him cooking. As he watched, he noticed that during the cooking the chef would break the rules of the recipe and would add unmeasured handfuls of extra spices and herbs, apparently at random to the meal. Surprised, he challenged the chef as to why he was not following the recipe and adding all these extra ingredients that didn't appear in the recipe. The chef answered simply that it was these extra ingredients that made the meal taste so good!

So in writing this 'recipe book' for therapy with children and families, I realise that it is quite limited. I realise that there are many more 'extra ingredients' to effective therapy that are not contained in this book and that these may vary across different professionals and different contexts. Furthermore you may not know what these 'extra ingredients' are until you meet the individual child that you are trying to help. Each child and adult are their own unique individual and each meeting is a unique inter-subjective encounter. For this reason it is important not to start from a position of complete certainty, but rather from 'one of unknowing'. When you don't know everything you make room for the client's knowledge and ideas, and these are certainly the most helpful. It is the willingness to let go of assumptions and the ability to look for freshness and newness in each human encounter that makes the therapeutic relationship work.

The audience of this book

Though the book draws its ideas from solution-focused counselling and therapy (and other strengths-based psychotherapies), it is not just relevant for counsellors and psychotherapists. The solution-focused model is very versatile and practical and is relevant for all professionals who work with children, adolescents, their parents and families to help them change and reach their goals. Thus, I hope the book is relevant for professionals from fields as diverse as social work, psychology, child care, family support workers, pastoral work, nursing and teaching, as well as psychotherapy and counselling.

I believe 'therapeutic work' is not the strict remit of qualified counsellors and psychotherapists, and this is borne out by the research evidence. For example, a recent review of the latest research data suggested that para-professionals with minimal counselling training were generally as effective as professionally qualified psychotherapists in helping their clients (Atkins and Christensen, 2001). My sense is that what counts is not simply your length of training, but rather the core values of respectful and responsible practice that you bring to the work.

This book is practice-based rather than theoretical, concentrating on the 'how to' of working with families. The emphasis is on developing strengths-based, collaborative practice that is family based and inclusive of the different perspectives of children, adolescents, parents and extended family. This book *briefly* describes the systemic and social constructionist theory and philosophy that underpins the practice ideas (in Chapter 1). But this is far from comprehensive and readers who are interested in exploring such theory can pursue further texts (for example, de Shazer, 1994; Gergen and McNamee, 1992; Street and Downey, 1996). To make the book accessible and practice-based I have illustrated the ideas using a variety of case examples and sample session dialogues.

Though the aims of this book are broad, the case examples are set within the bounds of my own professional training and experience, as a psychotherapist and social worker, and within my professional work context, in a child and adolescent mental health service. For example, you will notice that many of the chapters refer to the Parents Plus Programmes and to other groupwork interventions that combine cognitive/behavioural ideas with a strengths-based approach. These are the models that have evolved within the multidisciplinary context in which I work, but clearly there are other strengths-based applications and models as well as different professional contexts that raise different challenges. As you read this book, I encourage you to adapt the ideas to your own particular setting and context.

Overview of content and chapters

This book is divided into three parts. Part 1 consists of five chapters that describe the theory and practice principles of a solution-focused and strengths-based approach to therapy with children and families. Chapter 1 establishes the professional and theoretical of working with children and families, describing the principles that underpin the book. Chapter 2 outlines three core principles for strengths-based practice, notably establishing an alliance, elaborating strengths and focusing on goals, illustrating these ideas with a number of practical case examples. Chapter 3 describes the process of engaging and motivating children and families, in particular highlighting the need to establish a collaborative partnership from the outset. Chapter 4 considers how we can ensure that children and adolescents are included in therapeutic work by making our practice more child and adolescent centred, in particular by incorporating creative activities into the process. Chapter 5 considers the issue of completing a collaborative assessment and provides a guide to structuring a first session with a child or family. Chapter 6 considers the important but controversial area of diagnosis and formulation, and attempts to propose a strengths-based way of making formulations that recognises the benefits as well as the dangers of using formal diagnoses with children.

Part 2 of the book contains a series of chapters on specific applications of a strengths-based approach to working with children and adolescents and their families. Chapter 7 argues that groupwork is a naturally strengths-based intervention and describes how parenting groups can be established. Chapter 8 looks at groupwork with children and adolescents, and the specific issues and challenges that arise. Chapter 9 (co-authored with Grainne Hampson and Mary Fanning) describes the use of video feedback in a strengths-based early intervention programme with preschool children with developmental and behaviour problems. Chapter 10 describes the approach of externalising the problem, illustrating this with an extended case study.

Finally, Part 3 of the book contains two chapters that outline the application of a strengths-based approach to challenging contexts, namely suicidal behaviour and depression (Chapter 11, written jointly with Melissa Darmody and Brendan Madden), and child abuse and neglect (Chapter 12, written jointly with Declan Coogan).

Acknowledgements

Writing this book represents the work of many years and would not have been possible without the support of so many colleagues and friends. First I would like to thank Melissa Darmody and Brendan Madden, my partners at the Brief Therapy Group in Dublin, who inspire and challenge me in equal measure and who are great partners to share a vision with. I'm also indebted to Scott Miller, Chris Iveson and Michael Carroll for their constructive comments and mentoring as this manuscript developed.

Thanks also to all my colleagues at the Mater hospital, in particular Declan Coogan for his enthusiasm about Chapter 12 and to Matt McDermott for many helpful conversations about working with children. A particular word of thanks to my colleagues on the Parents Plus Programmes: to Grainne Hampson and Mary Fanning, who co-authored the Early Years programme and who have taught me how much fun it could be to work with preschool children; to Jean Forbes for teaching me balance in groupwork; and to Carol Fitzpatrick for her vision and constant encouragement. I would like to also acknowledge Suzanne Guerin and Michael Drumm for keeping the research going (though Michael was doing this remotely!). Thanks also to John Wheeler for his helpful ideas on engaging young children, to his son Matthew for providing the pictures in Chapter 3, and to Joshua Davis for locating one of my favourite quotes. I would like to acknowledge all the staff at Sage and in particular Alison Poyner for being constantly upbeat and constructive.

I am also very grateful to all my family and friends for their support as I was caught in the writing of this book.

Finally, I would like to acknowledge the many children, adolescents and families I have worked with over the years. It has been an honour to be a witness to your courage and triumph in the face of adversity.

A note on language

In an attempt to make this book as inclusive as possible, I have alternated many of the terms used. For example, I use the terms 'therapist', 'counsellor', 'worker' or 'professional' interchangeably to include all the different professionals who work therapeutically with children and adolescents and families. To avoid unwieldy uses of 'he/she' or 'him/her', plurals are used where possible when referring to clients and professionals. In specific case examples, an attempt is made to alternate between male and female clients and professionals.

PART I:
BASICS AND PRINCIPLES OF THE APPROACH

---

1   Establishing the Context

On Childhood

For children, childhood is timeless. It's always the present. Today is what they feel and when they say 'When I will grow up...' there is always an edge of disbelief – how could they be other than what they are?

Ian McEwan

There is always one moment in childhood when the door opens and lets in the future.

Graham Greene

On Parenthood

Becoming a parent brought me the greatest joy in my life, but also the greatest heartache.

A parent

My life completely changed when I became a parent. It was so hard because I wanted my old life back. It only became wonderful when I let go and went with the flow.

A parent

Working as a professional with families requires the ability to listen to and take on board different perspectives. The professional needs to be able to appreciate and see the world from a child or adolescent's eyes as well as from those of their parents.

Childhood and adolescence are times of first encounters and intense experiences in the present. They are periods full of joy and sadness, excitement and fear as well as rapid growth and new learning. They are also critical times when certain events and relationships greatly impact individual lives and determine futures. To engage children and adolescents as professionals, we need to take time to appreciate their experience and to understand the world they move in, while recognising their relationships with their families.

When we engage with children we also engage with their parents and the other significant members of their families. To be effective we need to be sensitive to and appreciate the experience of being a parent in its ups and downs, its joys and sorrows. The lives of children and parents are so inextricably linked that we almost cannot help one without helping the other. Parents who bring their children to therapy also bring their own needs, concerns and wishes. If we help parents with their own concerns, then we also help their children, and if we help children to change positively, then we also help their parents who care for them. When therapy is well done, it is hopefully a moment in the life of a child and their family when the door opens and a 'positive future is let in' that benefits each person in the family.

Working effectively with families also involves appreciating and understanding the professional context from which we operate. As professionals we bring our own perspective, and that of our profession, to the therapeutic process. This includes our personal style and beliefs as workers, the theoretical models we subscribe to, the standing and context of the agency we work for and the values and goals of our profession as a whole. The more self-aware and self-reflexive we can be of the theoretical models we bring to our work and the professional context from which we operate (both their strengths and their weaknesses), the better we can help our clients.

In this spirit of self-reflexivity and transparency, this chapter describes the guiding principles and theoretical context of this book, attempting to locate them within the context of professional knowledge (see Box 1.1). The chapter also describes how these principles can contribute to working with children and families, taking into to account the different and inter-connected perspectives of parents, children and significant others, including concerned professionals.

Box 1.1 Theoretical context and guiding principles

- Social constructionist framework.
- Developing strengths-based practice.
- Towards inclusive, multi-systemic practice.
- Appreciating the professional context.

Social constructionist framework

> *Truth is not what we discover, but what we create.*
>
> Saint Exupery

> *Nothing is good or bad, but thinking makes it so.*
>
> Shakespeare

Assumptions can be like blinkers on a horse – they keep us from straying from the road, but they block our view of other routes and possibilities along the roadside.

Armand Eisen

The underpinning philosophy to this book is social constructionism (Gergen, 1999; Gergen and McNamee, 1992; Hoyt, 1998): notably that people construct rather than uncover their psychological and social realities. Human knowledge and meaning is not absolute or universal, but evolves within specific contexts and communities of people. In human affairs there are many different systems of knowledge that could be derived to explain events and to guide meaning, that equally fit within the limits of the physical world and boundaries of historical facts and events. Taking the particular case of psychological knowledge, this implies that the ideas, theories and models that we as therapists, counsellors and other professionals hold about our work with families are not absolute, but rather social constructions that have evolved over time as discourses within certain communities of professionals. They may or may not be helpful in our work with the clients we might meet and could be in need of re-thinking and re-negotiation as we face the specific experience of an individual child or family. This means that guiding therapeutic principles, such as the medical principle 'that symptoms reveal underlying problems' or the solution-focused therapy principle 'that solutions can be created independent of original problems', are not true or false, but rather may or may not be the most helpful in guiding the therapeutic experience towards a positive outcome. Similarly, therapeutic constructs such as the DSMIV (American Psychiatric Association, 1994) diagnostic category of 'attention deficit disorder' or the solution-focused category of a 'visitor level of client motivation' do not necessarily exist as entities, but simply are more or less helpful ways of describing common patterns across distinct clients and families.

Social constructionism is not a licence for 'anything goes', nor theoretical anarchy. All ideas are not of equal value, either in terms of effectiveness or ethical quality. As Alan Carr states:

> Thus we can never ask if a particular diagnostic category (like DSM IV depression) or construct (like Minuchin's triangulation) is really true. All we can say is that for the time being, distinctions entailed by these categories fit with observations made by communities of researchers and clinicians and are useful in understanding and managing particular problems. The challenge is to develop integrative models or methods for conceptualising clinical problems that closely fit with our scientist-practitioner community's rigorous observations and requirements for workable and ethical solutions. (1999: xx)

Thus from a social constructionist perspective, we have a collective professional responsibility to ensure that our models are ethical to use and to conduct research to make sure that they are indeed beneficial to our clients.

The implications of social constructionism on the individual practice of therapists are quite profound. It means that when we engage in conversation with clients, we should be aware of the limits of our theories and conceptions. We should be prepared to revise them or to co-create better conceptions, should our models of the theories not fit with the unique experience of the clients in front of us. Frequently 'stuckness' in the therapeutic process stems from the therapist inadvertently holding on to a belief that is limiting progress or that does not fit with the client (see Case Example 6.4A in Chapter 6). Gillian Butler (1999) describes a systematic process whereby therapists, when faced by difficulty, can begin to deconstruct and analyse the therapeutic conversation to identify a disputed belief from their model that supports the difficulty, and then to be able to change this by drawing on another model. Social constructionism demands that we strive to be self-reflexive and self-critical. We are compelled to be theoretical-flexible and not to cling to 'pet' or favourite theories. For example, though solution-focused therapy is my model of choice, I strive to be flexible enough to abandon this approach if it does not work for a certain client. I remember one teenager who teased me, 'Ah, don't ask me another miracle question' (his previous social worker was also trained as a solution-focused therapist), to which I responded, 'What would you like me to ask about instead?' He answered, 'I just want to talk about how bad things are at the moment,' and so I followed his preferred direction.

Thus from a social constructionist perspective, the therapeutic relationship is a collaborative one in which therapist and client co-construct meanings, understandings, goals and treatment plans within the therapeutic conversation, operating from their respective knowledge bases, with the therapist cognisant of psychological models and best therapeutic practice research and the client as expert in the details of his life. The aim is to construct helpful understandings that fit both with the unique experience of clients' lives and the 'best known' psychological knowledge, and which satisfy ethical norms and broader societal expectations and which ultimately are of benefit to clients in achieving solutions to their problems.

Social constructionism and therapeutic conversation

> Life should be more about holding questions than finding answers. The act of seeking an answer comes from a wish to make life, which is basically fluid, into something more certain and fixed. This often leads to rigidity, closed-mindedness, and intolerance. On the other hand, holding a question – exploring its many facets over time – puts us in touch with the mystery of life. Holding questions accustoms us to the ungraspable nature of life and enables us to understand things from a range of perspectives.
>
> Thubten Chodron – on Buddhism.

From a social constructionist perspective, beliefs and meaning are mediated by language and constructed and perpetuated by the ongoing communications between people, whether these are in the form of individual conversations or collective communications such as writing, television or other media. Rather than providing us with a neutral description of reality, language in part creates and shapes reality. Put simply, how we talk about things influences how we feel, how we think and how we might act. Our beliefs, meanings and ideas are determined by the 'stories' we tell ourselves and each other.

In the context of therapy with families, this means that the 'stories' (and the underpinning beliefs) that children, parents and families tell about the problems that afflict them and the solutions that might help them are not absolute accounts, but ones that have evolved over time in the family and wider system. Coming to therapy is often about retelling stories in a different way that provides new perspectives, ideas and meaning which are more helpful for the children and family concerned. Like Chodron's quote above, the therapeutic aim is to engage in a therapeutic dialogue that eschews prescribing rigid answers and beliefs, and instead 'holds questions' in order to help clients understand things from different perspectives. This process helps clients generate new constructive meanings and beliefs that lead to action and change. The aim is to move from narrow stories of problems and oppression to empowering stories of strength and hope and liberation, that fit equally well with the evidence of the clients' lives.

Let us consider a concrete example of this process in therapeutic practice, where the mother is helped to construct a new understanding of her son and develop a new self-construct about her ability as a parent. A mother brought her six-year-old son to a child mental health clinic, due to her son's behaviour problems. The mother believed that there was something 'wrong' with her son, because he was 'so aggressive' and that she must be a 'bad parent' for not being able to manage him. Through careful dialogue with the therapist, who explored how the mother coped with the problem and also her positive influence on her son, different meanings and beliefs were negotiated. By the end of the therapy, she came to 'view' her son differently, realising that he was a sensitive boy who needed extra attention and encouragement. This new understanding, and subsequent change, helped her evolve a more constructive self-belief about her parenting. As she explained it to me, 'When I first came I felt a complete failure with my son. I felt I was responsible for his problems. What helped was realising that I wasn't a bad parent, but a good parent trying to do my best, and to realise that I could help my son.'

Sometimes the beliefs that limit and cause problems for clients are located in society's expectations that reflect a certain cultural and historical context. For example, 30 years ago a gay client presenting with depression at a psychiatric service would have been likely to experience a discourse that pathologised his lifestyle seeing it as a possible cause for his depression, whereas the same client presenting at a counselling service today would be more likely to have his lifestyle validated and affirmed. From a social constructionist perspective, the aim is to help clients understand the source of the ideas and beliefs that may define them as having a problem. For example, a teenager with eating problems may have a strong belief that she must be a certain weight or have a certain body shape. In therapeutic dialogue a strengths-based therapist may gently invite her to examine this belief and to consider its source in oppressive societal expectations. Through dialogue the therapist may help her to generate alternative beliefs and ideas (for example, that she can choose her own body image) that are more empowering to her to move forward. Groups can provide a powerful arena for this process to take place and this is the purpose of the Anti-Anorexia League (Grieves, 1998; Madigan, 1998). By bringing people affected by the same problems together, through sharing experience and strength, people can be assisted to generate new, more helpful ideas and beliefs, and then be empowered to challenge existing societal prejudices which reinforce the problem's influence.

Social constructionism and multi-cultural practice

A social constructionist framework has much to contribute to non-discriminatory multi-cultural practice. The challenge is for therapists to understand and appreciate the cultural factors that shape the lives of the clients they meet, while being self-aware of their own personal cultural identity and how this impacts their therapeutic practice. In addition, therapists are obliged to be aware of the societal forces and prejudices that may contribute to clients problems as well as the specific cultural context of the therapeutic model which is inherent in their own professional practice. This may seem like a tall order, but is the mark of a self-critical reflexive professional. Indeed, this is the reason why the practice of regular supervision and consultation that provides an arena to tease out these issues is universally seen as central (across all accrediting bodies) to good professional practice.

Case Example 1.1   The soft western way

A five-year-old boy whose parents were refugees in Ireland was referred to a child mental health service due to behaviour problems and a concern that he was displaying autistic type behaviour. During the first session the father reported his attempts to control his son using physical discipline. The therapist noticed her own feelings of unease at the father's description, and wondered whether she should challenge the father's use of physical discipline. When she began to raise other parenting strategies for managing behaviour, the father described how in his country of origin he would be expected to take control and to use physical discipline. This opened a discussion about culture and parenting, and the therapist acknowledged the father's positive intention to bring his son up in a responsible fashion and shared the ideas behind other strategies. Operating from a strengths-based paradigm the therapist asked, 'What are the good things about parenting in your culture that you would like to hold onto as you live here in Ireland?' The father thought about this and said, 'Well, I don't like how people want to find something wrong with my son here. In my country he would be looked after just the same as other children.' This opened a discussion about whether it was needed to name his son's difficulties and the importance and value of a culture that accepted different children as they are.

Later in the session, the father said he was looking for support on how to manage his son and agreed to try out an early intervention parenting group (see Chapter 9). As he made progress, the father reflected in the parenting group, 'When I started this course, I did not think that the soft western way would work with my son. It takes more time, but I see that he needs it.' When invited by the facilitator to say more about the 'soft western way', the father joked, 'But I also think you take things far too seriously here; you should relax more and take it easy.'

In Case Example 1.1, what made the difference was the therapist being sensitive to cultural issues around parenting. Rather than imposing her own cultural values, she strove to understand the parent's own cultural background and to appreciate its strengths and benefits. This helped build the therapeutic alliance and enough trust for the father to try out the parenting programme, which he interestingly dubbed the 'soft western way'.

It is important to note that non-discriminatory or multi-cultural practice is not limited to working with clients from different ethnic groups. There are many other groups in society that have distinct sub-cultures which require understanding and appreciation. For example, though my own background is a middle-class culture in which parents are usually educated and married, choosing to have children later in their lives, this is very different from many of the single working-class parents I work with, who are more likely to have left formal education earlier and to have children younger. As a professional, I have to work hard to understand this cultural experience that is different from mine, appreciating both the challenges (dealing with discrimination) as well as some of the benefits (for example, many of these parents have the support of grandparents and wider communities). The challenge as a professional is not to assume that we know what it is like to live life within the culture and experience of our clients, but to respectfully listen to what they say and to let them tell us what is important and helpful. I find it helpful to conceive of being a therapist as much like being a visitor to another country for the first time. Rather than being a stereotypical tourist who travels in a foreign country without a sensitivity to the local culture and who even seeks out examples of his own culture (for example, looking for the local Irish pub in the Far East!), it is better to don the role of being a respectful traveller engaged in getting to know the local culture and customs, and letting the local people show you the way.

Developing strengths-based practice

Many of the ideas in this book are inspired by the solution-focused brief therapy model developed by de Shazer and others in the 1980s and 1990s (Berg, 1991; de Shazer, 1988, 1991; O'Hanlon and Weiner-Davies, 1989). In developing the model, the originators drew heavily on the innovative therapy of Milton Erickson (Haley, 1973; Zeig and Munion, 1999) and the work of the Mental Research Institute (MRI) in Palo Alto (Watzlawick et al., 1974; Weakland et al., 1974). Milton Erickson was a highly influential therapist who evolved a resource focused way of working with clients that used creative and individual strategies to help them reach their goals. Erickson's creative and idiosyncratic approach was in direct contrast to the dominant psychoanalytic and behaviourist approaches of the day and his work spawned the development of many different therapeutic approaches such as strategic therapy (Haley, 1963), neuro-linguistic programming (Bandler and Grinder, 1979; Grinder and Bandler, 1981) as well as the MRI brief therapy model and solution-focused therapy.

Focusing on understanding the interaction and communication patterns between people, the MRI team evolved a model of 'brief problem-solving therapy' which essentially conceived of problems as 'failed solution attempts' which were reinforced and maintained in patterns of family communications. For example, a mother in an effort to get close to her son may bombard him with questions when he comes in from school. But this approach may have the opposite effect and cause him to pull away. The aim of MRI therapy is to identify these patterns and to help the family do something different, even if it was simply the opposite of what was done before. In the last example, the mother may find a solution by waiting for her son's initiative to communicate and then listening, rather than bombarding him as before. In many ways the solution focused therapy model replicated that of the MRI team, but instead of identifying problem patterns the Milwuakee team looked to identify already existing solution patterns – that is, times when the family, even to a small degree, are finding a solution to the problem. (Interestingly, this technique was already described by the MRI team but not emphasised in the same way.) With this subtle change of focus the solution-focused brief therapy model was born. The Milwaukee team spent the next few years expanding and refining this approach (Berg, 1991; Berg and Miller, 1992; de Shazer, 1988, 1991, 1994) and the model's popularity and appeal grew.

Part of solution focused therapy's appeal is in how its principles stand in stark opposition to a number of the 'self-evident truths' of many traditional and modernist therapies. For example, the approach questions the need to understand a problem before we find a solution, or the need to examine the past before building a future (see Table 1.1.) In fact, from its social constructionist perspective, solution focused therapy does not contend that the 'self-evident' truths of modernist (and largely problem focused) therapies should be replaced by the 'truer' and opposite solution focused ones. Indeed, any rigidly held or unquestioned beliefs held by the therapist can impede progress when these do not fit with those of the client. Rather, the contention is that for brief and focused therapy the solution-focused schema of beliefs generally, though not absolutely, is a better starting point for the therapy. The appeal of the model is also explained by its simplicity. Unlike the work of Milton Erickson, which is highly individualised and very hard to systematise, de Shazer and his colleagues took pains to develop a 'step by step' almost formulaic model of therapy that could be easily followed and implemented. This simplicity, however, is also the model's weakness and can lead to it being misunderstood to be insensitively applied in some clinical contexts. For example, novice therapists can over-rely on the techniques or the questions in the model and miss the respectful listening and relationship skills that underpin the approach (and which are essential to all successful therapy). Also, the model has been criticised for its lack of focus on social forces on such as oppression, disadvantage, and social inequalities, which curtail clients' freedom and their ability to make progress towards their goals.

Strengths-based thinking

In my own view, the greatest contribution of the solution-focused therapy model is the strengths-based thinking that underpins the approach. We are invited to think in terms of resources, skills, competencies, goals and preferred futures about our clients, their lives, the communities they belong to, the therapeutic

TABLE 1.1 *Comparison of problem/pathology and solution/strengths approaches*

Problem focused	Solution focused
Focuses on understanding fixed problem patterns in clients' lives.	Focuses on understanding how change occurs in clients' lives and what positive possibilities are open to them.
Elicits detailed descriptions of problems and unwanted pasts.	Elicits detailed descriptions of goals and preferred futures.
Person is categorised by the problems and diagnoses they have.	Person is seen as more than the problem, with unique talents and strengths and a personal story to be told.
Focuses on identifying 'what's wrong', 'what's not working' and on deficits in individuals, families and communities.	Focuses on identifying 'what's right and what's working', on strengths, skills and resources in individuals, families and communities.
Interprets and highlights the times that clients 'resist' or are inconsistent in their responses.	Highlights and appreciates any time the client co-operates or goes along with the therapists questions.
Therapy has to be long term to create enduring change.	Therapy can be brief in creating 'pivotal' change in clients' lives.
Trauma invariably damages clients and predicts later pathology.	Trauma is not necessarily predictive of pathology as it may weaken *or strengthen* the person. The therapist is interested in discovering how the client has coped with the trauma.
Centrepiece of therapy is the treatment plan devised by therapist who is the 'expert'.	Treatment plan is a collaborative endeavour between therapist and client, with their respective expertise. (Client as expert in their own lives and therapist as expert in therapeutic process.)

Source: Adapted from Sharry (2001b).

process itself and the professional context in which we find ourselves. We are invited to become detectives of strengths and solutions rather than detectives of pathology and problems, and to honour the client's expertise and capabilities as well as our own (Sharry et al., 2001a). The model also provides us with a practical method (via new questions and techniques) to make the conversations we have both with our clients and colleagues more constructive and collaborative, and to orient the therapeutic process towards solutions. As we shall see in later chapters, this strengths-based thinking has much to contribute to our work in difficult and challenging contexts, where pathological thinking may be reinforcing the problem and increasing the sense of difficulty.

The reorientation towards strengths and resources is part of a wider cultural shift in psychotherapy and the helping professions (Hoyt, 1998; O'Hanlon and Weiner-Davies, 1989). This has included the emergence of new popular models of psychotherapy such as narrative therapy (White and Epston, 1990), motivational interviewing (Miller and Rollnick, 1991), resource-focused therapy (Ray and Keeney, 1993) and possibility therapy (O'Hanlon, 1998), all of which share a strengths-based orientation. This reorientation has also affected traditional models of professional practice, leading to a focus on resilience in family therapy (Walsh, 1996) and psychiatry (Haggerty et al., 1997), the emergence of strengths-based approaches in social work (Saleeby, 1996), and also the development of 'appreciative inquiry' as a method of organisational consultancy (Hammond, 1998).

Though the solution-focused model is located within a social constructionist philosophical paradigm, the ideas have a strong resonance *in practice* with many traditional psychological therapies. For example, the focus on goals, measurable change, and helping clients think more constructively is shared by the cognitive behavioural traditions of therapy (Beck, 1976; Ellis, 1998). In addition, the person-centred approach emphasises the core therapeutic attitude of acceptance (or unconditional positive regard), whereby the therapist strives to hold on to a positive view of the client as a person of 'unconditional self-worth' despite any negative behaviours or feelings the client may display (Rogers, 1961: 34). This notion of acceptance resonates strongly with the core values of a strengths-based approach. Indeed, as I shall explore in Chapter 2, a strengths-based approach can be conceived as building on the foundational work of the person-centred approach, offering set techniques and conversational strategies that can help cultivate and maintain the attitude of unconditional positive regard.

Evidence for a strengths-based approach[1]

Several research studies have shown that substantial numbers of clients who are awaiting psychotherapy or who receive minimal treatment (on average 43 per cent) experience 'spontaneous remission' – that is, they overcome problems by their own resources without any formal professional help (Assay and Lambert, 1999; Lambert and Bergin, 1994). Other studies have shown that in the general population, many people overcome problems through their own efforts and resources, without coming into contact with professional services at all. For example, there is extensive research that many people with addiction problems (such as alcohol or smoking) recover by themselves without recourse to professional help (Prochaska et al., 1992). In addition, there is evidence that many children or young people who might have received a diagnostic label do, in fact, 'grow out' of their problems without professional help. For example, Cohen et al. (1993) found that while as many as 17.1 per cent of children meet the criteria for Attention Deficit Hyperactivity Disorder (ADHD) in childhood, this has fallen to 11.4 per cent in mid adolescence and 5.8 per cent in late adolescence.

The above studies suggest that many people overcome problems by their own strengths and resources. It is this 'self-healing' process that a strengths-based approach to therapy aims to enhance. Even when people access professional support, there is evidence that it is their own actions and resources that make the vital difference, rather than those of the therapist. For example, in a comparative study of parents attending therapist-led group parenting sessions and parents working

---

[1]This section looks at some general evidence for a strengths-based approach. Further evidence for specific principles, for example establishing a therapeutic alliance and goals, is explored in Chapter 2.

through the video-based material by themselves (completing exercises and suggested homework), both groups showed similar levels of positive change (Webster-Stratton et al., 1988), suggesting that the client's agency and actions, rather than those of the therapist, are the most significant contributor to success. In addition, many clients improve by increasing their access to social support. For example, Mallinckrodt (1996) found that that clients' perceptions of increased social support outside of the psychotherapy was more important in terms of symptom reduction than growth in the strength of the therapeutic alliance. These studies lend evidence for strengths-based approaches to therapy that aim to build upon clients' own actions, resources and social supports in the process of positive change.

There is also evidence that the reverse is true, that a focus on client deficits and highlighting problems in therapy can actually lead to poor outcome (Miller et al., 1997; Miller and Rollnick, 1991). For example, confrontational group therapy, focused on highlighting client deficits, has been shown to lead to poorer outcome and more harmful effects than other more supportive approaches (Lieberman et al., 1973) and that, alarmingly, such approaches may be particularly unsuccessful or damaging for clients with poor self-ego strength or self-esteem (Annis and Chan, 1983). Contrast this with the work of the Plumas project, which used a solution-focused group intervention (focused on helping participants identify personal goals and strengths) with 151 perpetrators of domestic violence (a client group that has high levels of poor self-esteem). On completion of the programme, only seven clients (4.6 per cent) had re-offended, and in a recent six-year follow-up which tracked 90 of the clients in the study, recidivism rates amounted to 16.7 per cent (Lee et al., 2003). These results are very impressive when compared to recidivism rates at five-year follow-up for traditional treatments, which are as high as 40 per cent (Shepard, 1992).

Underpinning a strengths-based approach to therapy is a belief that clients possess (either personally or within their social networks) most of the resources and strengths they need to change and reach their goals. This is consistent with belief within the person-centred approach in the existence of a self-healing potential in all people (Rogers, 1986). Psychotherapy is simply about providing the right conditions, notably an empathic and supportive therapeutic relationship, for this self-healing potential to be brought to the fore. Or as Prochaska et al. state: 'in fact, it can be argued that all change is self-change, and that therapy is simply professionally coached self-change' (1994: 17). Perhaps the best endorsement for a strengths-based approach is given by researchers Bergin and Garfield who, reflecting about the extensive research evidence compiled in their book, concluded that 'as therapists have depended more upon the client's resources, more change seems to occur' (1994: 826).

Towards inclusive, multi-systemic practice

It takes a village to raise a child.

African Proverb

Professionals often experience a dilemma as to who should be involved in therapeutic work with families. Different schools of thought propose different answers. Historically, children tended to be seen alone for child psychotherapy (Klein, 1957; Axline, 1971), almost to the exclusion of parents. In the original conception of behavioural parent training, the therapist supported and worked directly with parents without necessarily including the children. With the advent of systems theory and family therapy, parents and children were seen together, though many writers have suggested that the therapy often, albeit inadvertently, became dominated by parental concerns and goals (Wilson, 1998). Young children in particular were often excluded from sessions or included only if they were 'seen and not heard' (Selekman, 1997). In wider systems (for example, school and child protection services) the focus can easily centre on professional and parental concerns, and the child's voice can be lost as they become the last person to be consulted, even about critical decisions affecting their lives. Such a 'splitting' of child, parent and professional perspectives has not been helpful in trying to construct effective therapeutic interventions.

In recent times, there has been a growing desire to be more inclusive and 'multi-systemic' in professional and therapeutic work with children. Many family therapists have been concerned with developing a more 'child-focused' practice, realising that the inclusion of even young children's perspective in the therapeutic process is not only more ethical but more effective in terms of outcome (Wilson, 1998). In addition, many child psychotherapists and play therapists now conceive of parents as partners in the therapeutic process, realising that their constructive involvement is essential to helping the child in therapy. In filial therapy (Kraft and Landreth, 1998; Schaefer and O'Connor, 1983), parents are included in play therapy sessions and encouraged to use play therapy techniques directly with their children. Even if the parent is not present during the child's therapy sessions, many child therapists now are much more likely to organise frequent review and feedback meetings with parents to ensure their supportive involvement in the process.

In the field of parent training, it been shown that treatment is much more effective when social skills training is offered to the children as well as parent training to the parents (Webster-Stratton and Hammond, 1997). Not surprisingly, it has been shown that outcome is further increased when teachers are also directly included in the programme (Webster-Stratton and Reid, 1999).

The consensus seems to be that the more significant people we constructively include in the therapy, the better the outcome. As illustrated by Figure 1.1, parents, children, teachers and peers all have direct influence and capacity to create change in a particular child's life. The more people who are supportively involved and committed to bringing about positive change, the higher the likelihood of success. Multi-systemic therapy, which builds on this premise, has demonstrated particular success in working with 'difficult' cases such as young people at risk of criminal behaviour (Henggeler and Pickrel, 1995; Henggeler and Smith, 1992). Multi-systemic therapists adopt a practical and flexible approach to working with each young person, drawing on the resources of all the different systems that affect him or her. If the problems occur in school, then they will support the teacher; if the problems are within the peer group, then they may

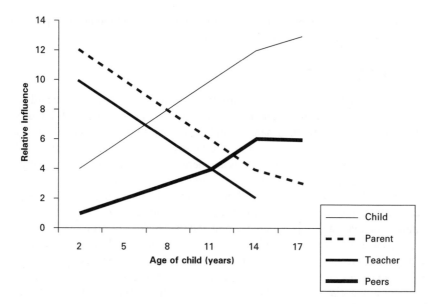

FIGURE 1.1   *Contribution to change*

either work with the peer group or collaborate with the youth service to re-direct this young person to more pro-social activities and groupings. If the parents are not involved and find it hard to discipline the young person, then the therapists will support the parents in assuming a more involved parental role. The multi-systemic approach recognises that problems (and solutions) exist within may different systems, and the more inclusive and flexible you can be, the better for the young person.

In this book I argue that the more multi-systemic and more inclusive we can be in our practice with children and families (given the limits and strengths of our own context), then the more effective we can be. There is no 'right' modality or best way to help children. Parent, family or child psychotherapy, working with teachers, other professionals and community groups, all make a contribution. Indeed, the most effective practitioners of each discipline are sensitive to and aware of the contributions of others. It is not a case of 'either/or' when it comes to finding effective ways to working with children and families, but rather 'both/and'. What counts is being able to find a way of intervening that is sensitive to the needs and preferences of the child and family you are dealing with. From a collaborative or strengths-based perspective, the best route forward is often simply the one that best emphasises the family's resources and the one that they are most willing to travel. As we shall see in Chapter 3, in deciding which way to move forward it is best to engage in an open and transparent discussion with the family and to be led by their preferences and wishes. The more they are involved in setting not only the content and aims of treatment, but also the method of treatment (for example, whether family of individual therapy), the more likely it is that they will fully participate.

Who to include?

Whereas an adult can present for counselling or therapy of their own accord and without the involvement of another person, this is not the case with children. Children are brought by their parents, and often referred by professionals such as teachers. Indeed, the arrival of a child and family to a therapeutic session usually involves a number of concerned adults and networks who have interacted to make this possible. For example, a teacher, concerned about a child's disruptive behaviour in her class may discuss this with the parents, who then contact a child mental health centre for help. Or a health visitor, concerned regarding the welfare of a small child, may raise this with the parent and then make a referral to a child protection social worker. To be effective when we work with children, adolescents and families we must take into account these systems and networks that directly affect their lives and recognise the respective contribution to change. Figure 1.1 provides a pictorial representation of how the relative influence of major figures in a child's life can change as the child grows older.

Though they bring their own temperament and genetic disposition, the lives of young children are largely determined by their parents' actions and responses. Parent–child relationships are the most significant factors in their wellbeing and children have much less responsibility than their parents in bringing about change in a family. Once they start preschool, their teacher becomes an important person in their lives, and given the large amount of time a child spends at school, this environment has a large bearing on a child's life. In addition, starting preschool brings children into contact with other children and so starts the influence of peers and friends on their lives. As a child grows older, we expect these respective ratios to change. The child begins to develop their own personality and history and slowly begins to become much more influential and more able to make decisions to determine their own lives. Coupled with this increasing autonomy is a reduction of the direct influence of parents and teachers and an increase in the influence from peers. As children grow older, and especially when they hit adolescence, they begin to spend more and more time with friends and peers and these relationships become very influential in their lives. Parents and teachers can find it harder to directly influence and direct the children in their charge, or certainly the locus of control has shifted dramatically, and the responsibility for creating change has moved much more to reside with the child. As professionals hoping to work constructively with families in order to bring about positive change, we must ensure that we involve and include those who have the most power in the system, notably those who can bring about positive change. This varies across families and across the lifecycle.

Who are the child's family?

Reflecting on research carried out in the US, McGolderick et al. (1993) explore the changing nature of families and what is regarded as the 'normal' childhood experience of family life. Available research indicates that people are marrying later and less often, having fewer children and divorcing more, and that an increasing number of couples are having children without ever marrying. Emerging trends also indicate that 12 per cent of young women will never marry, 50 per cent of young women will end their marriages in divorce and 20 per cent will have two divorces. It is no longer unusual to encounter families where children are cared for by separated and single parents and other family structures that do not fit the traditional stereotype. For example, McGolderick and her colleagues note that six per cent of households include gay or lesbian couples (1993: 416). Such households are usually made invisible by what would traditionally be regarded as a 'normal' environment for the care of children.

Thus in considering who are the major figures in a child's life it is important for professionals to be cautious about applying a narrow definition of family and to take into account the many different significant people who could be important in a child's life, for example:

- live-away parents;
- foster parents;
- step parents;
- grandparents;
- aunts, uncles;
- younger and older siblings; and
- child minders and babysitters.

A child's family is better defined as 'the collection of people to whom he/she is emotionally attached and connected and who provide care, support and nourishment'. Professionals need to be sensitive to the unique circumstances of each child and family they meet, appreciating the various significant people who make a contribution in their lives. For example, a six-year-old boy may live with his mother during the week, see his father at weekends, be child-minded by his grandfather every afternoon, and have a significant connection to a cousin of the same age. Often it can be surprising as to who is a significant person in a child's life and as to who can be the most helpful to them in overcoming a problem, as in Case Example 1.2.

Sometimes, even very young children can make a real difference when they are included in the therapeutic process. For example, four-year-old Peter, who was referred for behavioural problems, behaved very well in school and at home when he was by himself. It was the arrival of his brother John, now two years old, that caused him the most anguish. The relationship with John had the biggest impact on Peter and indirectly on the whole family. During therapy, what made the most difference to this family was the inclusion of John with Peter in joint play therapy sessions with their mother. These meetings supported the mother in guiding Peter and John in how to get on with one another and in managing more effectively when they didn't.

Case Example 1.2 The baby-sitter helps out

Some years ago, a mother brought her eight-year-old son, Paul, to therapy. She was concerned about how he was coping with the death of his father two years previously, as he had never spoken about it. In the first session, the mother brought Paul and the 15-year-old babysitter Fiona. The therapist initially suggested that he would see Paul and his mother alone, but the mother said she would like Fiona to sit in on the meeting as she knew Paul very well.

In the meeting, Paul was very anxious and closed down when his mother raised the subject of his father dying. Later in the session, Fiona revealed that her father had also died when she was eight. Paul listened intently as Fiona talked of her experience and how she had come to terms with it. She had also gone to 'see someone' about it and found it very hard to talk, but she eventually did and felt better. When asked how to help Paul, Fiona suggested that one could not rush Paul to open up, and that he might feel better talking to his family. At the end of the session the family took away a storybook designed to help children cope with death, which they planned to read by themselves and with Paul.

At a follow-up meeting, things had moved on. Both Fiona and the mother had read the book with Paul and this helped everyone talk about the father's death. In particular, the mother made a helpful connection with Paul, understanding how he felt. Though Paul did not open up to the therapist in the session, he did so at home with his family, which was much more important. And surprisingly, the person who was most helpful in bringing out this pivotal change was the 15-year-old babysitter. The therapy might have had a very different result if the therapist had not trusted the mother's judgement and Fiona had been excluded from the sessions.

Appreciating the professional context

Though many professionals share therapeutic guidelines, the nature, scope and outcome of their work can be very different depending on their professional context. For example, the work of a child protection social worker on a statutory team differs fundamentally from that of a therapist in a child mental health service or a resource teacher in a special school. Just as the 'system' of the family and the context in which they find themselves has a large bearing on how therapy proceeds, so also the professional system and context in which workers find themselves equally makes a large contribution to the therapeutic process. What problems professionals encounter, what methods and models they can employ and what way they can engage clients are all largely determined by the context in which they work. While a strengths-based philosophy can contribute to therapeutic practice, it needs to be sensitively applied to the professional context. (In Chapters 11 and 12 we will consider the application of the ideas to the particular contexts of working with suicidal clients and with child abuse and neglect, where particular ethical and practice constraints are raised.) A good to way to reflect about the strengths and challenges of a particular professional context is to consider the following questions:

- Who are the clients?
- What types of problems/goals will the clients present with?
- What are the best services the professional agency can provide?

Who are the clients?

This is not as straightforward a question as it might initially seem, as there may be many more stakeholders and interested parties concerned with professional work than the child and parents referred for a service. For example, if a school counsellor is referred a child due to disruptive behaviour in the classroom, then the teacher concerned is likely to have specific goals for the work and be interested in the outcome. Or the work of a therapist in a community drugs team may be accountable to the state funders of the agency who have specific goals in terms of reduced or safer drug usage. Or society at large is likely to have an interest in the work of a child protection social worker and expect that it leads to increased safety for children. Depending on their context, the remit of professional work is not just determined by the goals of the child or the family, but also those of the professional agency, the referrers, the funders and society at large. While the children's and parents' goals may be the most important, they are not the only ones involved and the goals of other stakeholders and interested parties, need to be taken into account. For example, for a counsellor working in a general practitioner (GP) or medical setting, it is not just enough that she carries out good work with clients because the referrers also need to value the work and see it as achieving a goal they identify if they are to continue to refer people, and thus the work is to survive.

Strengths-based thinking can contribute to the process of establishing who your clients and stakeholders are and in negotiating goals with them. For example, instead of complaining about the huge number of referrals from teachers to a child mental health service, therapists can ask 'How can I use this great resource of teachers, concerned and motivated enough to make a referral, to help the children?' Or instead of feeling overwhelmed at the number of community referrals to a child protection team, the workers can wonder 'How can I utilise this increased community awareness of the needs of children to create a safe environment for children?' By thinking in these resource-focused ways it is possible to come up with new methods of empowering children, parents, other professionals and people in the community to take action against the problems that concern them and to make progress towards their goals.

The goals of clients, professionals and stakeholders can appear to be in conflict or at odds with one another. For example, the child protection social worker is tasked with the dual goals of protecting children while also respecting the rights of the parents and the privacy of the family. From a strengths-based perspective, the aim is to find a 'win-win' way of meeting the goals of all concerned. As is the case when working with family members with different goals (see Chapter 3), the aim is to co-create a common goal that is centred on the child and the parents' wishes, which takes into account the agency context, the requests of your referrers, the funders and stakeholders. Of course, any negotiation must take into account the hierarchy of goals that are determined by agency policy. For example, a client goal is usually considered more important than that of a referrer, and a goal for a child's safety overrides the personal goal of a parent. It is important to emphasise, however, that individual goals are usually best met when the interdependent and collective goals of significant others are also taken into account. For example, the goal of a child's welfare and safety is usually best met when the goals of those who care for him or her are also acknowledged and validated.

What types of problems/goals will the clients present with?

The professional context is also determined by the fit between the agency's goals and those of the families that attend. Different communities of families require different approaches. In Case Example 1.3, the professionals have to adapt and redefine their service to ensure that it is centred on the families' goals.

Case Example 1.3   Adapting a service to what the clients want

A community-based child and family centre was set up to provide services to 'families at risk' in a deprived area. Families who had been repeatedly referred to child protection services due to concerns over neglect were highlighted as those most needing services and particular help in improving their parenting.

To respond to this, the workers sent fliers to their clients about a parenting group, but very few people attended, especially the 'at risk' clients they hoped to reach, and the group stopped.

As a result they went out, over a period of weeks, and visited a number of the families to discover what services they thought the family centre should provide. The parents identified three things:

- a 'drop in' centre where they could go and chat and have tea;
- educational classes for themselves such as cooking, knitting and needlework; and
- play groups for their children.

Acting on this feedback, the workers set up these services. They linked them together; for example, parents could attend the 'drop in' or educational classes while their children were in the play group, and the programme proved to be very successful. Word spread and more and more families attended. Over time a core parents' group was established in the centre, which welcomed many of the new families who attended. The workers consulted with this group about developing further services. After a year the parents identified that they would like a course on parenting, but one they were involved in setting up and which was not just 'telling them what to do'. The workers supported this genuine innovation and within a short time a successful self-help parenting group was established.

In Case Example 1.3, even though the initial goals identified by the parents (cooking and knitting classes) were not the overt goals of the agency (child welfare), they indirectly led to them. By attending and learning how to knit or cook, the parents were gaining essential support and developing themselves as people, all factors that would directly and indirectly improve the wellbeing of themselves and their children. Further, once the agency had listened to the parents and established a working alliance, the parents were able to take on board and respect the goals of the agency.

Many problems with professional agencies are not functions of the skills or deficits of the workers themselves, but are how the overall agency functions and is perceived by the clients. Though it is a long-term process, professional agencies need to work hard to be closely allied with the communities they serve, ensuring a fit between the agency and community goals.

What are the best services the professional agency can provide?

From a collaborative perspective, it is best to follow clients' preferences in deciding what way to intervene to help them (as we shall discuss in more detail in Chapter 3). Of course, this is not without limits, as professional responses to client(s) goals are largely determined by the function and context of the professional agency. From a strengths-based perspective, it is important to consider the strengths of the professional context (and not just the limitations). The question becomes 'How can the strengths of the professional context be used to the advantage of the clients?'

For example, working in a school it might be more useful to run a series of therapeutic groups with the children, who are a captive audience, rather than with the parents, who could be harder to engage. The reverse is often true in work within an adolescent mental health setting, where the parents are keen to attend while the adolescents would rather stay away. There are many different therapeutic models and ways to provide therapeutic services (see Box 1.2), all of which have a validity. For example, behaviour problems can be improved by either working with the parents, or with the children, or with both as a family unit. Reviewing the research (Kazdin, 1997) shows that parent management training, social skills training with children, family therapy and multi-systemic therapy (which includes a range of interventions) all have proved promising in the treatment of conduct disorders in children. Other comprehensive research reviews have shown that generally all the major psychotherapy models are equally successful in helping clients (as cited in Garfield and Bergin, 1994; Hubble et al., 1999; Miller et al., 1997).

Thus it is important not simply to ask which is the right intervention, rather it is more useful to pose some other questions such as:

- Which intervention will fit best with this specific family, at this specific time, in this specific context?
- Which will best meet this family's needs and goals?

- Which will build on their strengths and which will they be willing to take part in?
- Which intervention does the professional have the ability, training and confidence to deliver?

Box 1.2   Possible therapeutic interventions

- Family therapy – seeing the whole family.
- Individual work with children (for example, play therapy).
- Individual work with adolescents.
- Individual work with parents.
- Drug therapy/medication.
- Couple/marital work with parents.
- Groupwork with children and adolescents.
- Groupwork with parents.
- Drop-in groups (for example, at a family resource or after-school service).
- Consulting/liaising with other professionals (for example, teachers).

All of the above can be offered either in the home or in a clinical setting such as child mental health setting, or indeed in a community setting such as a school or after-school service.

Summary

In this chapter we have outlined the theoretical foundations and practice principles that are inherent in the ideas of this book. We have briefly described the social constructionist principles that provide the philosophical framework, and outlined the development of solution-focused and strengths-based principles that provide the orientation for collaborative practice. We have also described the challenge of multi-systemic practice that attempts to be inclusive of the needs of children, adolescents, parents and families taking into account the wider systems such as the school and community. Finally, we have acknowledged the professional systems in which the rationale for professional practice is constructed, involving the needs of referrers, funders and other stakeholders.

2   Guiding Priniciples of Practice

A Lion was awakened from sleep by a Mouse running over his face. Rising up angrily, he caught him with his paw and was about to kill him, when the Mouse cried
'Forgive me this time and I shall never forget it.'
The Lion took pity on the Mouse and let him go. As he was leaving the Mouse said
'Who knows but I may be able to do you a good turn one of these days?'
The Lion laughed at this idea saying
'How could you a little Mouse help me the King of the jungle?'
Some time later the Lion was caught in a trap by hunters who wanted to take him alive to a zoo. The Lion roared out in fear and he was heard by the little Mouse who came to his aid. The little Mouse quickly gnawed through the ropes that bound the King of the jungle and freed him.

The Lion and the Mouse, Aesop

The story of the Lion and the Mouse illustrates some key aspects of a resource and strengths focused approach to helping people. Even though the tiny mouse appeared to have little to offer the great Lion, in a different context the mouse provided the ideal help – a little friend that proved to be a great friend. When working with children and families, often the most helpful ideas can come from the youngest or least powerful person in the family. Some time ago I was working with a mother and her three children, referred because of the aggressive behaviour of the eldest son who was 12. A turning point in the third session was when I arrived late to see that the youngest girl, who was six, had sat in what was normally my seat and I was left to sit in her smaller 'child' seat. This prompted me to ask 'Would you like to run the meeting?' In a playful mood she answered yes. 'Well, what do you think we should talk about?' I asked her. She thought for a moment and then said 'I think we should talk about why Dad doesn't come home very much.' This opened up a conversation in the family about how they felt about their father's absence and it freed up the older son to talk a little more about his feelings, which proved to be of great benefit to him. This little girl, who might have been excluded from the therapy because of her age, was able to make a valuable contribution.

Similarly, people in the system who have been previously 'written off' or deemed to be a negative influence in a child's life can, when included more constructively or within a different context, become a resource to a child. Many times I have worked with families where a live-away parent, because of allegations of violence or abuse, has been excluded from therapy, only to discover that this person can make a contribution and return to a more constructive role with their children. For example, one father who had left the family home after a violent relationship and who had limited contact for several years, rose successfully to the challenge of caring for the children full-time when they were about to placed in residential care. Even parents who have seriously abused their children can make a contribution to creating a constructive path forward. For example, one father I worked with who had sexually abused his two children began letter contact with them, where he took responsibility for what happened and apologised to them. This small act was of enormous value to the children and very helpful to them in coming to terms with what had happened.

The Lion and Mouse fable also teaches us another helpful lesson. In the story, the mouse returned to help the great Lion because of the mercy the Lion had originally shown him. If the Lion had killed the mouse, then the mouse would have not been there to help him. The kindness or mercy the Lion showed was repaid (with interest!). As therapists, it is important that we should treat all people in the system with respect and kindness, not only because it is the 'right thing to do', but also because this respect is often repaid in kind. So often I have seen therapists get into unnecessary conflict, either with members of the family or with the professional system. These conflicts, which could have been healed by respectful dialogue and understanding, severely hamper collaboration and reduce outcome. For example, we could be critical (and inadvertently dismissive) of a teacher who has referred a child to be assessed on account of his behavioural problems, because we believe the problem is related to her classroom management skills. Yet such an attitude will diminish her cooperation in any treatment plan and not be in the child's best interest. Alternatively, we can go that extra distance to understand and appreciate the difficulties she experiences in the class with this boy and to value the steps she has taken to solve it (for example, contacting you). This respectful approach is much more likely to elicit her cooperation and involvement. The respect you show to her is likely to be repaid – and she is likely to forgive the many errors you make in your therapy! (We all need this level of compassion and understanding!)

In this chapter we consider three of the basic principles (see Box 2.1) of working with children and families, from a collaborative, client-centred and strengths-based perspective.

Box 2.1   Principles

- Building a therapeutic alliance.
- Focusing on strengths, skills and resources.
- Making client goals and preferences central.

Building a therapeutic alliance

Being able to form a collaborative relationship or alliance with children and the key members of their family is essential to effective therapy. The necessity of a therapeutic alliance as a precondition of an effective helping relationship is one of the few undisputed conclusions from outcome research over many years (Bachelor and Hovarth, 1999; Garfield and Bergin, 1994). Specific research studies have repeatedly found that a positive therapeutic alliance is the single best predictor of positive outcome (Krupnick et al., 1996; Orlinsky et al., 1994). This result is independent of the model of therapy or its mode of delivery, whether family or individual. Even in group therapy, there is compelling evidence that the analogous concept of group cohesion – namely the sense of belonging or attraction a client has for the group – is essential to gaining effective outcome (Hurley, 1989; Yalom et al., 1967 as cited in Yalom, 1995). So central is the therapeutic alliance that many writers argue that all other aspects of helping relationships process such as gathering information or carrying out assessments should also be secondary. As Alan Carr states regarding an initial psychological assessment:

> All other features of the consultation process should be subordinate to the working alliance, since without it clients drop out of assessment and therapy or fail to make progress. (1999: 113)

So as a therapist, how do you establish a therapeutic alliance with the family who comes to see you? How do you create enough trust so that they will become partners in the therapeutic process?

In trying to answer these questions, it is important not to be proscriptive or definitive. At the heart of the therapeutic encounter are human relationships that bring together the unique mix of the clients' and therapists' personalities and histories. These therapeutic relationships are always unique interchanges between two or more people and it is impossible to generalise about what will work in all cases. A way of connecting with one client may not work with another. Two different therapists are likely to connect differently with the same client and two different clients are likely to call for different styles of connecting from the same therapist.

There are five principles that can help guide this process:

1 Empathy, acceptance and genuineness.
2 Respectful curiosity.
3 Problem-free talk.
4 Humour.
5 Self-awareness.

These principles should only act as guidelines to you as you attempt to form alliances with your clients. What counts is being sensitive to each client you meet and finding what works in each individual situation.

Empathy, acceptance and genuineness

Carl Rogers, one of the most influential figures in modern counselling, pioneered the studies into the qualities of an effective therapeutic relationship. Initially he focused on the therapist skills which could contribute to this process and conceptualised a 'non-directive' approach to counselling that emphasised active listening on the part of the therapist. Active listening included skills such as reflecting back, summarising, paraphrasing and so on. In his later work, he reframed his approach as Person Centred Counselling and moved from a focus on therapist skills to a focus on the quality of the relationship. He came to realise that what was essential was not necessarily the listening skills the therapist used, but the core attitudes of empathy, acceptance (or unconditional positive regard) and genuineness that these communicated to the client. If the client felt empathically understood, accepted unconditionally and that the therapist was genuine in their responses, then therapy could begin. Active listening skills would not work if they did not communicate these core attitudes (for example, if they were parroted, undertaken rigidly or disingenuously, and were not sensitive and responsive to the client) and conceivably other modes of communication (such as humour) could also be effective if they were imbued with empathy, acceptance and genuineness.

Interestingly, many studies show that it is the client's perception of the therapeutic alliance as opposed to that of the therapist or external observers (who rated video-taped sessions) that is most linked to successful outcome (Bachelor, 1991; Gurman, 1977). As therapists, we need not to rely just on skills and ensure that the core attitudes are actually communicated to the client; what counts is not whether we judge that we are being non-judgemental, accepting and empathic, but rather whether our clients actually *feel* supported, not blamed, accepted and understood.

When counselling families, we have the challenge of communicating these core attitudes to more than one individual at the same time. It is not effective to empathetically understand a child if this understanding alienates a parent. Nor is it effective to construct a position where you are 'on the side' of the parents if this pits you against the child. When working with families it is important to seek deeper understandings which are inclusive of both children and parents and to construct positions where you are 'on everyone's side'. You are seeking to understand each person's perspective and to construct ideas and ways forward that include everyone's needs and preferences. For example, when meeting a teenage girl and her mother who are in conflict over the teenager staying out late, you can seek to understand both the mother's need to ensure her daughter's safety and the daughter's need for independence. From an inclusive understanding you can begin to construct mutually beneficial ways forward. Often this process is described in family therapy as remaining 'neutral' (Jones, 1993), though this can be misleading as neutral can sound as though you are uninvolved or that you 'don't care' as the therapist. Perhaps a better conception is that you do care, but that you care for all people at the same time.

Maintaining this stance towards all members of a family can be very difficult, especially when there is a lot of conflict. It is essential, however, in order to be effective. Sometimes it is not possible in a family meeting to establish an alliance with all family members. In these situations, individual meetings can be arranged to give you time to build up an alliance and understanding of each viewpoint before a family meeting is embarked upon.

Respectful curiosity

A strengths-based or solution-focused approach to therapy builds on Rogers's three basic attitudes of empathy, acceptance and genuineness, while adding one other – respectful curiosity. Interestingly, Rogers himself alludes to this attitude as he describes the development of a 'sense of awe' towards the client:

> As therapy goes on the therapist's feeling of acceptance and respect for the client tends therapist's to change to something approaching awe as he sees the valiant and deep struggle of the person to be himself. (Rogers, 1961: 82)

Strengths-based therapists attempt to cultivate this sense of awe towards their clients by adopting an attitude of respectful curiosity towards their lives and the stories they tell. They are interested in them as people who are more than the problem; they want to find out more about their talents and strengths, and they are interested in their values, desires and preferences for their future. Much of this respectful curiosity is communicated by the questions that the therapist asks to guide the therapeutic process, such as:

- I'm interested in how you managed to get through that difficult situation?
- I'm curious about what you would feel when things were different (or better)?
- I wonder what was different last week when things went well?
- Suppose things were to get better next week, what would that look like?

Even if these questions aren't directly asked of the client, the wonder and respectful curiosity that underpins them is what changes the dynamic of the therapeutic relationship.

Strengths-based therapists start from a position of 'not knowing' and see each session as an opportunity to learn from the clients who are the real experts in their lives. In preparing to meet a new family, Jonathon Prosser (2001) describes a number of preparatory questions that therapists can ask themselves to free their minds from the negative expectations of a problem-dominated referral letter and to replace this with a respectful and more optimistic curiosity. These questions include:

- What new, wonderful and surprising things will I find out about this family in the next session?
- I wonder what I will learn, and how much I will be inspired?
- I wonder how much fun I will have in the process?

These questions can help free us as therapists from a problem-focused mindset and give us a freedom to discover new perspectives and ideas that are more useful in helping the family move forward. For example, many of the children referred to child and family clinics are described exclusively in terms of their problems, such as 'failing at school', or being 'aggressive' or 'oppositional'. Yet on closer examination, we may discover that they also have many positive qualities such as being a great cook, having a specific talent for football, or being very caring towards an invalid grandparent. In addition, we may discover that many parents labelled as 'limited' or 'deprived' have their own unique strengths, as is illustrated in Case Example 2.1.

Case Example 2.1   A talent for singing

When working as a community social worker, I was referred a family from a very deprived area, headed by a single mother who had a mild learning disability. There was a long history of concern about her ability to be a parent and the school would frequently report that her children were neglected in very basic ways (for example, being inappropriately clothed, poor hygiene, regularly missing school and so on). However, the mother was also very suspicious and hostile towards services and rarely engaged with workers for long periods. Frequently the case would be closed, without substantive change, only for new concerns to emerge at a later date. On reading the long 'problem focused' file, it was easy for me to feel pessimistic about engaging the family in a helpful way.

However, a turning point in being able to establish an alliance with the mother came from a conversation at the beginning of a session when she explained her interest in singing. It turned out that she had a great singing voice and people in her family reported that she could 'sing like Mary Black' (a traditional Irish singer). She spoke about her long-standing interest in singing and how she was pleased that her ten-year-old daughter was taking an interest in singing (this was one of the few areas where the daughter succeeded in school).

This new information helped change the nature of my relationship with the mother and helped me 'see' her differently, as not simply a deprived limited single parent, but as an individual person with talents and aspirations. As a result the context of our interaction began to change. By not only focusing on her problems but also valuing her talents in a more balanced way, my therapeutic alliance with this mother was transformed and our work together could begin. Over time she trusted me enough to co-create with her a practical child protection plan for her children to establish routines in their care.

Problem-free talk

An important way of establishing an alliance with clients in solution-focused therapy is to start the session with problem-free talk (George et al., 1990; Walsh, 1997). This means that the therapist engages the family in a conversation about things that are going right in their lives and which do not necessarily have a connection to the problem that has brought them to therapy. The aim is to get to know the clients as people, who are distinct from the problem and who have talents, hopes, values, hobbies and interests just like other people. On meeting a family for the first time, the therapist may spend some time talking to them about what they like to do as family, what trips and holidays they like, and even what they like about each other. This may be done informally, as part of a 'getting to know you' conversation or it can be done as an exercise or a fun game; for example, family members could be invited to name a favourite family trip or work together on drawing a picture of their strengths or motto as a family.

Informal problem-free talk can resemble social chitchat, though it has a constructive orientation; a skilled therapist is listening carefully for strengths, skills and resources that can be useful later in solving problems. For example, in a recent case working with a family who was referred on account of the son's out-of-control behaviour, the therapist engaged the father by talking about his work as a carpenter, rather than immediately talking about the presenting problem. This conversation revealed that the son also shared a strong interest in his father's work and liked to help him on jobs. This problem-free talk identified a connection between father and son that became central to the eventual solution.

As well as identifying strengths and resources, problem-free talk often has a subtle effect on the therapist's view of the family and thus the therapeutic relationship. Many children and families referred to professional services are surrounded by a negative story that details failure deficits and layers of problems. It is very easy, as therapists, to connect into that story and to become deflated and pessimistic about change (in turn adding to the family's pessimism). Problem-free talk allows therapists to connect with clients as people who are much more than the problems that bring them to therapy, and to note the many positive aspects of their lives that may often be overlooked and undervalued. This is often the beginning of a different positive story emerging that points to new hopes and possibilities. In this way, the therapeutic relationship can be altered to one that is based on an appreciation of strengths rather than just deficits and one that inspires optimism for realistic change.

Humour

> *Laughter is the quickest distance between two people.*
>
> L.G. Boldt, 1997

Humour is probably the most common way that people connect and join with one another. Many interpersonal relationships, whether intimate or otherwise, are built upon or sustained by a shared sense of humour. Indeed, it is hard to conceive of any effective human relationship that is devoid of a sense of humour. In fact, making jokes and sharing laughter is probably a more frequent human interchange than rational argument or active listening. Despite the omnipresence of humour in human relationships, it is notably absent in the literature describing the therapeutic relationship. If you were only to read the literature, you would be led to believe that therapy is exclusively a serious, worthy and weighty process, when in practice it is not always this way.

In my experience, humour is a very useful way to connect with clients and to communicate a sense of non-judgemental understanding. A moment of shared laughter can cut through a sense of being blamed, can even reduce the oppression of the problem and crucially can help build the therapeutic alliance. In addition, the lightness, creative imagination and positive energy that underpins humour is very useful when it comes to a creative envisioning of goals or solution building with clients. Therapy that is marked by an exclusively serious or heavy approach can often inadvertently reinforce the heaviness and seriousness of the problem and restrict access to the client's imagination and creativity that is needed to solve the problem. It is my experience, whether with children or adults, that therapy characterised by a lightness of touch and a playfulness as well as seriousness and earnestness is the most effective.

Of course, we're not talking about any type of humour (as much is about belittling people and putting them down). Consider the following sample dialogue to illustrate this process, taken from a child mental health setting. Many parents feel very blamed and judged when their children have problems. In fact, this is often the greatest obstacle to forming a therapeutic alliance as it causes them to be defensive or feel oppressed (naturally this is not helped by the fact that many mental health professionals actually do blame parents in how they diagnose and treat childhood problems!). In the following dialogue the therapist uses humour to overcome this defensiveness of a mother who has brought her six-year-old son to the child and family clinic because of his behavioural problems. When she goes into the therapist's office, the child sits quietly while the mother talks at length about their problems.

Mother:	He's really a demon at home, he throws tantrums all the time and never does what I ask. [*She looks at child sitting quietly*] Of course he is making a fool of me here, sitting so quietly here, good as gold.
Therapist:	Would you believe that this often happens here.
Mother:	What?
Therapist:	When parents bring their children here, they often behave very well in my office, even though their parents are coping with really bad behaviour at home.
Mother:	[*Interested*] Really?
Therapist:	And to be honest, I'm glad that your child is behaving well in my office. [*Pauses and then adds self-mockingly*] I really don't think I could cope if he threw a tantrum in my office.
Mother:	[*Laughs*] You'd find it hard to cope, too.
Therapist:	Absolutely!

The above joke indirectly communicated to the mother that the therapist understood how difficult it was to manage tantrums and how he understood what it was like to feel incompetent in the face of them. This helped break the mother's sense of being judged and create an alliance that helped her let go of engaging in problem talk (to make sure the therapist understood how bad things could be) and move to consider solutions with the therapist on her side.

Probably the reason that humour is not often cited as a way of connecting in the psychotherapy literature (unlike listening) is the fact that humour is risky. It can be taken up the wrong way or add to a sense of being misunderstood. What is essential is to use humour in a sensitive and skilled way, that builds people up, reduces isolation, makes the problem look small and ridiculous and helps communicate to clients that you understand their predicament and are on their side.

Self-awareness

A therapeutic relationship is based upon a two-way human connection between the therapist and the client(s). As a therapist you bring your own personality, feelings, thoughts and personal history to the process. Often this is very helpful, providing you of a way of being empathic, identifying with or understanding a client's experience. Sometimes, however, it can act the other way and cause you to have negative feelings towards clients. As Wilson notes:

> Therapists may experience powerful feelings such as a desire to punish a child for behaving badly or to rescue a child from negligent parents. (Wilson, 1998: xx)

Depending on our own personality and history, certain children and certain families will hook us in and cause us to feel strong negative (and positive) feelings and be tempted to react in unhelpful ways. For example, our ability to respond constructively is compromised if we feel strongly critical towards a parent that is likely to be communicated through our tone of voice or body language. Equally, our anxiety or expectation of problems may cause us to react too quickly and thus we can contribute to the likelihood of a child acting out in a session. As a result, therapists need to be self-aware of their input to the therapeutic relationship; they need to work hard (through self-reflection, supervision and consultation) to be aware of how their own thoughts and feelings are contributing to the process. The more self-aware we are, the more we can make choices about how best to respond. For example, if we realise that the critical feelings we feel towards a parent stem from the fact that her behaviour reminds us of patterns from our own childhood, then we can work hard to put these feelings to one side and to understand the unique perspective of the parent in the room. Or if we realise that the feelings of criticism are a reflection of how professionals often react to this parent, then we can use those feelings to empathically understand the parent's perspective and to respond more constructively.

In psychodynamic terms, this process of teasing out the therapist contribution to the therapeutic relationship is framed as analysing and understanding countertransference. From a strengths-based perspective the aim is first to be aware of and understand these feelings and then to try and respond to them in the most constructive way to help the client and to maintain the alliance.

Focusing on strengths, skills and resources

> *The real voyage of discovery consists not in seeking new landscapes but in having new eyes.*
>
> Marcel Proust

When I first trained as a therapist, I was taught how to understand and diagnose problems. Much of the theoretical input on the courses was focused on describing in detail the symptoms and effects of the problems and sub-problems. Depending on the theoretical orientations, a huge variety of causes were proposed to explain children's problems such as poor attachment between parent and child, dysfunctional family communication, or individual factors such a parent's depression, alcoholism or skills deficits in their parenting skills.

Sometimes external factors were proposed, such as homelessness, poverty or deprivation. Case presentations were concerned with putting together a jigsaw of causes and effects to create a complete picture of the problem. This could include intergenerational factors as causes could be traced across the extended family, with grandparents and even great-parents sharing similar presentations.

Whatever the merits of problem analysis and formulation, it is not sufficient in itself to help families solve or move beyond them. In addition, excessive problem analysis can have some unwanted effects: families can feel hurt, defensive and demoralised by the pejorative descriptions that such categories contain. For example, if we say that a child has an attachment disorder, this can suggest to a mother that she has not been able to create a supportive relationship with her child and thus that she is to blame for her child's problems. Even if we don't discuss our categorisations and thoughts with the families we work with, they can be communicated indirectly and their pejorative nature can compromise the therapeutic alliance. For example, it would be hard for us to believe in our clients abilities, or maintain an attitude of unconditional positive regard towards parents, when much of our professional thinking has been engaged in exploring how their actions have contributed to the problems in the family.

From a strengths-based perspective it is important to include an appreciation of strengths in our work with families, and arguably this approach is much more useful when empowering families to change. Rather than exclusively putting together the jigsaw pieces to get a picture of the problem, it is also important to put together the different jigsaw pieces that form the solution. The pieces of the 'solution jigsaw' include the unique experiences, strengths, resources and skills of the children, the parents, the family and even the community in which they live. Such strengths-based information provides vital 'clues' to the solution that is likely to best fit the family's unique circumstances. For example, one mother, referred because of child protection concerns, was labelled as chaotic and disorganised, yet she put great value on celebrating religious milestones in her children's lives, such as their first holy communion. When this motivation was acknowledged and appreciated, this mother accepted a child care plan that included practical daily support and coaching (which she had refused up until now) as it was focused on helping her prepare her children for their first holy communion, which was an important family event. Frequently, the family strengths that provide the vital clues to a solution are surprising and have little to do with the original problem, as was the situation in Case Example 2.2.

Case Example 2.2   A hidden family strength

A ten-year-old boy and his family were referred to a child mental health clinic due to the boy's significant behaviour problems at home and at school. The referrer noted that many of the difficulties appeared to centre on a hostile relationship between father and son, which alternated between 'flaming rows' and periods of coldness and distance.

In the first family session, when exploring how they coped with difficulties, the father relayed his interest in Tai Chi, which helped him calm down and manage stress in his work. This opened up a surprising range of ideas and principles that the family could use to manage their conflict. Most surprisingly, however, was the interest the son took in these ideas. He had for a long time wondered what his father was doing when he practised Tai Chi (in the living room in the house). As a result of the family meeting, the father took the step of including his son in his practise and began to teach him some of the ideas. This developed into a shared connection between them and a metaphor for them in resolving differences.

The father's interest in Tai Chi thus became a significant piece in the solution jigsaw and in helping this family connect with each other more supportively.

From distress to healing

Generally, intimate and family relationships are both the sources of people's distress and the source of their healing. Even in the most healthy relationship there are times when the relationship is a source of hurt and distress for all parties and even in the most dysfunctional relationships there are sometimes moments of connection and better communication. A strengths-based approach to therapy is about paying attention to and cultivating the moments of connection and healing. By understanding these positive moments in more elaborate and rich detail, they can become more real and more readily accessible. In addition, people can learn how it is that they can bring about these moments, and these insights can be used to diminish the power of the difficult times. Often the switch between a relationship being dysfunctional or damaging to one that is more supportive and satisfying is a small one – the aim is to help clients learn how to 'flick the switch' in their favour! Case Example 2.3 illustrates this.

Case example 2.3   A potential resource

One stressed single parent I worked with as a child protection social worker, found her own mother over-bearing and critical and as a result had cut off contact with her. The grandmother contacted me on a couple of occasions, complaining about her daughter's care of her grandson.

Rather than 'taking a position' on the grandmother's contact either by dismissing her concerns as 'interfering' or by using them as simply further evidence of the mother's inability to parent, I attempted to view the grandmother's contact positively as a potential resource to the family. I acknowledged the grandmother's desire to help her daughter and her grandson and explored with her what she hoped would happen for them. We also discussed how she had tried to help in the past (the grandmother had offered advice, which had been spurned by the mother) and she expressed frustration at her help not being accepted, but she understood that the mother might feel undermined. I sympathised with her and asked her to think how she could give her daughter help in a way that she wouldn't feel undermined. After much discussion, the grandmother remembered that in the past when she had offered to baby-sit her daughter's children at the weekend when she was going out, this help was often accepted. She decided that this help might be the best help to offer. With this insight confirmed, we discussed how the grandmother would talk to her daughter about the help she wanted to provide and about her contact with me (I had explained that I would have to relay her concerns to the daughter), and she met with her daughter the next day.

Though the mother was initially suspicious of the grandmother's motivations, she was willing to give her 'another chance' and the new babysitting arrangement started. Over time the grandmother became much more supportively involved in her grandson's life, and her relationship with her daughter became a cooperative rather than a conflictual one. Interestingly, this led to healing on all sides (this is one of the fascinating results of working in a resource-focused way) in that not only did the daughter get some extra help, but the grandmother was given an opportunity to feel useful and valued and to develop a better relationship with her grandson. Further, the grandson was given access to another adult who genuinely cared for him.

The strengths-based approach to therapy helped facilitate this to happen: by treating the grandmother's contact as a potential resource rather than simply as 'another problem report' and by channelling her motivation to seek a more supportive connection with her daughter rather than accepting her initial characterisation as over-bearing and an extra pressure for the mother, a more mutually satisfying outcome was achieved for all.

There are (more than) two sides to every story

A strengths-based approach to therapy is about viewing families through a different lens, notably one that takes into account a more empowering description of their life situation. From a social constructionist perspective, the ideas, hypotheses or 'stories' we have about ourselves and others aren't necessarily true or false (indeed, there are often many different accounts, stories and theories that would fit the data equally well). But the ideas we have and communicate to other people do have impact. They do shape and create the reality we describe. This is analogous to the traditional idea of a 'self-fulfilling prophecy' – people will be formed by their reputations and the predictions people make about them. The more important the person who makes the prediction, the more powerful the prediction. This is a sobering thought for us to bear in mind as professionals who have far-ranging powers over our clients – our reports and ideas can stay with people and determine the expectations of other people and what services these families will have access to. People will live up to (or rather live down to) the negative ideas people have about them. From a strengths-based perspective, the aim is to invite clients to generate more helpful accounts, descriptions and stories about themselves that fit equally with the facts and reality of their lives, but which are more empowering to them in reaching their goals. The aim is to have positive 'self-fulfilling prophecies', which are genuine, fitting the data equally well and which are hopeful rather than pessimistic, inspirational rather than imprisoning, and empowering rather than limiting.

For example, there is a prevalent idea that 'people who were abused as children will have a tendency to replicate this upbringing and abuse their own children in some way'. This idea has strong currency not just in professional circles (where many empirical studies appear to give it credence), but also in the general public and in circles our clients move in. Whether true or false as an idea, however, it is not necessarily a useful point from which to start therapy. It says nothing about the efforts of the many people who try to break the pattern of abuse and to create a more positive future. This has been brought home to me by the stories of the many parents and families I have worked with, for example of Sheila described in Case Example 2.4.

Case example 2.4   An alternative understanding

Sheila was a 24-year-old single parent. She had a very traumatic childhood, suffering physical abuse and neglect by her parents, before being received into care at the age of ten. She had two children by different fathers, neither of whom were supportively involved in the children's care. Recently, there had been concerns about Sheila's own care of her children, in that the eldest had appeared at nursery with bruises and the neighbours had heard shouting. Sadly, this was very similar to the reports made about Sheila's own mother when Sheila was a child herself.

As a social worker reading this referral about Sheila, I felt pessimistic. It was easy for me to conclude that Sheila's own inadequate upbringing was coming to bear on how she was bringing up her own children and to feel that 'the past' was relentlessly reproducing itself on the present generation. I was lucky, however, not to let this thinking prevent me from hearing a different story that Sheila told me about her life.

Sheila was also devastated by the prospect that the past was 'catching up on her'. Given her own childhood, she had resolved to be different as a parent. She wanted so much to give her children a different childhood and to be there for them in a way that her own parents were never there for her. As a result she tried to give them everything that was denied her. In particular, she tried to be all-giving to her older son, never saying no to him, and giving him everything she could at great expense to her. Under this permissive parenting, however, her son began to run riot, particularly in school. This led Sheila to feel very frightened that he would be taken away and she 'snapped' one day and got really angry with him. What horrified her the most was that she found herself saying to him all the horrible things that her own mother told her.

From this more understanding account of Sheila's circumstances I was able to acknowledge and honour her great intentions to 'do things differently'. I was able appreciate and explore her values to be a caring and sensitive parent and how she aspired to be there for her children. This appreciation of her strengths, born out of a more empathic account of her circumstances, helped create an alliance between us and provided the starting point for therapy. From here Sheila was able to open up about the difficulties she had, and to identify what supports she needed to help her keep to her own goals as a parent. Working cooperatively with her, she agreed to access support at her local family resource centre and this helped her 'get back on track'.

Rather than accepting a simple pathological explanation of events, it is more important to seek a richer, more empathic and more strengths-based account of events that is more empowering and linked to future possibilities and goals. It is this strengths-based understanding that provides a bridge between the problem and the solution. Once understood in this more empathic light, the client is more likely to trust the therapist and the therapeutic process and consider options for change. Even if solutions are not forthcoming, a strengths-based understanding can provide the best way to garner the client's resources to cope with the problem and/or create the best platform on which to implement a professional plan of action. In Case Example 2.3, if Sheila's child care had not improved, in spite of her intentions, then a child protection plan for the children to come into care may have been considered, however, a strengths-based approach to this process may provide the best opportunity for this action to serve the children's long term interests. For example, if Sheila views herself not exclusively as a failed parent, but also as a brave parent (for facing her own difficulties and letting her children live elsewhere) who still loves her children though they live elsewhere, then there is a better chance that she will remain supportively involved for her children's sake (for example, in terms of access). By maintaining a collaborative, respectful and strengths-based approach as a professional rather than an exclusively authoritarian or expert one, you create possible conditions for an ongoing alliance and working relationship to be maintained.

Coping with Problems

One should not deny the verdict, but one should defy the sentence.

D. Saleeby, 1996: 303

When people are initially introduced to a strengths-based or solution-focused way of working, they often see it as being a form of positive thinking or being out of touch about the reality of problems in clients' lives, or being in denial about the many external oppressive forces that burden marginalised groups (such as poverty, racism and so on). This, however, is an oversimplified view. A good strengths-based therapist is not problem-phobic and takes very seriously the reality that problems do exist in clients' lives, and the fact that many people are battling with oppression and prejudice. The difference is the belief that strengths-based solution building rather than deficit-focused problem solving is the most effective time-sensitive way to help clients. In particular, the shift is from exploring the nature of problems and how they affect or damage clients to exploring how clients have responded and coped with these problems. Such a reorientation of the conversation can be more empowering, in that it assumes an active coping response on the part of the client, rather than a passive reaction to life problems. Consider the following example of a parent coping with difficult behaviour from her son Peter:

Client: When Peter throws a tantrum, he can really lose it, I can really feel at the end of my tether.

Therapist: I'm sorry to hear that, it sounds difficult.

Client: Yeah.

Therapist: When he throws a tantrum, how do you get through it?

Client: I don't know … I just try and not let it get to me.

Therapist: You try and not let it get to you?

Client: Yeah, it's hard, but I try and remain calm.

Therapist: You try to remain calm?

Client: Yes, I used to lose it at him always, but I found that this made him even worse.

Therapist: Ah, I see, you've learnt that being calm works better.

Client: Yeah.

Therapist: I know it can be really hard to remain calm in those situations … how do you do it?

Client: Well … I think to myself, 'this won't last forever, he will calm down soon'.

Therapist: I see, so you remind yourself that the tantrum will lift and that it will be better soon. What else do you do?

Client: Sometimes, if I can, I walk away from him, you know, put a bit of space between me and him …

Therapist: Ah, I see … a bit of space during those difficult times can make a difference.

Focusing on coping highlights the fact that despite having problems clients still have access to a number of strengths and resources which allow them to survive and manage their lives. These coping strengths, which are often forgotten or not fully accessed, provide 'clues' to creating the solution and/or helping the client live even more resourcefully in the face of the problem. In addition, the shift in the therapeutic conversation from 'impact' to 'coping' can in itself be beneficial to clients. Such a strengths-based conversation can be experienced as more liberating and empowering as it gives voice to the 'story' of clients' creative coping in the face of the problems that afflict them.

Focusing on coping gives us a different 'lens' with which to view difficult past events that have occurred in client lives. For example, if a client describes her parents as being very cold towards her as a child, rather than simply asking 'How cold were they to you?' or 'How did this make you feel?' or 'How did this affect you', we can ask 'How did you cope with/deal with what happened' or 'What did this experience teach you?' or 'Given the type of childhood you had, what decisions have you made about the type of parent you want to be?'

Allan Wade (1997) takes this approach further in working with clients who have experienced violence and severe trauma. He has found people 'resist' the violence that has happened to them in everyday simple ways (which he calls 'small acts of living'). For example, a woman who is raped may deal with what is happening by freezing her body and putting her thoughts elsewhere, or a child who is sexually abused by her father may respond by being defiant and troublesome to her parents. Such responses or 'resistances' are often undervalued and unappreciated, and if they are described in therapy they are often thought of as maladaptive coping responses or symptoms (for example, as dissociation in the first example and as a behavioural problem in the second), rather than appreciated as heroic acts of resistance. Wade argues that shifting the therapeutic conversation from asking how clients have been damaged or affected by a past trauma to asking how they have responded to or 'resisted' this event can uncover a story of creative coping and 'resistance' on the part of the client, which in itself is liberating and therapeutic to express. Wade argues that through this process people begin to experience themselves as stronger, more insightful, and more capable of responding effectively to the difficulties that brought them to therapy.

Though a focus on coping inherently conceives that people can be strengthened and learn from negative and traumatic experiences (as well as damaged by them), this is not to justify or approve such experiences. Furman and Ahola use the metaphor of healing bones to illustrate this:

> Even if fractured bones may sometimes become stronger after healing, it does not justify fracturing bones. However strong a bone may become from recovering from an accidental fracture we do all in our power to protect ourselves and others from such injury. (1992: 37)

Such an approach is pragmatic: we cannot reverse the adversities we have experienced or the terrible things that have happened to us, all we can do is choose our response to what has happened. We can choose to learn from it, choose to let it make us wiser and more compassionate and we can choose to endeavour to bear witness and give support to others who have experienced similar events.

Making client goals and preferences central

> *The Hare was boasting of his speed before the other animals. 'I have never yet been beaten,' he said, 'I challenge any one here to race with me.' The Tortoise said quietly, 'I accept your challenge.'*
> *'That is a good joke,' said the Hare. 'I could dance round you all the way, it will be easy.'*
> *The race was fixed and the Hare and Tortoise lined up. The Hare shot out ahead at the beginning of the race, leaving the Tortoise behind. But he couldn't resist playing to the crowd. To make a fool of the Tortoise he ran back and forth and around him. He even stopped and had a nap. 'Look I can beat him easily, I can even take a rest in the middle.'*
> *The Tortoise simply ignored the Hare and concentrated on the race, plodding forward at his own pace, his eyes fixed on the finishing post. In taking his nap, the Hare forgot the time, and awoke suddenly to see the Tortoise nearly at the finishing line. He charged forward to try and catch up, but it was too late and the Tortoise won the race.*
>
> *The Hare and the Tortoise*, adapted from The Fables of Aesop

In the above story, the Tortoise beat the Hare by ignoring the Hare's flash attempts to distract him, by plodding along at his own pace, however slow, and by keeping his eye firmly fixed on the finish line. This could also be a metaphor for counselling and psychotherapy. Even the therapeutic models essentially conceptualised as being 'brief', such as solution-focused therapy, work best when the process moves gently at the client's pace towards the client's goals. The aim is not to rush ahead of the client or to distract from the process using 'flashy' techniques or exercises, but rather to stay with them, keeping their goals central to the process and to make progress at their own pace. Like the Tortoise in the above story, the aim is to plod along making progress, with your eye firmly on the finishing line.

In this way, an overall guiding principle for the recent strengths-based collaborative therapies is a focus on client goals and preferences. The shift is from considering problems and unwanted pasts to elaborating goals and preferred futures. What the client(s) wants and wishes to happen by coming to therapy becomes the compass that guides the entire process. In the reformulation of brief solution-focused therapy, distil it down to core principles and start each session with 'What are your best hopes for coming to these meetings?' (George et al., 1999).This becomes the central question of the entire therapy and the subsequent conversation is focused on elaborating these hopes and goals in evermore rich and meaningful detail.

The importance of therapeutic goals is borne out by many outcome studies. Orlinsky et al. (1994), reviewing the literature, reported that having clear goals that are agreed between therapist and client is strongly associated with positive therapeutic outcome. A process study of solution-focused therapy (Beyebach et al., 1996) found that clients who had formulated clear goals in the first session were twice as likely to complete the therapy successfully. Other studies have shown that tailoring drug and alcohol treatment programmes to client goals and preferences (rather than having a 'one size fits all' approach) means that clients are more likely to enter treatment early and to complete the course successfully (Miller and Hester, 1989; Sanchez-Craig, 1980).

A focus on client goals and preferences has also run like a thread through many of the traditional psychotherapy models, such as cognitive therapy and rational emotive therapy (Beck, 1976; Ellis, 1998). Carl Rogers (1961) conceptualised that individuals had a preferred or ideal view of self and experienced distress when there was a gap between this ideal and their perceived self. In others words, people experience misery when their life is out of sync with their aspirations, values and life goals. Strengths-based therapy aims to help people articulate these goals and values and in doing so to discover how these preferred ways of being can happen in their lives. Shifting the focus from problems to goals has a number of other benefits, as is illustrated in Case Example 2.5 (originally explored by Sharry, 2001b).

Case example 2.5   The power of goals

Paul was 15 years old when he was referred to me on account of his long recurrent history of joyriding and theft. He was described on his report as having a cynical attitude towards social services and having no remorse about his crimes. When I met Paul for the first time, instead of going over his problem history we started talking socially about different things he was interested in. I asked him about what work he thought he'd like to do in the future. For some reason Paul took this question seriously, thought for a while and then gave a clear answer: he would like to be an airline pilot. I was surprised by the answer. Paul was poorly educated and barely literate. It was hard to imagine that he had the skills to be a pilot. But I resisted the temptation to dismiss the idea and suggest a more suitable career, realising that this is probably what usually happened. Instead I asked what attracted him to be a pilot. This opened up a long conversation and he spoke non-stop about the interest he had in planes, stemming back to his childhood. Over the next few meetings, the subject of planes and other vehicles became our dominant discussion. I took seriously his interest in becoming a pilot and we discussed the steps he'd have to take to move towards this career, for example returning to education. We negotiated a goal of him gaining an apprenticeship as a mechanic, which he achieved within the next two months. When my work with him ended he was working happily in this position. He still spoke of wanting to work with planes, though he had now modified his goal to working as a mechanic with them.

This case illustrates how much energy and motivation for change can be released when we identify client-centred goals, as opposed to those imposed from the outside or formulated from problem descriptions. Large, idealistic goals that are important to clients are highly motivating and once these are understood and supported, 'small' focused goals, which are realistic in a therapeutic contract, can be negotiated. Once Paul's desire to be a pilot was validated and supported, the more realistic goal of an apprenticeship could be negotiated. Coincidentally, this satisfied many of the referrer's goals, since working as a mechanic, Paul did not commit crime. Most importantly, this was a goal that motivated him and one he was willing to work hard for to achieve in the short term.

Establishing therapeutic goals and helping clients elaborate their preferred views is by no means always an easy process. Steve de Shazer, the co-founder of solution-focused brief therapy, has described therapy as two people in a small room trying to find out what the hell one of them wants!

When working with families, the process is further complicated by the fact that you have to help several individuals articulate their goals, some or all of which may appear to be in contradiction with one another. Family members often start out with problems statements such as 'he never listens to me' or negatively formulated goals such as 'I just wish he would stop being so moody,' which often attribute blame and create conflict and counter charge. The aim is to help family members reformulate their goals to a format that is more positive and inclusive and which other family members can support and even take responsibility for. When goals appear to be in conflict it is often a case of seeking a formulation of a goal which takes into account both party's needs and wants. For example, in working with a couple where one party feels swamped and wants space and the other feels distant and wants more intimacy, the question becomes 'What would it be like when there is both space and intimacy in your relationship in a way that both of you feel happy?'.

When working with families, often goals go through stages of development as they are formulated in more positive and inclusive ways. For example:

1 'I just wish he wasn't so moody' (critical problem statement).
2 'I wish he would be more cheerful' (positive but focused exclusively on another's actions).
3 'I wish we had happier conversations' (positive, specific, shared responsibility).
4 'I love the times we joke together after dinner and would love there to more of these times' (positive, more specific, shared responsibility, meaningful and rich detail).
5 'I want to be more cheerful and positive when we spend time together after dinner' (positive, specific, meaningful and focused on what client can do to bring about goal).

Goal formulations 4 and 5 are particularly effective, as not only are they positive, clear and meaningful to the client, they also focus on the client's thoughts, actions and feelings and thus what he or she can do to bring it about.

Even when goals appear to be diametrically opposed there can still be a way of establishing an agreed therapeutic goal which respects the needs of both parties. For example, when working with a couple where one wants to leave the relationship and the other wants the relationship to survive, the therapeutic goal can be to help both parties understand their differences and to reach a decision about how to move forward.

When families are in a great deal of conflict, it can be very hard for them to move from a critical problem focus and to formulate positive goals. Indeed, it can be very hard for them to sit in the same room without descending into damaging rows or negative communication. In these cases, it may be better to work with family members in individual sessions, at least initially, before embarking on family work. Similarly, individual sessions are often the best way forward when the goal concerned is private to an individual family member, for example, a parent wanting to come to terms with her childhood abuse, or a parent in a violent relationship wanting to make plans for her safety, or a teenager wanting to 'fit in with' and meet new friends.

To illustrate some of these ideas, consider the following case of the Walsh family, consisting of a mother, father and a 14-year-old son, Gerry, who come to therapy with different goals.

Therapist: [*Addressing family*] So what are your best hopes for coming to these family meetings?

Mother: Well, I just want Gerry to start studying again and to stop hanging around with those friends of his. They're bad news.

Gerry: [*Mutters under his breath*] You don't know what you're talking about.

Mother: See what I mean, he never used to be like that.

Therapist: [*Addressing mother*] What do you hope would happen by Gerry staying in and studying a bit more?

Mother: Well, I want him to get on better in school, I want him to pass his exams – to have a future.

Therapist: Ah, I see, you want him to have a good future ... [*Pause*] Gerry, what do you hope for, coming to these meetings?

Gerry: I just wish she'd get off my back.

Therapist: You'd like your mother to give you some space?

Gerry: Yeah, I'd like her to realise that I have to make my own decisions.

Therapist: So you'd like to be able to make some of your own decisions ... [*Pause*] And Mr Walsh, what would you hope to get out of these meetings?

Father: I just wish the rows would stop at home.

Therapist: I understand ... What way would you like things to be going in the home?

Father: Well, I'd like everyone to be getting on better.

In the above sequence, the therapist has attempted to get each family member to articulate their goals in a way that is less contentious and more likely to be accepted by each other. The mother has moved from simply stating that she wants Gerry to stop hanging around with his friends to her deeper and more positive goal that she wants him to have a better future. Similarly, Gerry has moved from stating that he 'wants his mother off his back' to a wish to make more of his own decisions and the father has moved from wanting 'no rows' to wanting 'everyone to be getting on better'.

Elaborating goals in rich detail

The more a goal is richly described and elaborated in concrete detail, the more likely family members will work towards it. A goal that is compelling, attractive and personally meaningful to the family is likely to inspire them to move forward and to work together. In addition, the process of elaborating a goal (rather than complaints or problems) is likely to transform conflict between family members and to help them develop a common purpose which they are willing to work on together. In solution-focused therapy the 'miracle question' in its various forms (Berg, 1991; de Shazer, 1988) is often cited as a useful way to achieve this. Consider now the above example continued along this track:

Therapist: Let me ask you an unusual question ... Supposing you all go home tonight and a miracle takes place, that means the problems that brought you here have all disappeared and all of you have reached the goals [that we just talked about]. But overnight you don't know that this miracle has taken place. So what would be the first thing that you'd notice in the morning that would tell you that you had reached your goals?

Mother: Well ... Gerry would be up for a start, he would be on his way to school.

Therapist: Mmmh, what would be different for you?

Mother: I guess I would feel happier, not as stressed.

Therapist: What about you Gerry, what would you notice in the morning that would tell you the miracle had taken place?

Gerry: I dunno ... I guess there would be less hassle.

Therapist: What way would the morning go instead?

Gerry: I suppose we would have breakfast together.

Therapist: Ahh, a family breakfast.

Gerry: Yeah, there would be time.

Therapist: And what would you notice about your Mother that would tell you the miracle had taken place?

Gerry: She wouldn't be rushed, she would have time to have breakfast.

Therapist: And you Mr Walsh, what would you notice?

Father: Maybe, we would have time to sit and have a good chat together. We'd have a bit of a laugh together.

Therapist: So if the miracle took place you would have time to sit down as a family and have a laugh together.

The process of elaborating a goal in detail is highly motivating to clients. Specific, highly meaningful details, such as 'having a laugh together' or 'sitting down and having a good chat' in the example above, can make all the difference to transforming conflict and making the goal compelling and attractive.

Scaling progress

Once a future goal has been established in clear detail it is important to make a link back to the present and to explore the progress the family have already made – to look for the parts of the miracle that are already happening in their lives. One of the most useful ways of doing this is by using scaling questions (described in much more detail elsewhere, for example, Sharry, et al., 2001a). Consider the example continued below:

Therapist: So how close are you to these goals, say on a scale of one to ten where ten is the miracle happening and one is the furthest away you have been?
Mother: I'd say two, I still feel pretty far away.
Therapist: What makes you say two instead of one?
Mother: Well ... I think because we are all here today?
Therapist: So the fact that you got organised as a family to come along together is a sign of progress?
Mother: Yes.
Therapist: What about you, Mr Walsh, where would you rate things on the scale?
Father: About six.
Therapist: Oh, and what puts you at six?
Father: We used to have nice family dinners together, not so long ago. And last Sunday wasn't so bad ... we seemed to all get on OK.
Therapist: Right, what happened last Sunday?
Father: We watched a soap on the box together, had a bit of a laugh together.
Therapist: Do you remember last Sunday, Mrs Walsh?
Mother: Yeah, I do, wasn't so bad. I had a bit more time, wasn't as stressed about work.

By using scaling in the above example, an exception to the problem has been identified. From a strengths-based perspective, it is these exceptions that deserve special attention in the therapeutic conversation. Essentially, they represent examples of solutions that are already occurring in the family's lives; they illustrate times and events when the family, by their own resources and strengths, were able to make progress to their goals. By exploring these exceptions the family can gain insight into how they can be brought about or made to happen on a more regular basis.

Scaling questions also facilitate the breaking down of goals into small manageable steps. The question becomes: 'What would it take to move one point (or half a point) ahead on the scale?' The aim is to help the family describe what would things look like or what would be happening if things were just a little bit better in their family, or if they had made a small step of progress towards their goals. By helping the family envision and describe this next step in rich meaningful detail, perhaps even helping them recall times in the past when they made similar steps, progress can be established as both compelling and realistic.

Living out of your dreams

For us, there is only the trying. The rest is not our business.

T.S. Elliot

When therapists first encounter a goal-focused way of working, it is initially perceived as providing the best way of helping the client make progress and take the next step towards what they want to happen. However, this is to overlook a much more subtle effect of a goal-oriented way of working. Focusing on goals, preferences, values and aspirations rather than problems and complaints positively impacts a person *whether or not external progress is made towards the goal.* The goal/value reorientation holds many benefits in itself, for example, the person lives out of their values rather than their problems and they begin to notice and attend to examples of their goals and preferences already occurring in their lives. Thus the therapy is partially done when we help clients articulate personally meaningful goals and values in the therapeutic conversation. This is the profound though subtle shift we seek in therapy. The act of thinking differently and more constructively has a subtle effect on the thinker and not just the object of the thinking. Just as we influence the reality we experience in how we think about it (see discussion on social constructionism in Chapter 1), so the act of thinking in a certain way constructs the thinker. This means that over time we are formed by our habitual thoughts and what we think about. Goal-oriented and constructive thinking over time has an influence on the person.

To use a simple example, a powerful technique that is suggested to parents as a way of changing negative behaviour in their children is for them to go out of their way to praise and reward any small examples of their children's positive behaviour. While this idea is based on the behavioural principle that the child's good behaviour will increase because it is now positively reinforced, this misses the subtle effect on the parent carrying out the praise and rewards. By reorienting their thinking and attention to their child's good qualities and by expressing these 'new thoughts' repetitively (and with genuine intention), both the parents' relationship with the child and their sense of self as a parent are positively affected and changed.

Thus much of the process of therapy is about tapping into clients' goals and ideals, resources and strengths, and helping them articulate their vision for their lives, without necessarily a focus or action plan as to how they will make the necessary steps towards these goals. Ironically, of course, it is the articulation of clear positive proactive goals that is the best possible way to make progress and is more effective than negative strategies.

These principles can also be applied to our work as therapists and to how we engage with the clients. When sitting in the room with a client I try and focus on the core principles of therapeutic work, for example, of being respectful, constructive, optimistic and empathic, rather than being attached to outcome or to how things should evolve or change for the client. As T.S. Elliot, the poet, said: 'For us, there is only the trying. The rest is not our business.' Ironically, of course, it is these core attitudes communicated in the therapeutic alliance that are the most likely to empower and inspire the client and thus to help positive change come about.

Summary

In this chapter we have described three over-arching principles that are at the core of a strengths-based approach to working with children and families. We have focused on the need to establish the therapeutic alliance that forms the platform on which all therapeutic progress is built, the lack of which is the source of many problems. We have also described the strengths-based thinking that is at the heart of the approach and which runs like a thread through all the therapist questions and responses in the therapeutic conversation. It is through this strengths-based conversation that helpful understandings are created, the skills necessary to make progress identified and the resources and supports needed are accessed. And finally, we have outlined how a focus on client goals and preferences acts like a compass for the work. The goals of the child, the parents, the family and the other stakeholders in your work (such as those of the referrer) supply the rationale for your intervention and form the yardstick against which progress and success will be measured.

3   Engaging and Motivating Families

The North Wind and the Sun had a quarrel about which of them was the stronger and agreed that the one who could remove the coat from a man travelling below would be deemed the victor.

The North Wind went first and immediately sent a howling blast that shook the traveller's cloak. But he immediately wrapped it closely around him, and the harder the Wind blew, the tighter he held it to him. The North Wind tore angrily at the cloak, but all his efforts were in vain, because the traveller firmly held on to his cloak, fighting the North Wind.

Then the Sun began to shine. At first his beams were gentle, and in the pleasant warmth after the bitter cold of the North Wind the traveller unfastened his cloak and let it hang loosely from his shoulders. The Sun's rays grew warmer and warmer. The man took off his cap and mopped his brow. Soon he became so warm that he gently took off his coat and sat down by the side of the road to enjoy the lovely sunshine.[1]

The North Wind and The Sun, adapted from The Fables of Aesop

A collaborative strengths-based approach to counselling children and families is characterised above more by the approach of the Sun rather than the North Wind. The North Wind rushed ahead of the traveller and worked with great effort to try and force the traveller to take off his cloak. This led the traveller to resist and the harder the North Wind tried (using more of the same unsuccessful approach), the more the man resisted. In contrast, the Sun's approach was more patient and gentle. He shone in the background and created the right conditions for the traveller to take off his cloak. Rather than taking over he gently 'invited' the traveller to do the work himself and he waited patiently for the traveller to decide to take off his own coat. The Sun did not make that decision for him, but waited for his participation. In addition, the metaphor of the sun reveals other key aspects in this process. The role of the therapist is make clients feel warm and respected and by 'shining a light' to help them take a different and more helpful view of their situation. The therapeutic hour can literally be conceived as an invitation to clients to pause instead of rushing, to take time to 'sit by the side of the road and to enjoy the view'!

Establishing a collaborative partnership

The story of the North Wind and the Sun provides us with a good metaphor of the process of engaging children and families, particularly in the first session. (Indeed, I sometimes remind myself of the story when I find myself in a session

---

[1] I was inspired to use this story by a presentation by John Prosser (2001).

taking too much control or saying too much. I pause and say to myself, 'Be the sun, not the wind'.) Good therapists do not rush ahead of their clients or work 'too hard' to get them to participate. Rather they go slow, taking time to understand and tune into where the client is at. Like the failed efforts of the North Wind, if you are working harder than the client, then you are working too hard, and they are likely to resist all your ideas and strategies, simply because these are not their own ideas and strategies. Crucially the aim is to invite clients to take part fully in the therapeutic process and to become full collaborators with you as the therapist.

The process of engagement and assessment can be best seen as a collaborative partnership between the therapist and the child and their family. Each party brings their own expertise and knowledge. As the therapist, you bring an expertise (hopefully!) in therapeutic interviewing and often some general knowledge of the types of problems children and families face and the types of solutions that are helpful. The child and the parents are experts about their own lives. Only they know the unique and specific details of their family life that are important in understanding the problem and in creating a solution. In deciding what could be helpful, only they know what would 'fit' with their families and what they would be prepared to try out as a therapeutic strategy.

In a therapeutic session the therapist and child and family bring together their respective expertise and knowledge in an attempt to put together something of use for the family. Collaboration, consultation and negotiation with the child and all key members of the family about all stages of the therapeutic process is critical to ensuring that everyone is on board, such as determining:

- Who should be involved and included?
- What problem should be worked on?
- What is an agreed and satisfactory goal?
- What the process of therapy would be. (For example, which model and what mode – individual or family and so on.)
- What an agreed result is?

For example, on seeing a family for the first time you may ask, 'Who would like to start?' simply as a way of giving the responsibility to the family. Even young children can be invited into the process in this way; for example, in the first session you can ask them, 'Would you like to start and tell me why you have come here or would you like your mum to tell me?' Even if children choose the latter, you can strike a deal with them as follows: 'Well, if your mum starts, will you tell me what you think afterwards? Or make sure to tell me if your mum misses something out or if there's something you don't agree with?' The more agreement you can get at the beginning of a session about what is to follow, then the more likely everyone is to take part. Rather than simply deciding the structure of a session, a period of negotiating what will happen will make a big difference to the family's participation.

Consider Case Example 3.1 where the therapist, after initially getting into difficulty, was able to recover by taking time to consult with the teenager and their family about the best way to proceed. The final plan worked best because it had been arrived at by consultation with both of them and both of them were on board and committed to it.

Case Example 3.1   Who should be seen first?

Joan made contact with a child and family clinic looking for an appointment for her 14-year-old daughter, Susan, whom she was concerned was anorexic. Without clarifying what was the best way to proceed, the therapist arranged to meet mother and daughter together and attempted to establish goals. Joan, the mother, launched into describing her worries regarding Susan's eating. Susan was immediately offended and denied everything. A row ensued with the mother confronting and Susan denying. The therapist at this point suggested they take a break and that he meet with mother and daughter separately.

The therapist first consulted with the mother, who described long-term difficulties in her relationship with her daughter, her recent worries regarding her eating and her difficulty in getting through. When asked what was the best way to proceed, the mother said she felt that Susan 'should be seen alone' to give her the best chance of opening up. When meeting with Susan individually, she complained of her mother always being on her back about food, when there was nothing to worry about. She also said that she wanted to get on better with her mother. When asked what way she would like things to proceed at the clinic, she said she didn't see much of a point in coming along, but would if she thought it was 'going to keep her mother off her back'. The therapist then asked who she would like to come along to the therapy and she mentioned her older sister Petra, who she was close to at home.

The therapist finally met with mother and daughter together to try and agree a plan going forward. He fed back to them, briefly, the content of the individual meetings, focusing on their goals and wishes for one another rather than their complaints and upsets. A plan was agreed that they would both come to therapy for a mixture of individual and joint meetings and that Petra, the older sister, would also be invited. This agreement was honoured and over time substantial progress was made in the communication between mother and daughter, mainly with the help of the older sister as intermediary. By the end Susan felt she was getting on better with her mother and Joan felt more reassured about her daughter's welfare and that she did not have an eating disorder.

Attending to motivation

When a client does not engage in therapy or drops out of it altogether, a common explanation that many therapists offer is that the client was simply 'unmotivated' and not willing to participate. This explanation, however, is not always the most helpful as it implies that the responsibility for the therapeutic failure lies with the client (and thus lets the therapist 'off the hook'!) when in reality it is more likely to be a shared responsibility between therapist and client and a product of the context in which they are working together. From a strengths-based perspective, there is no such thing as an 'unmotivated client'. Everyone is motivated to achieve something or desires things to be a certain way, though these goals may differ from the implicit goals of therapy. In addition, motivation is not fixed but open to change over time. It can take a long time for a client to generate a goal and then to develop the willingness to work towards it. If you meet a 'motivated' client in a first therapeutic session, this is usually due to the large amount of work he or she has already done prior to coming to therapy in the form of developing an awareness of a problem, clarifying a goal for themselves and deciding on a method to achieve it (for example, coming to therapy). The therapist is benefiting from the many steps a client has already taken along the path to change. From a strengths-based perspective, it is important to appreciate the client's motivation and to work hard to establish goals that are centred on their desires and preferences and thus compelling to them. It is also important to be sensitive to where they are at with respect to possible goals. A client who has clearly formulated a goal will require a very different approach than a client who only has a vague sense of what they want to be different, or one who was sent to therapy by another a person.

The solution-focused therapy model describes three levels of motivation that categorise the therapist–client relationship at any given time, notably customer, complainant and visitor (Berg and Miller, 1992; de Shazer, 1988), which require a different approach if therapy is to be successful:

1   At the *customer* level of motivation the client has established a goal that they believe they can move towards by changing their own thoughts and actions. The therapeutic relationship is collaborative with therapist and client working together.
2   At the *complainant* level of motivation the client thinks there is a problem, is motivated to change it, but sees it as something beyond their control and to do with how other people are behaving and thinking. The therapeutic relationship can often be conflictual as the client frequently wants the therapist to 'do something' on their behalf or to persuade someone else to change.
3   At the *visitor* level of motivation therapy the client either doesn't feel that the identified problem is an issue for them or they are uninterested in the identified goal of the therapy and thus are not really motivated to take action. If they do get to the counsellor's or therapist's office it is generally because they are sent or coerced by a third party.

An example of a complainant is a mother who is very concerned about her teenage son, who is dropping out of education, and insists he attends counselling. The son in this case, who believes his leaving school is not a problem, could be described as a visitor.

In seeing families or couples in therapy, it is important to remember that different family members could be at very different levels of motivation with respect to a certain goal and the process of coming to therapy. This often leads to conflict and these clients can be experienced as 'warring' with one another. It is important that the therapist does not contribute to this conflict by 'taking sides', becoming a judge or valuing one position over another. Rather, it is important to become multipartial; that is, to find a way of accommodating and understanding the different perspectives and positions. The therapist needs to find a way of establishing an alliance with each family member that accommodates their level of motivation and perspective. Consider now Case Example 3.2, which will be used to illustrate this process for the remainder of this section.

Case Example 3.2   Different levels of motivation

A six-year-old-boy, Joe, is brought to therapy by his parents on account of concerns expressed by Joe's teacher about his behavioural and attention problems in the classroom. The teacher finds him 'impossible to manage' and wants him assessed, believing he may have ADHD. She also wonders if many of the problems are caused by his parents being over-permissive and letting him 'rule the roost' at home. Mother is very upset by the teacher's report. She is critical of how the teacher handles her son in school, feeling she is 'on his back' all the time. She is also concerned, however, about the 'aggressive streak' she sees in her son when he throws tantrums at home. She also wants him assessed. Father thinks the problems are exaggerated (particularly by the teacher) and thinks Joe is just being a normal active six-year-old. This leads to a lot of conflict between the parents, with the mother accusing the father of being uninvolved and undermining and the father accusing the mother of over-reacting and not being able to manage her son. Joe seems confused by the business of coming to therapy and 'tunes out' during the family assessment meeting, playing with toys in the corner.

In Case Example 3.2, all the participants are at different levels of motivation with respect to the therapy. The teacher and the mother are both at the complaint level of motivation. They recognise problems, notably 'attention and behavioural problems', but these problems (and thus the solutions) are framed as being out of their control and influence. Both are critical of one another, suggesting that the other 'needs to change' to solve the problem. In addition, by wanting Joe assessed, they implicitly suggest that Joe also needs to change or 'be fixed' to bring about the necessary change.

The father and the son are at the visitor level of motivation with respect to coming to therapy, perhaps with Joe being most so. The father acknowledges that there are some problems but sees these as being a normal part of childhood and certainly not warranting any particular professional intervention. Joe appears to be the least involved and least consulted about the problem and the unusual suggested means of solving it – coming to talk about it with a stranger!

Engaging the family

As is the case in the family in Case Example 3.2, individuals at different levels of motivation about the same problem are often in conflict with one another. Different complainants blame one another about the source of the problem. Complainants frequently criticise visitors about their laziness and irresponsibility and visitors frequently see complainants as 'causing the problem' by their over-reactions or how they approach the situation. These negative interchanges are rarely helpful and lead to increased defensiveness and polarisation. In order to engage the different participants in this drama, it is important that the therapist does not reproduce any of the above 'critical dynamics'. Inadvertently, many therapists resort to cajoling and haranguing visitors to become more involved in the therapy and to 'confronting' complainants to take responsibility for their own actions and to see their part in the problem. Such dynamics are 'more of the same', only repeat unhelpful patterns that go on in the clients' lives and are unlikely to be bring about change. Indeed, they are likely to cause clients to drop out of therapy, feeling more defensive and blamed and less likely to engage again. More subtle and personalised approaches, tailored to the clients level of motivation, are called for. The aim is to create the conditions for complainants and visitors to move into a customer level of motivation.

Engaging Complainants

People at the complainant level of motivation can feel burdened and powerless in the face of the problem. They need first to be supported, nurtured and understood by the therapist before they can become customers. They are not ready yet (as customers are) to consider how their own actions 'cause' the problem (or the solution) and unlike customers will experience any 'do something differently' tasks as an extra burden. The first stage for the therapist is to constructively understand where the client is at and to establish a supportive alliance with them.

In Case Example 3.2, both the mother and the teacher are at the complainant level of motivation. It is important not to 'take sides' and to rather adopt a non-blaming, empathic response towards both their positions. You can empathise with the mother about how difficult it is to manage a small child and how upsetting it can be when you worry about whether something is wrong. You can compliment her on her concern for her son, which has led her to take action to sort things out (and come to therapy). You can empathise with the teacher about how difficult it is to have one child disrupting a whole class and how unsupported she can feel in managing this. You can appreciate how she has initiated the referral, the detailed report she has provided and how she has helped motivate the family to attend.

It is important to appreciate the different views that the mother and teacher have about the issues, and to do that in a strengths-based, multi-partial way that opens possibilities for teamwork and collaboration. For example, you can agree with the teacher that a firm as well as positive parenting is necessary for Joe at home, and you can agree with the mother that Joe needs to be positively supported and given every chance at school. In addition, you can acknowledge with both the teacher and the mother the fact that despite their differences they have already worked together as a team for Joe's sake in initiating the referral.

Transforming complainants into customers often involves a painstaking re-examination of the data; the aim is not to ask the client *to do differently*, but *to think differently*. The search is for exceptions and coping skills, not previously noticed or thought important, but which reveal the client's effectiveness in the face of the problem. The therapy is like a journey through the desert looking for an oasis, or a long search for 'buried treasure' (George, 1998), which the therapist inspires the client to believe is there, waiting to be discovered. Once these gems have been found and client credit taken for them, workable positive customer goals are easier to establish.

In Case Example 3.2, to elevate the mother's level of motivation, it is important to take her initial goal of wanting her son assessed seriously (rather than argue with it). You can agree that it is a very good idea to try and get a helpful understanding of the situation, but explain that you need her help in doing this. As you explore the situation, be on the lookout for exceptions – times where she was able to manage and cope with Joe's behaviour (for example, she might find that if she sits with him and guides him how to play with other children, there is less aggression) and co-construct with her helpful ideas about what was happening during these times (for example, understanding that Joe was not simply 'aggressive' but rather particularly shy and awkward in dealing with other children, or that Joe has particular attention problems, such as ADHD, which cause him to act in this way). Make sure that she gets credited with these exceptions (for example, for her skill in guiding Joe in play and her sensitive understanding of him).

A similar approach can be adopted when consulting with or providing feedback to the teacher (either on the phone or in a face-to-face meeting). The aim is to include and value the teacher's contribution in an assessment and in any plan to create a solution. For example, if a diagnosis of ADHD is used to explain Joe's special needs, you can explain to the teacher that in your (as well as research!) experience, teachers make a critical contribution to helping children with these special needs in how they structure their classrooms and relate to the individual child. (A diagnosis such as ADHD can also be very helpful in getting extra resources for a teacher, for example, a teachers assistant.) As with the mother, in consulting with the teacher it is important to search for exceptions – times the teacher does make a difference in the classroom with Joe – and to give her credit for these.

Engaging visitors

Rather than confronting the visitor about being 'not motivated' about a certain goal, the solution-focused therapist works hard at trying to validate and understand their underlying positive intentions. The aim is to uncover a goal they are willing to work on, to discover what they want to do, rather than clarifying what they don't want to do. In Case Example 3.2, the father's perspective can be validated – he does not want his son to be labelled negatively and he wants to try and sort out the family problems independently of therapy. His perspective does not have to be validated in opposition to that of the mother, but rather as different and equally valuable: she wants to find ways of understanding and managing her son's behaviour and he wants to do it in a way that does not negatively describe his son and which fosters the family's independence – both valid parenting goals.

Though visitors can often be viewed as 'not cooperating' with the therapeutic process, this does not take into account the 'small steps' of cooperation they have already made. For example, in Case Example 3.2 the father, despite his reservations, has come along to the first session (or if he does not attend this meeting, it can be acknowledged that he has not blocked his son's attendance). His motivation to do this can be explored constructively: perhaps he is there to support his partner in managing his son, or because he has an open mind to try something new.

Engaging children

A special group of clients who are generally at the visitor level of motivation are children. Like Joe in Case Example 3.2, other people have decided for them and they often feel 'tuned out' in the therapeutic process. We need to be especially accommodating, as therapists, to engage them. Simple things like showing them around the therapy room and the selection of toys can make a difference. When interviewing a family with a one-way screen or video, it can be fun and put children (and the parents) at their ease by taking time to show them this in operation. The therapeutic process needs to be sold to children in a way they can understand, for example, 'When you come along we have time to play with whichever toys you want, and we have time to talk about worries and anything you want to make better in your family.' In addition, many children fear they will be 'told off' in therapy. Taking in problem-free interaction, in play or in conversation, finding out what they are good at or enjoy doing can help create a different expectation and thus an alliance from which a customer contract can be established.

As discussed in Chapter 1, the more often therapists can use children's language and slow the session down to proceed at their pace, the more children are willing to become involved. Directing a family therapy session at the child's level often benefits the parents as well as the child. It helps parents appreciate their child's perspective (often the most valuable aspect of therapy), and simple child-like language can ensure that everyone is on board. Being child-like as a therapist can benefit all the family members (at least that is my excuse!).

The initial positions adopted by young children

As well as generally being at the visitor level of motivation, young children respond with varying degrees of openness to the therapeutic process and to the questions of the therapist. John Wheeler (2001) has described three positions that young children initially adopt towards the therapist:

1   **Hello Mister! What's your name?**

Though these children may be unclear about the reason they are here or what 'therapy' is all about, they are friendly and sociable with the therapist and ready and open to answer questions. They like the attention the therapist gives them and are generally cooperative, willing to do activities and to try out what the therapist suggests.

2   **You can play with me if you want to.**

These children are a little bit more wary of the therapy and the therapist. They are often reserved in the session, as they feel nervous or out of their depth. They tend to tune out and play by themselves with any toys in the room. As they are often undemanding and seem not to be interested in the therapeutic process, they are often inadvertently excluded from the conversation. It can be easy for therapists to inadvertently ignore these children as they engage in 'important adult conversation' with their parents.

It does pay great dividend, however, to take time to engage these children and to work hard to include them in the therapeutic process. They prefer the therapist not to be too direct, nor to ask too many questions, as this can make them feel under pressure and cause them to withdraw further. To engage these children, it is important to give them plenty of time to settle in the session and to proceed gently and indirectly. For example, it can be useful to join with them in a play activity of their choice or to sit alongside them as they play with toys, gently joining in by making comments on their play or asking to help. These children usually appreciate creative and activity-based ways of communicating (see next section) rather than simply answering questions. They take a little time to open up and to be drawn into the therapeutic process.

3   Go away and leave me alone!

These children are usually set against the idea of coming to the therapy and actively set about 'tuning out' or sometimes being disruptive. Because they can be difficult in the room, they are often excluded from the meetings as therapists arrange 'easier to handle' meetings with their parents. It is much more effective, however, to work hard to include them. It can help to acknowledge how difficult it is for them to participate and the worry about being blamed or punished that may underpin this. It is important that you accept their position and tell them that they don't have to answer questions if they don't want to. Trying to strike a deal with them by giving lots of choices can help gain their cooperation. For example, if the child doesn't respond to any questions or comments, you can ask 'Would you like to answer questions or would you prefer your Mum to tell me first what happened?' It is helpful to try and put them in charge as much as possible, for example, you can say 'If I ask a question that is too hard or too upsetting, will you tell me and I will ask another?' Your aim is to be as sensitive and respectful as possible to encourage them to open up and participate. Sometimes you have to 'prove yourself' to these children. For example, one eight-year-old boy I worked with, who did not want to come to the session, finally agreed to talk if the video to the team room was turned off. A few minutes into the session, he made an excuse to go to the toilet, and doubled back into the team room to check that indeed the video was turned off. I commented on this when he returned, 'Oh, you wanted to check that I had turned off the video as agreed?' and he nodded. After this he became a little more cooperative in the session. It is also useful to use rewards with these children. For example, if they answer a couple of your questions, they will be able to then play their favourite game. Or if they cooperatively complete the session, they can get a treat such as soft drink (agreed with the parents in advance).

If a child does 'act out' or become disruptive in a session, rather than simply ending the meeting, it can be beneficial to work collaboratively with the parent to manage this problem. If you stay with the parent and child in the room, remaining calm, respectful and firm, this can provide helpful modelling to the child and great support to the parent (see Chapter 9). Sometimes a short time out or five-minute break from the session can help. Children often change their stance quite quickly and are prepared to re-engage after a short break. At a later stage, it can be helpful to reflect with the parent and/or the child (if he or she is open for this), about what happened. Parents often find it useful if the therapist acknowledges how they felt during the disruption. For example, I might share how difficult I found the disruption and use this to empathise with the parent. In my own experience, these moments, when handled correctly, can be turning points. The parents can feel supported by the fact that I have witnessed some of the behaviour that they deal with all the time and the child can feel glad that we got through it to the other side in a respectful way. This can result in a deeper alliance with both parent and child.

For example, when doing a home visit with a five-year-old boy and his mother, the boy threw a big tantrum and refused to go to school. Though this was difficult, I stayed with the mother and child to support them through this. Eventually the boy calmed down and we were able to strike a deal with him about going to school. Later I met briefly with the mother to reflect about what happened and I acknowledged how difficult the situation was, complimenting her on how she coped. At a group session, the mother spoke about it to the other parents, saying how supported she felt because she knew that wasn't just her, that she knew other people would find the tantrum difficult too. The fact that she got through to successful resolution was a breakthrough for her.

Summary

In this chapter we have considered the process of engaging families both before and during the first consultation. We have discussed how critical it is to establish a spirit of collaborative partnership from the outset and to see decisions regarding the goals, methods and contexts of the therapy as joint ones between you and the family. We discussed the importance of being sensitive to client motivation, acknowledging that different family members may be at very different levels of motivation or engagement with the therapeutic involvement and will call for quite different responses from you as the therapist or professional. We then considered the special case of children and adolescents who almost always are brought to the therapy at the request of another person and thus require a special sensitivity and professional approach so that they can be invited to become full participants. In the next chapter we will further consider how to engage children and adolescents, in particular by using play and structured activities.

4 Becoming Child and Adolescent Centred

I liked therapy best when there was a lot of playing and only some talking.

An eight-year-old girl

I preferred it when I didn't have to answer too many questions. I hated that. I liked it better when we did stuff on the computer together.

A 14-year-old boy describing his experience of coming to counselling

Counselling or working with children and adolescents therapeutically is a very different process than counselling adults. Children inhabit a different world than that of the adult and are at a different developmental level. They don't share the adult preference for language and verbal communication and the rules of adult conversation just don't apply to how children relate. Children like to communicate through play and creative activities as well as through conversation. Even adolescents who may appear to be more able to engage in adult conversation are at a transitional stage in their lives and share many of the preferences of younger children for structured activities and indirect and imaginative forms of communication.

In this chapter, we discuss how therapists and professionals can make their practice more sensitive to the developmental level of children and adolescents by including structure and creative activities in their work. Making therapeutic practice more child and adolescent centred is advantageous even when working with parents or other family members present for a number or reasons: first, by simplifying the language and slowing down the pace of the session, we ensure that all adults are on board and that they understand what is going on. Second, child-centred language and activities can be much more fun and playful and it gives the family a space to enjoy each others company – an excellent fringe benefit of effective family therapy. Third, parents often find it valuable to observe the therapist communicating in a child-centred way with their children, and they can learn a lot from this skills modelling. Finally, by making the session child-centred, you give parents an insight into the feelings and inner world of their own child, which is often the most valuable aspect of a therapy session.

Communicating and talking to children of different ages and developmental levels

A child of five would understand this. Send someone to fetch a child of five.

Groucho Marx

Grown-ups never understand anything for themselves, and it is tiresome for children to be always and forever explaining things to them.

Antoine de Saint-Exupery

Below, we describe three broad developmental levels for children and the particular issues raised in trying to communicate with them. Though age ranges are given, these are to be taken very flexibly as there is much overlap between groups. For example, many six-year-old children have significant speech and language difficulties (even if not formally assessed) and relate to adults in a manner that is more appropriate for a younger child. The converse is also true and many preschool children are able to engage in imaginative reflective exercises and to ask challenging verbal questions. What counts is that we tailor our communication style to the child, in front of us. In my own experience, therapists and counsellors tend to over-use verbal language and adult communication styles and do not take into account the developmental level of the child.

Young children aged two to five

The verbal language of preschool children is underdeveloped and most of their communication is non-verbal, via gestures, facial expressions and behaviour (including crying and tantrums!). When engaging with preschool children, therapists need to be sensitive to the way they communicate and be prepared to join with them at their developmental level. This means simplifying verbal language as much as possible and backing it up with gestures, body language, facial expressions and so on. Indeed, many problems between parents and preschool children are simply based on misunderstanding communication. For example, one mother relayed a story of how she was trying to give her three-year-old child a spoonful of medicine and he kept spitting it out. The mother continued to tell him to swallow it and he kept spitting it out. She was becoming frustrated, when it suddenly dawned on her that he didn't know what the word 'swallow' meant. As a result she then demonstrated what she meant, by taking a spoon of water and swallowing it herself, emphasising the throat action to the amusement of her child. Her child eagerly then followed suit, swallowing the medicine, and delighted at having a new game with his mother!

In addition, preschool children are concrete in their thinking and immediate in their behaviour. It is difficult for them to make links between past and present behaviour. For example, if you see a child sharing and you want to reward them, unless you do this immediately or shortly after (using verbal and non-verbal language), the child is unlikely to make a connection between the two events and the lesson is lost. Working therapeutically with preschool children it is generally more effective to focus on here-and-now interactions rather than recalling previous events. For example, in the Parents Plus 'the Early Years' Programme (see Chapter 9), when working with a parent whose goal is to 'manage better their child's oppositional behaviour', we try and enact this in the therapeutic room (by asking the parent to play with their child and then tidy up) and then support the parent and child in the here and now in managing this problem (and making a video to review later). Alternatively, if a parent is having difficulty with a breakfast or homework routine, it can be useful to do a home visit to witness the problem as it happens and thus support the family in the here and now.

Video review is very helpful to parents, but it can also can have a powerful effect on young children, even those with little language. For example, a two-year-old boy (referred due to behaviour problems and attachment difficulties) became fascinated by a video of him playing and sharing with his mother, and he would play the video over and over again, reinforcing the happy experience between him and his mother. The mother and therapist further reinforced this experience by naming and commenting on what was happening as he watched, for example, 'Oh look, you are smiling at your Mum and she is smiling back' and so on.

Children aged five to ten

Though children at this age have a better understanding of verbal language, they can find the cognitive questions, often used by adults talking to them, taxing to answer. Depending on their ability, they may find it difficult to answer therapeutic questions such as 'What were you feeling then?' or 'What would you like to happen next?' and therapists might receive quite a few 'dunnos' to verbal questions. Often it is better to approach these questions creatively. For example, you could show children pictures of different feeling faces and ask them to pick one that matches how they feel now or yesterday. (You could make an initial game out of the feeling faces, asking them to match the facial expressions themselves or to guess which face matches a character in a story.) Alternatively, rather than cognitively asking children what they want to happen next, you could ask them to paint what they see in a crystal ball or read a story that matches with different endings asking which one they like the best.

At this age, children like to communicate through play and imaginative activities and will engage in lots of creative therapeutic activities such as artwork, playing with puppets and figures and role play. In many ways, this is the ideal age for play therapy, as children are old enough to grasp the purpose and meaning, and young enough not to feel inhibited or awkward. Children at this age are also able to talk and reflect about what is happening in their play and this is a crucial part of therapeutic work. For example, when a child is role-playing with puppets she may talk about what is happening and it may be similar to an event in her own life. Gentle therapeutic comments and questions can be helpful. For example, if one of the puppets is being bullied or attacked, the therapist can ask how the puppets are feeling or what does the puppet need to happen to feel better?

Thus, working therapeutically with children between five and ten involves having a balance between playing and talking, between activities and discussion, and between structure and free time. The children are able to communicate both symbolically and through talking, and it is best to include both in a session. As the eight-year-old girl quoted at the start of the chapter said, 'I liked therapy best when there was a lot of playing and only some talking.'

Adolescents aged 11 to 16

On entering adolescence, children gain the ability to think about the world in much more complicated ways and can become more verbal and accustomed to exclusively using language to express themselves. Coupled with this is a period of intense change for the adolescent as they struggle with issues such as independence from their parents, sexuality, self-identity, peer pressures and friendships and pressures about study and school. Friends and peers play a critical role in the lives of adolescents and they will often seek support and information from these circles rather than the adult world. In addition, adolescents are generally more willing to challenge and confront their parents and other adults as they seek more involvement on the road to independence.

Though they may be intellectually more able to communicate, they may also become more private, self-conscious and awkward. While an eight-year-old boy may be relatively open and trusting with adults, the same adolescent might be more suspicious, confrontative or secretive. One 13-year-old boy would become awkward and embarrassed when asked personal questions in a face-to-face conversation. Building on his interest in computers, he was much more predisposed to answer the questions when they were part of an interactive computer questionnaire, with the therapist sitting beside him as a support rather than in front of him asking questions.

Generally, adolescents like to be treated as adults and thus be full partners in the therapeutic process. More than younger children, it is important to consult and involve them in the decisions about how the therapy proceeds, for example, whether it is family or individual (see Case Example 3.1 from Chapter 3). Confidentiality is an issue that needs to be thought through carefully. As the adolescent is becoming an adult, their privacy from their parents needs to be respected and the professional needs to think through if and how information is reported back to parents. This issue is quite dependent on the context in which you are working as a professional. For example, children often see school counsellors without parents necessarily being informed, while in a child mental health setting, parents are generally involved from the outset.

Accommodating adolescents in the therapeutic process is about accepting where they are at developmentally, and using this as an opportunity rather than as an obstacle. For example, with a rebellious adolescent who challenges every step of the therapeutic process, it is important not to be defensive or rigid, but to take time to listen carefully to their objections and to negotiate alternatives with them. Transparency and a negotiation of the 'rules of the therapy' is an important process with adolescents. Indeed, this often becomes a substantive part of the therapy, hopefully helping them learn respectful negotiation! Alternatively, if an adolescent is extremely awkward or unforthcoming in a conversation about feelings, it is important not to see this simply as a contra-indication, but to change track and use other indirect forms of communication. For example, one 11-year-old boy would simply answer 'dunno' to every question the therapist asked about his rows with his parents, but he was elaborate in conversation when asked about football and his successes on the field. The therapist later used the football as an indirect way of talking about managing conflict. For example, he explored with the boy how he was able to keep his cool when tackled on the field or how he was able to be team player, or how he was able to accept instruction from his coach. This became a metaphor for managing his conflict at home.

Finally, though adolescents are more verbal than younger children, it is important not to over-rely on conversation and to include activities and exercises as well. For example, many adolescents will consider doing art or answering a questionnaire or even doing a role-play during a session.

Engaging children and adolescents with creative therapeutic activities

Play therapists are experts in using creative media to engage children in therapeutic conversation. Ideally, they work within a designated play therapy room that has access to sand and water play, painting and artwork, dress-up materials, dolls, puppets and construction play materials. While as a professional working in a different context (such as a child protection worker or a family therapist) you may not have access to a designated room or such an elaborate range of materials, it is still important to have access to some creative activities to complement verbal conversation in order fully to engage children and adolescents. In my own work in child mental health I have a 'toy cupboard' that contains a number of versatile activities that I draw upon in my work with children and adolescents, which I list in Box 4.1. Far from being comprehensive, the list reflects some of the ways I routinely use to use to engage children and some of the 'tools' I draw upon to advance therapeutic work. For readers interested in exploring in more detail the use of play and creative materials with children and adolescents, please see some of the excellent texts such as Geldard and Geldard, (1997) and Schaefer and O'Connor (1983).

Box 4.1 Creative therapeutic activities

- Construction materials.
- Artwork and drawing.
- Reading and story books.
- Worksheets and workbooks.
- Puppets and figures.

Construction materials

Construction materials such as clay, play dough, blocks, building bricks (for example, LEGO) are probably the most versatile of toys giving children an opportunity to interact with tangible objects and to make things without pre-defined rules. They are highly appealing to a broad range of ages from preschool children and even to young adolescents (who often love to manipulate clay). They can be used by very young children, who simply like to feel and manipulate the materials, and with older children who can construct things and use the materials imaginatively to tell a story. Therapeutically, they can be used to engage children in relaxed play and are excellent ways to provoke language and communication. In the Parents Plus 'the Early Years' Programme (Chapter 9), we recommend construction materials for parent–child play as a means of helping parents and children connect in a relaxed way, opening up communication and thus promoting children's language and development.

Artwork and Drawing

Artwork and drawing are very versatile therapeutic activities and appeal to children and adolescents. This can range from 'free art', when children are invited to draw from their imagination anything that comes to mind, to 'structured art exercises', when children are invited to draw about certain situations that are the concern of the therapy. For example, a child may be asked to paint a picture of their family, a happy time at home, or a picture of a happy time in the future. A very useful resource in structured artwork is *The Anti-colouring Book* (Striker and Kimmel, 1979). This contains a huge number of imaginative drawing and art exercises, whereby children are invited to complete a picture with ideas from their imagination. Some of these exercises have obvious therapeutic benefits, for example, when the children are invited to complete a picture of their family crest, or to draw a picture of the future in a crystal ball, or to draw a picture of their nicest dream or worst nightmare. Other pictures have more subtle benefits, such as the invitation to draw a picture of the possible front of a newspaper, when the child has performed a heroic deed or for the child to draw a picture of a trophy he would like to give someone. Other pictures are simply designed to be fun and stimulate the child's imagination, such as the invitation to draw what the flowers might look like on the moons of Jupiter or to draw a picture of an exotic fish just discovered by explorers. As a way of building rapport with a child it can be very useful to let them thumb through the book and select one of the drawings he or she would like to try. Case Example 4.1 illustrates the benefit of drawing.

Case Example 4.1 Drawing out a solution

William was a seven-year-old boy who was cared for by his maternal grandparents, as his mother was a drug addict who lived a chaotic lifestyle on the streets. The mother did not have any regular access to William and periodically would drop in on the family 'out of the blue' (about once every six weeks). His grandmother had tried to regularise access but to no avail, and was very concerned about the effect on William of these unorganised visits as he often would get distressed afterwards and have nightmares, though say little verbally. The grandparents wondered about stopping the visits and brought William to therapy looking for advice on how to proceed. After an initial meeting alone with the grandparents, the therapist saw the family together for subsequent meetings (though it was not possible to include the mother). William was shy about talking, so the therapist invited him to do some drawing. William responded to this readily and in the first meeting drew two pictures of things he liked at home. In the second session, the therapist suggested he do the following sequence of solution-focused drawings:

1 Something you enjoy doing or something you are good at.
2 A special wish that you would like to happen.
3 Draw a happy time recently when you were closest to the special wish.

The therapist gave William time and space to draw each picture in turn and then gently invited him to talk about them. For the first drawing William drew a picture of himself playing football with his brother and his grandfather. He spoke readily about this, much to his grandparent's pleasure (who witnessed the discussion). For the second drawing, William drew a picture of his family including his mother at home together around a table eating dinner, and for the last drawing he drew a picture of his mother being by the door of the house, with him being in the inside window looking outside. He spoke a little about the pictures, identifying each of the people in them.

The grandparents acknowledged that they, too, wished that the mother could come home to live with them and that she had 'broken their hearts'. They recognised that the third drawing might represent the last time his mother had called unexpectedly. They had not let her in as it was late and they thought it would upset William. They thought he had not noticed that she had called.

After the session break, the grandparents said they had reached a decision. They said they felt they should try to make the most of whatever contact the mother made. They will keep trying to organise things in a stable way, but felt it would not be in William's interest to turn her away.

Reading and story books

Story books centred on a therapeutic theme are very useful when working with children of all ages. The combination of pictures and words, the act of storytelling by the therapist or parent, and the fact the story can be read many times, all make the experience memorable for children. Working with children as young as two, books can be used to help cope with life transitions, such as, for example, going to preschool (Garland, 1995), learning to use the toilet (Ziefert, 1999) or learning to sleep in their own bed (Perversi and Brooks, 1998). Books can also be used to help children learn social skills, such as sharing with other children (Hughes, 1993), understanding their own feelings (Anholt and Lawrence, 1994), or making friends (Thomas, 2000). Specialist books can also be used for specific therapeutic problems, such as helping children cope with serious medical problems (Mills and Chesworth, 1992) or to understand their transition to foster care (Blomquist and Blomquist, 1990).

Books can be read to the child either by therapist or parent (or both, as repitition is very helpful for young children). A useful model is for the book to be introduced by the therapist in the session and then given to the parent to read with the child at home. In reading the book, it is important to give the child time to interact with the experience, to look at the pictures, to read as many of the words that they can and to raise their own comments and questions. Essentially, the book acts as prop, to facilitate children in expressing their feelings and in providing them with an opportunity to talk to the therapist (and to their parents) about certain issues.

Though books are generally not used in the above way with adolescents, similar therapeutic advantages can be gained by watching and reviewing videos. For example, in a 'social skills group' snippets from videos of popular teenage films that highlight issues of friendship and relationships (positive and negative) can be shown and then debated and discussed in the group. A skilled therapist can use the adolescents' knowledge and interest in the films to encourage sharing and self-reflection within the group.

Worksheets and workbooks

Worksheets or workbooks that combine questions and art for the reader to complete are excellent therapeutic tools, especially for older children and adolescents. These can be used as a way of building up a therapeutic relationship with a child, or to encourage children to reflect about events, or to help them build up a picture about their lives. The 'All About Me' workbook, developed in Dublin, invites children to answer a series of questions and to draw pictures about their lives and family backgrounds, such as 'Who is in my family?', 'What are my likes and dislikes?', 'Where is my favourite place?', 'Who do I most like to talk to?', 'What are three things I like best about myself' and so on. These workbooks are particularly relevant in life story work with children in care, to help develop a sense of themselves and their family background and to maintain connections with important people (Ryan and Walker, 1993).

Worksheets can be adapted to any therapeutic theme to suit a child you are working with and can be imbued with a strengths-based theme. For example, a child can be invited to write out (or draw) his three wishes for the future, to list his strengths and the people in his life who are his supporters, and then to draw on a 'road map' the various stages on a journey towards his goals and hopes. In addition, there are many workbooks on the market that creatively combine pictures and thoughtful scenarios to engage a child around a particular theme, such as bereavement (Heegaard, 1988) or parental separation (Heegaard, 1992).

The only caution about using workbooks is that they require a degree of cognitive ability on the part of the child and thus may be less suitable for younger children or for children with special needs.

Puppets and figures

Puppets and figures of people and animals are very helpful therapeutic tools for a number of reasons. First, children naturally will play with these toys without instruction or prompting from adults. Second, they encourage the child to be creative and imaginative; any games they create with the figures are their own and don't follow predefined rules. Third, they invite the child to tell stories that are about their own lives; children will naturally project their own feelings and thoughts onto figures and puppets and enact scenarios which mirror scenarios in their own lives. Finally, they require less cognitive ability than worksheets and can be used therapeutically with very young children.

These toys can be used in free play with children, when the therapist simply follows the child's lead, commenting on his actions with the toys, 'Oh, you are putting the man in the doll's house', and interpreting when appropriate 'I notice you have locked the door to keep the Mummy out'. The therapist can invite the child to talk about feelings and to tell a story with comments such as 'I wonder what the Mummy feels being lock out?' or 'I wonder what the Mummy wants to happen next?'

Therapists can also use puppets and figures to guide or influence a therapeutic session. For example, a therapist can invite the child to choose an animal from the box that is most like him (or another significant member of his family) and then ask, 'Tell me about the tiger (or whatever animal is chosen); what is the tiger like?' Such an indirect approach can help a young children talk about themselves and their relationship to their family. Alternatively, the therapist can start a story with the figures, for example, 'This bear is sad, because the other animals won't let him play with them,' and then invite the child to continue the story. In the Dinosaur Programme (see Chapter 8), a highly-structured social skills intervention for groups of children aged six to eight, the therapists use puppets with predefined personalities to communicate with the children. For example, rather than the therapist talking directly to the children about the group rules, Dina the dinosaur (who is in charge) is brought out to discuss the rules and to reward the children for keeping them, while Wally and Molly (brother and sister puppets) are brought out to discuss (and role play) the problems they have getting on with one another. The use of puppets in this way can be more compelling and engaging to children, rather than adult conversation alone. Case Example 4.2 illustrates communication using role play with a telephone.

Case example 4.2   Phoning home

Jenni was a seven-year-old girl who was taken in to foster care two years earlier due to neglect and who was now being considered for a move to adoptive parents. There was concern that she was ready to move on and she was seen by her social worker for a number of therapeutic sessions. Jenni would readily play with all the toys and materials in the play room, but would rarely bring up her feelings about changing home or what she wanted for the future. The social worker tried to engage Jenni in these conversations using different worksheets or books, but she showed little response.

During session two, she discovered two phones in the cupboard and became quite excited by them and asked 'Who can I telephone?'. The social worker said that they were magic phones and she could pretend to phone anyone she wanted. Jenni picked up the receiver and said 'I want to phone Amy (her birth mother)'. The social worker entered into the game and pretended to be the mother on the other phone. Jenni engaged in a conversation asking her mother how she was and to make sure she was well. She then asked, 'Why aren't you looking after me at home?'. This opened a brief conversation as to how Jenni had come into care. After a minute, Jenni put down the phone and returned to playing with other games.

Jenni returned to the 'magic phones' in other sessions and they became an important way for her to indirectly ask questions about things that worried her. On one occasion she phoned her mother's social worker, wanting to know that she was doing her job to make sure her mother was being looked after, and on another she phoned her adoptive family saying what she wanted when she came to live with them. The phones became a safer way for Jenni to ask questions and one she was in control of. If she wanted to end the conversation she simply put the phone down (and the social worker learnt not to push her with questions when she was not on the phone).

Summary

Children and adolescents communicate in different ways than adults, and professionals need to accommodate this in their approach if their work is to be successful, either seeing the child alone or in the context of their family. In this chapter, we have briefly outlined the stages of development, of preschool children, school-age children and young adolescents, suggesting how therapeutic conversation could be adapted to include them. We have also described some structured activities and creative media, such as art, worksheets, books, puppets and figures, that therapists could easily integrate into their practice in order to make it more child and adolescent centred.

5 The Structure of a Strengths-based Session

When meeting children or families it is a good idea to have a 'map' in mind for how to structure the meeting. Whether you are a psychologist conducting a formal assessment in a child mental health clinic, or a social worker providing a brief telephone consultation with a distressed parent, or a care worker having an informal meeting with a young person in a residential home, having a sense of the overall shape of the meeting helps to ensure a therapeutic benefit. Indeed, much research suggests that the contribution that psychotherapeutic models make to client change is less to do with their techniques or theory *per se* and more to do with the helpful therapeutic structure they give to the meetings. As Miller et al. (1997: 184) state, 'Studies conducted to date suggest that one of the best predictors of negative outcome in psychotherapy is a *lack* of focus and structure' (Mohl, 1995). Thus it seems that the fact that a professional sets time and space aside to be with a client, with a specific focus and a specific structure such as a beginning and end, in itself can be very helpful. Though session maps provide therapeutic signposts for conducting a meeting, it is important not to over depend on them. They remain as flexible guidelines to help a professional proceed therapeutically, and always they must be adapted and tailored to the client's needs and priorities. In addition, as a collaborative strengths-based professional you can be fully transparent about the 'session map' you are using. If it is helpful to the client, it can be useful to discuss your approach and to negotiate changes if necessary.

A 'roadmap' for a strengths-based session

In this chapter, we outline a simple 'roadmap' that you can use to structure a strengths-based consultation with a child or family member. The map can be used to give an overall shape to all types of professional consultations, whether this is a two-hour formal family assessment or a five-minute telephone consultation with another professional. The map consists of the four stages as shown in Box 3.1.

Box 3.1   A 'roadmap' for a strengths-based session

Stage 1: Joining
Stage 2: Establishing goals
Stage 3: Reviewing progress
Stage 4: Clarifying next steps

The steps described are not always in this sequential order and there is considerable overlap. For example, after reviewing progress at Stage 4, the client may decide that he wants to revise a goal and thus you return to Stage 3. Or when at Stage 4, reviewing next steps in a family session, you may return to Stage 1 to join with an adolescent who has only now begun to speak. The stages really provide essential elements of a strengths-based session, rather than a sequential or step-by-step guide.

Progress through the stages can be aided by a series of reflexive questions for therapists that let them know whether the therapeutic session is on track. For example:

- Have I joined/connected sufficiently with each person present?
- Have we established a well-formed goal that we are working on together?
- Have I clarified and appreciated what progress the clients have already made?
- Before we finish, are we clear about what the next steps are, both in terms of the clients goals and the expectation for ongoing professional contact (if any)?

In the remainder of this section, we describe in more detail some of the issues involved at each of the different stages. We also highlight a number of sub-stages which are often helpful, though not essential, to consider.

Stage 1: Joining

As discussed extensively in Chapter 2, a critical variable in successful therapy is the ability of the therapist to join with and form an alliance with the family. The quality of the therapeutic alliance is the platform on which all therapeutic progress is built. As discussed in this chapter, the forming of this alliance starts well before the first session. Thinking carefully how you engage families in the context of their communities, ensuring that you have respectful and inclusive initial conversations with referrers and family members as you decide how best to proceed, and ensuring that this attitude of respect and collaboration comes across in any appointment letter and advance information, are all important 'pre-steps' in the formation of a constructive alliance.

Coming to see a professional can be an unnerving experience for clients, especially if they have never attended a similar service in the past. Even if they are 'therapy veterans' they may not know what to expect from your service, or if they do they may have unrealistic expectations about what you can and can't provide. For this reason it is very important to explain the process to them in advance, whether this is in the appointment letter or verbally before the session begins. Sometimes both are necessary and valued by clients. In my own practice in a child mental health clinic I find the following explanation useful at the beginning of a first consultation. The explanation usefully comes after introductions and some problem-free talk with the clients.

> Thank you for coming in today. Let me explain what will happen in our meeting and see if that is OK with you. Generally we initially talk for about 45 minutes. We talk about the problem that has brought you here today and what you would like to be different. We also talk about solutions you have tried and discuss what you think needs to happen next. We then take a break, which gives you a chance to think about what we said and think how you want to take things forward. We (the team) will also have a discussion and try to answer any questions you have and see how we can be helpful. We will then come back together and share ideas and discuss what way you want to proceed. The whole process should take about one and a half hours.

Even when conducting a brief consultation over the phone with a parent it is worth taking a few moments to connect with and join with this person before beginning the business of the conversation, whether this is enquiring about and appreciating things that are going well in their lives (see Chapter 2) or taking time to explain the process above. For example, one parent who felt generally blamed by professionals for her son's extreme behaviour problems, really appreciated when I took time to ask her about her parenting of her other children, who were succeeding in school and making her feel proud.

Stage 2: Establishing goals

Clarifying the problem to be worked on
Sometimes clients, immersed in the presenting problem, are not immediately able to shift to establishing goals. In these cases, it can be useful to listen carefully to their narrative to understand the problem from their perspective. While in solution-focused therapy the focus is mainly on moving to the solution, in my own experience it is often necessary to have built up an empathic connection with clients before they will shift from 'problem talk' to considering goals and exceptions. Carl Rogers (1951, 1961) described how it was necessary to have created the core conditions of empathy, unconditional positive regard and genuineness in the therapeutic relationship before growth and change could be facilitated in the client. For some

clients this can be a quick process and a solution-focused working alliance can be established early on, while for others it can take some time and more 'problem talk' before they feel understood by the therapist. This is especially the case if there has been mistrust between the client and therapeutic services in the past. In my own work context, it is very common to meet parents who feel very dissatisfied with their previous contacts with child mental health services, for example, if they did not get diagnosis when they sought one, or if they felt blamed for their child's problems, or if they did not get the practical help they sought. In this situation a mother may describe her experience as below:

Mother: No one seems to understand how difficult he is to manage. Do you know that yesterday he smashed my only remaining piece of china, for no reason at all?

Therapist: That must have been terrible; it sounds like the china was important to you.

Mother: Yeah, it was. [Pause] He's just so impulsive and unpredictable.

Therapist: Sounds like things can be very difficult at times.

Mother: Yes, and I want to get something sorted, this can't go on.

Therapist: You really want to get things sorted, you want things to change.

Mother: It has to change both for his and my sake.

Therapist: [Pause] You sound very motivated to make a difference for, as you say, both your sakes.

A strengths-based approach to listening contributes greatly to overcoming blame, to the creation of trust and to establishing a working alliance. The therapist listens carefully and sensitively within the clients' narrative for strengths, skills and resources, for what they are doing right rather than what they are doing wrong. Every therapist statement to the client should reflect and imply these potentials and strengths. In the last example, instead of the therapist simply saying 'This is a very difficult situation for you' he can add 'and it sounds like you have been persisting and trying to make a difference for many years now.' The latter statement frames the parent's stance as a resource and begins to identify 'persistence' and 'motivation' as qualities that can be used to build a potential solution.

Goal setting In Chapter 2 we described how helping clients formulate positive, detailed, realistic and personally meaningful goals is a key aspect of a strengths-based approach to therapy. These client-centred goals become a compass to guide the entire process. When clients start with problem descriptions, the aim is to uncover the goals and preferences that are inherent in their stories. The aim is to 'gently nudge' or orient clients towards thinking about goals, rather than the effects of the problem they are immersed in. The question becomes, 'What way would you like things to be different?' or 'Instead of the rows, what way would you like things to go each evening with your child?' As discussed in Chapter 2, the aim is to elaborate these goals in as much meaningful detail as possible. Consider the above example continued below:

> *Therapist*: Sounds like a very difficult situation at the moment ... what would you like to be different?
> *Mother*: I would just like some peace.
> *Therapist*: Some peace, that's sounds nice ... What would this peace look like? What will you be doing when you are peaceful?

Therapeutic goals As well as establishing the clients' goals and preferences that emerge from the problems and difficulties they are facing, it is important to establish what their goals, hopes and expectations are for the professional help they are seeking from you at this time. Essentially, you are trying to establish and agree a realistic goal for your work together; you are trying to determine your part in helping them reach their life goals. Much confusion occurs in therapeutic work, when clients and professionals have differing expectations about the work. For example, the work will run into conflict if, as a professional, you believe you are providing family therapy to help the parents communicate more effectively with their children, when actually the parents are seeking a psychological assessment of their child which they can use to get educational help in school.

When consulting with another professional, much confusion is caused when there are conflicting expectations for your respective work. For example, a psychologist may be consulting with a teacher believing that his role is to provide consultation and support regarding classroom management, while the teacher believes the role should be about doing direct work with some of the identified children. Therapeutic progress can be curtailed unless respective roles are clarified and an agreed therapeutic goal established.

Stage 3: Reviewing progress

In this part of the consultation, the therapist begins to explore some pathways to a solution that the family have attempted thus far. The focal question becomes: 'How have you tried to solve the problem/make progress towards your goal in the past – what has worked best?' The therapist is interested in exploring with the family the best solutions and ideas that the family already have access to. Coping questions can be asked to elicit the strategies that clients have already taken to solve the problem. In the last example, useful questions might be:

- How did you manage when he broke the china?
- How do you cope when he throws a tantrum?
- What happens eventually?
- How do you get him to stop?

Exceptions to the problem can also be identified and explored in elaborate detail. Supposing, for example, a mother remarks that her child is a little quieter in the evening, the therapist can become curious about this and elicit more detail with questions such as:

- That is interesting, isn't it – what do you think makes him quieter in the evening?
- How do you bring this about?
- Tell me more about your routine in the evening. What exactly happens then?
- Who else notices that he is quiet then, what do they notice?

As discussed in Chapter 2, the attitude on the part of the therapist is one of respectful curiosity. The therapist dons the role of a respectful investigative journalist, who views the client as the 'expert' in their own lives and who asks questions to elicit and learn about the client's knowledge about managing the problem in their lives.

When having a follow-up conversation or meeting a family for the second time, the stage of 'reviewing progress' becomes particularly significant. Questions are centred on what progress clients have made since the last meeting, and the orientation of the therapist is to explore and elaborate each example of positive change that the family describe. Change can be identified and reinforced using the EARS technique (Berg, 1994), meaning the therapist should first *Elicit* examples of progress, then *Amplify* and *Reinforce*, and finally *Start* again with a new example:

- *Elicit*:   What has been better? What's different?
- *Amplify*:   Who else noticed this change? How did you get the idea to do this?
- *Reinforce*: Wow, that's quite an achievement! How did you do it?
- *Start over*: What else is better? What else is different?

Formulating an understanding

> *In the beginners mind there are many possibilities; in the expert's mind there are few.*
>
> Shunryu Suzuki

Therapeutic progress often centres on helping clients generate constructive understandings and meanings that are more useful to them in making progress towards their goals. Referrals to therapy are often initiated when a particular question is raised or a particular understanding sought. For example, a parent may bring her family to therapy because she wants to understand why her teenager has suddenly become withdrawn or sullen. Or a teacher might seek consultation with a psychologist because he wants to understand what is underlying the poor progress of a child in his classroom. In some professional contexts, this search for meaning is very explicit and part of the therapeutic contract. For example, when children are referred to a child psychiatric service, the parents are often looking for an assessment of their child's developmental level or a diagnosis or explanation for the emotional or behavioural problems they see occurring. In the latter examples, the expectation is often that the professional will be an 'expert' and be able to provide a helpful opinion, assessment or diagnosis.

From a strengths-based perspective, formulating an understanding is conceived as a collaborative endeavour between therapist and client. Ideally, the aim is to facilitate clients to generate their own understanding, explanations and plans, though in many instances therapist ideas and input have a place, for example, where clients are explicitly seeking a professional assessment of their family's circumstances. Even in these situations, it is best to take time to elicit the client's understanding and ideas first by asking questions such as 'How do you understand what is going on in your family?' or 'What do you think is at the bottom of your son's behaviour?' before respectfully offering therapist explanations and formulations. Because formulation and diagnosis is such an important and controversial area in child adolescent mental health, we will cover it in more extensive detail in Chapter 6.

Stage 4: Clarifying next steps

If a professional consultation is to be useful, it must have some impact in the client's life outside the duration of the meeting. Thus, it is useful to allow some time near the end of a session for clients to think through how they want to move forward or what they want to happen next. Such a reflective or planning phase of the consultation can be introduced simply by stating something like:

> We are coming to the end of our meeting, so lets take a moment to pause and summarise what we have discussed, and to think how you want to move forward.

Or it can be introduced more formally by taking a therapeutic break (Sharry et al., 2001a, 2001b), for example saying:

> I'm going to suggest we take a five-minute break now. This is to give you time to think and reflect about what we have discussed, to pick out the important ideas that came up, or to make any decisions or plans. You might also like to think about whether this session has been useful and how you would like us to be further involved. While you're thinking, I will also think about what we have discussed (and consult with colleagues for their thoughts [if working as part of a team]). If you would like to hear some of our ideas and thoughts, please ask me when I come back.

Evaluate client ideas first   After an informal pause or a break it is important to follow this up with some exploratory questions, such as:

- So far, what ideas or thoughts have you had that you think you would like to take away from this meeting?
- Over the course of our conversation what has struck you as being important?
- What sense have you as to how you would like to move things forward?
- How did you find our meeting/conversation today? Was it helpful to you? (If so, what helped? If not, what could have been different?)
- What further contact would you like with me to help you continue to progress?

It can be useful at this point to make case notes. Recording client ideas in a written form gives them a special validation and status. Equally the act of writing slows down the process, reinforcing the key insights generated by giving them extra time and attention.

In many instances, time given to clients' own ideas is sufficient for them to gain insight into their situation and to establish a plan as to how to move forward. For example, frequently parents seeking advice on how to manage difficult behaviour in their children come up with the best cognitive behavioural ideas on how to proceed, with minimal input from the therapist, when they are given a little time to think through what has worked for them. Indeed their own ideas work better because they are formulated in their own words and are tailored to their own situation. For example, one 11-year-old boy who was in trouble over aggression at home (and who was also a good footballer), when given time to think during the break came up with two ideas on how to manage his temper. He said he would have to be like his football coach and 'talk himself down' when he got angry and also decide to go to his room if he felt things were about to flare up. In this way he had developed his own formulations of two ideas similar to many from cognitive behavioural anger management courses (such as positive self-talk and taking a time out), but these ideas were more effective to him as they were in his own words and they linked in with one of his strengths (being an able footballer).

Provide professional feedback if need be
Post-break also provides an opportunity for the professional to give particular feedback to the child and the family, whether this is in the form of a written formulation, a message from the therapy team, or an appraisal and summary of the session from his or her perspective. As we shall discuss in more detail in Chapter 6, from a strengths-based perspective this feedback works best when it is balanced, positive and empowering. In many settings it is appropriate for professionals to provide explicit suggestions and ideas for going forward.

Decide on what's next for professional involvement
Finally, the time post-break provides an opportunity to discuss with the client 'What's next?' and whether there is to be an ongoing treatment plan. Depending on the context, your work in this can include follow-up meetings to evaluate progress, or a range of therapeutic options from individual play therapy, to groupwork with parents, to referral to another more suitable agency (see Chapter 1).

Often it is useful to have outlined some options to the family prior to the break so they have time to consider the issues. In addition, they don't 'have to decide' during the meeting, and giving people a few days to think through the issues or simply planning to meet again before finalising a course of treatment is often the best way forward. Once again the spirit of collaborative partnership with the client is the overriding principle, and the decision of which course of treatment and what comes next is a joint one between you, the child and the family, best taken with deliberation at their pace.

Evaluate session with family   A final useful step at the end of a consultation is to 'check in' with the family members as to how they found the session. This can be done with a simple statement like 'I hope the meeting today was helpful to you; how did you find it?' before listening carefully to their responses and asking for extra details if appropriate. Not only is it useful to gain feedback from clients which can help improve professional practice, the simple act of checking with the family as to whether the session was useful is generally experienced as very respectful by them and maintains a collaborative therapeutic alliance.

Brief consultations with professionals

As discussed in Chapter 1, when working with families there are often many different professionals and services involved. Successful therapeutic work with families is generally based on successful collaboration between professionals and agencies. Many of the strengths-based principles that are crucial in creating collaboration with families are also helpful in collaborating with other professionals, even when there appears to be conflicting agendas and expectations. For example, it is useful to take time to join with and get to know a professional and to appreciate their unique perspective. It is also useful to emphasise common goals and intentions (such as the welfare of a child) and to draw on the respective strengths of each agency, rather than being critical of specific agency weaknesses or deficits.

Collaboration is aided when, as a professional, you seek to share credit for therapeutic progress and avoid attributing blame for 'stuckness' and problems. For example, just as we would seek to explain an improvement in a child's behaviour in terms of the child's or the parent's resourcefulness when talking to the family, so we would explore the teacher's contribution to this positive change when talking to the teacher (as well as reflecting about our own contribution as a therapist). Credit for successful change, exceptions or individual strengths can be shared among all those involved, and this is an important factor not only in reinforcing and celebrating change, but also in creating cohesion and collaboration.

The 'roadmap' for a strengths-based consultation discussed in this chapter can also be used a guide when structuring a meeting with another professional. Case Example 5.1 describes a telephone consultation with a teacher about the management of a child with behaviour problems.

Case Example 5.1   The 'carrot and stick' in the classroom

Pete was a seven-year-old boy brought to a child mental health clinic by his parents due to behaviour problems in school. Realising the critical purpose of Pete's school teachers in making progress towards a solution, the therapist was keen to gain their cooperation in the therapeutic process and to seek their support as potential allies to Pete. When the therapist spoke to the class teacher, she first relayed the numerous problems that were experienced in the class with Pete. She described how he was demanding, that he hated being told what to do and that he could 'lose it' without warning. The teacher was clearly stressed and the therapist empathised with her how difficult it was to manage a child who was acting out in a large classroom. A dialogue about explanations for the problems followed:

Teacher: 'Why do you think he is acting out the way he is?'
Therapist: I'm not sure ... from your experience of teaching him for the last four months, what is your sense of it?
Teacher: [Thinks] I think he has a problem with authority. He has a problem being told what to do ... there is a bit of an angry streak to him.
Therapist: And in your experience, because I'm sure you have come across boys who are similar to Pete before, what do you think is the best way to manage him?
Teacher: Well, I think he needs a carrot and stick approach ... he probably needs more carrots than sticks, because the sticks don't work.
Therapist: I think you have hit the nail on the head. He needs a balanced approach, but with a lot of positives or 'carrots'.

Continuing this direction in the conversation, the therapist began to explore how the teacher actually managed the problems on a daily basis. The teacher described how it helped if she gave him a lot more space. Pete responded well to being given choices, rather than being told exactly what to do. She also noticed that he responded well to responsibility and being given chores to complete in the classroom. She also noticed how she needed to keep him busy and to make sure he had something to do, such as a puzzle, if he finished his work early. The therapist listened carefully to these strategies and asked questions to elaborate them in more detail. They also explored what 'sticks' might work with Pete, for example, him having to leave the classroom and go to the head's office for a brief period.

The therapist then went on to explain the therapeutic work with Pete, describing how it was going to build on the 'carrot and stick' approach by giving Pete a space to reflect about his actions and by providing some extra 'carrots' for Pete to behave well, in particular helping Pete's mother set up a reward system whereby Pete would get stars for periods of good behaviour and special treats when he gained sufficient stars. The teacher made a comment in a light-hearted way, 'You (the therapist) get to provide the carrots, while I end up being the stick.' The therapist shared this joke and acknowledged that he realised that the teacher had the more important and influential role, and that is why he needed her support in making the therapy work. They went on to think through how in practical terms this might happen. The teacher agreed to set up a parallel reward system for Pete in the classroom. They also agreed upon regular telephone meetings to give feedback on the therapy and to supporting positive classroom strategies. During later consultations, Pete's behaviour had improved as reported by his mother and his teacher. The therapist made sure to identify each person's contribution for the change, in particular exploring with the teacher how her classroom management strategies had managed to work.

The consultation in Case Example 5.1 highlights a number of aspects of the important work of consulting with teachers. If the therapeutic process is going to have a positive impact in the classroom, then the inclusion of the teacher is critical to this. It is best to design the therapeutic approach to fit in with the teacher's 'carrot and stick' approach.

Some people might say that it is unethical to meet with the teacher separately, that such meetings should have the child and/or the parents present, that otherwise there is the danger of collusion or pitting one perspective against another. These are delicate issues. In my own experience, I think it is much better to be flexible about the type and attendance at meetings and to make these decisions collaboratively with the family. I believe it is equally 'unethical', or at least unhelpful, to insist on a family meeting with a teacher when the parents would prefer individual consultation.

Finally, it is possible to be non-collusive when meeting different parties from a family or system even when they are in serious conflict with one another. What counts is that you remain respectful and inclusive, both to the client in the room and to the client not present. You are seeking a deeper, more inclusive understanding that includes all the important perspectives. You are seeking a 'win-win' understanding rather than a 'win-lose'. In fact, I would suggest that maintaining a respect for clients not present will gain you respect and trust from the client in the room. A parent will be unnerved if you readily 'take their side' against a teacher. Rather than this increasing your alliance with the parent it may, in fact, diminish her trust in you, as on a deep level she may fear that when you have an individual meeting with the teacher you will take the teachers side in a similar way.

Summary

In this chapter we have described a versatile and simple four-stage guide for structuring strengths-based consultations and sessions with children, adolescents and their families. First, you need to ensure that you have joined with the clients and that you have an alliance with them. Second, it is important to establish a goal for the consultation that is meaningful and relevant for the client. Third, you need to devote time in the session to reviewing and making progress towards the goal, emphasising client strengths and resources. Fourth, it is useful to spend some time evaluating the session, reflecting on the ideas raised and identifying any next steps. These four stages are overlapping and thus best considered as elements of a session rather than a step-by-step guide. In the final section of this chapter we discussed how this model could be adapted in briefer consultations, in particular when consulting with other key professionals such as teachers.

6 Constructive Understanding – Formulation and Diagnosis

When you label me you negate me.

Soren Kirkegaard

Know your enemy well. Only then can you defeat him.

Anon

When I first worked as a solution-focused therapist in child mental health, I was very cautious of using expert diagnoses and labels, particularly those characterised by DSM-IV (American Psychiatric Association, 1994) and ICD-10 (World Health Organisation, 1992). Though such categories were dominant in the field of psycho-therapy, psychology and psychiatry, they struck me as pathological, limiting and unhelpful in working therapeutically. I preferred to work with the family and child who came to see me and collaborate with them in trying to reach a solution to whatever problem they arrived with, without having to use a psychiatric label to categorise and name the problem. Indeed, this was a view shared by many of my psychiatrist colleagues who were reluctant to diagnose a child, especially young children, with a label that could have long-term consequences. This 'unknowing' approach generally worked well and parents were happy to focus on getting help for their child without recourse to a formal diagnosis.

Over the years, however, this situation has begun to change. There has been a growing 'globalisation' and 'standardisation' of psychiatry and pressure to follow international standards set down in DSM-IV and ICD-10. The managed care system in the US requires labelling and diagnosis before a service can be provided, and the 'evidence-based practice' in the UK suggests that a child needs to be diag-nosed before they can be matched with a corresponding 'empirically validated treatment' for that disorder. While it is easy to take a critical stance towards such global directions (for reasons to be explored later), they have had an impact on the awareness and understanding of the families and children who attend services.

In clinical practice, there have been a growing number of parents who are aware of the various disorders and labels and actively seek them when attending services. For example, it is now very common when parents present with their children for them to have a question in mind such as 'Do you think my child has Attention Deficit Disorder?' or 'Do you think his social difficulties mean he has Asperger's Syndrome?' or 'Does his school difficulties mean he has a Specific Learning Difficulty?' Indeed, many parents arrive with their children at a clinic with a label already applied, looking for the appropriate treatment. For example, a parent might arrive asking for medication or social skills training for her child with ADHD. It is clear that labels such as ADHD or Asperger's Syndrome are very much alive and well known in the community. They have emerged as pretty strong social constructs and are widely used by parents and children as well as professionals to describe childhood problems. And rather than this being all bad, in some instances the label has been meaningful and beneficial to parents. For example, one mother I worked with who was struggling with very difficult behaviour from her 11-year-old son described how at times she would feel like 'strangling' her son. But then she would remember that he had 'ADHD and can't help himself'. This would help her be more patient with her son and get through a difficult incident. Another teenager I worked with described how, in retrospect, the label of 'clinical depression' was helpful for her because the problem had been named and it stopped her feeling that everything was her fault.

I came to realise that a simple critical stance towards such labelling or not taking part in the process of diagnosis was not necessarily the most helpful stance. As David Nylund (2000) suggests, trying to stop the labelling process is like stopping a fast-moving truck by standing in front of it! What is needed is to take a more understanding approach and to engage in a more respectful dialogue with the labelling ideologies. In clinical practice, it is foolish to ignore the diagnosis questions of clients and more respectful to start with where parents and children are at and to listen more carefully to them about the positive and negative impact of such descriptions in their lives. Then it is possible to collaborate with them in a search for constructive understandings that are more fitting and more tailored to their unique circumstances.

In this chapter we explore a strengths-based approach to formulation that centres on the creation of constructive understandings that may or may not include diagnoses but which aim to be helpful to children and families in moving towards solutions. First, we explore the implications of two important diagnoses: Attention Deficit Hyperactivity Disorder (ADHD) and Autism Spectrum Disorders (ASD).

ADHD – biological disorder or social construction?

Nowhere is the issue of labels and diagnosis more contentious in the field of child mental health than with the diagnosis of ADHD. This diagnosis has emerged as a popular category for children who present with such behaviours as impulsivity, over-activity, difficulty in sustaining attention, being easily distracted, and difficulty in following instructions, particularly when these difficulties occur in an educational or classroom context. The most common explanation is the biological/medical one, best exemplified by the work of Barkley who proposes that 'ADHD is a largely biological disorder that has a substantial genetic/hereditary basis' (2000: x). From this perspective, the 'disorder' is best assessed and diagnosed early and treated primarily with stimulant medication such as Ritalin, combined with social skills training and behavioural parenting techniques.

There are many critiques of the medical biological construction of ADHD. For example, the naming of the problem as biologically located within the child fails to take into account environmental factors such as those within family and school systems. The growth in the diagnoses of ADHD could simply represent the failure of family, school and society to accommodate and value the different ways of relating that highly-spirited, energetic and active children present with. The use of a pathological diagnosis like ADHD has a number of long-term negative implications for children, such as making them feel that there is 'something wrong with them' and they have no personal control over the symptoms. Furthermore, unlike other diagnoses which receive psycho-social treatments, the biological explanation of ADHD ensures that it is primarily treated by medication. Rightly, there is a real concern about medicating children, given the side effects and long-term implications. Often the dominance of the medical model is backed up by the claims of it being based on science or research studies. But when you examine these studies further, you can see that the results are not as solid and the claims are over-generalised (Nylund, 2000). Indeed, there is something compelling and attractive about brain-based or biological explanations, which appear to have the approval of an objective science, which cause to overlook more subtle and more individual explanations. In addition, many of the vested interests in the biological/medical model are often not examined. For example, the idea that ADHD needs to be diagnosed earlier and more widely can be viewed as a call for more psychiatry and more business for pharmaceutical companies. In the US, one of the national support groups (Children and Adults with Attention Deficit Disorder: CHADD) is funded by Novartis, the manufacturer of Ritalin, which arguably biases the organisation towards viewing ADHD as a disease that requires medication.

The social constructionist perspective challenges the notion of ADHD as a fixed biological entity. Rather, ADHD is conceived as a social construct that has evolved over time within our culture to explain a set of behaviours and inter-relationships which are open to other meanings and interpretations. As ADHD is neither a biological entity or an interpersonal problem, both explanations have a degree of validity. As Nylund states:

> Moving beyond a reductive, either-or distinction, I understand ADHD as a construct that is produced in a social context, which may include institutional, interpersonal, and biological factors. This view makes room for a wide range of solutions to ADHD symptoms and behaviour problems.(2000: 44)

The over-employing of the ADHD diagnosis to name certain behaviours, and the privileging of the biological explanation for these behaviours, does not allow for the emergence of more individual formulations and overlooks many alternative explanations that are equally valid and which may be more empowering to children and families.

Further, the cultural meaning of the diagnosis of ADHD, as distinct from other psychiatric diagnoses, is such that the diagnosis is likely to become fixed and long-term. For example, if a child receives a diagnosis of depression, generally parents and carers expect that with the appropriate support and treatment this will be a temporary problem and do not expect that their child will still be depressed in a year's time. If a child receives a diagnosis of ADHD, there seems to be the expectation that the child will continue to have ADHD in a year's time and so there will be continuing problems. This is not due to differing scientific evidence about differing rates of recurrance between children diagnosed with depression and ADHD. In fact, there are different studies that suggest that a significant number of children with either diagnosis will go on to have recurrent problems and be re-diagnosed with the same label as older children. (Just like there are other studies that show that many children originally diagnosed with either depression or ADHD do not receive this diagnosis as older children, as the problems have diminished. From a strengths-based perspective these are the children to study, as their experiences would shed light on how children and families overcome substantial problems.) What seems to be at issue is the cultural construction of diagnoses and labels, and thus the beliefs and meanings that surround them. Some labels are more fixed than others and have more serious long-term social implications for the holder. It is these labels that we must be cautious and judicious about using.

From a social constuctionist point of view, the aim is not to disband the biological/medical view of ADHD. Rather, the aim is to challenge its dominance as the only objective explanation and to allow parents and children access to a diversity of explanations and wisdom. Indeed, you do not have to use a formal diagnosis such as ADHD with a child and family in order to be helpful to them or to ensure that they access the appropriate support. Nor is the aim to argue that medication should never be used, but that it be presented as one of many possibilities, and be ethically administered. Put simply, the aim is to challenge the simple chain causality that moves from problem to diagnosis of ADHD to medication, and instead to open up more meaningful discussions.

Finally, while the social constructionist perspective may differ from the medical/biological/scientific one in its understanding of how diagnoses are created and maintained, the concern is often shared within practitioners of both paradigms to ensure that clients draw the most empowering conclusions from any diagnosis used. For example, Barkley, citing the genetic evidence, suggests that like qualities height and weight 'ADHD may simply represent an extreme form of a normal human trait and not a pathological condition in most cases' (2000: 74). He goes on to suggest to parents that they understand ADHD in the following way:

> Understanding that ADHD is just an extreme form of a trait we all possess and that it is something people 'come by naturally' should help everyone view ADHD from a kinder perspective. Your child is born with this problem; it is through no fault of his own that he lies at that position in the continuum. Likewise you should neither assign blame to yourself nor accept it from others. (2000: 74)

From Barkley's perspective the aim is to be non-blaming, to empower parents to become well informed and scientific, so they can make the best decisions regarding their child's difficulties, so they can take charge of their child's condition to ensure the best possible results. Whether you agree with the genetic biological model or not, the above understanding is a much more empowering and constructive version to take of the diagnosis, rather than the more limiting conclusions and meanings which abound.

Being on the autistic spectrum – disability or difference

I like being different. I would prefer being different to being normal. I am glad to have AS and I am proud of who I am.

Kenneth Hall (2001: 64) as a, ten-year-old boy
diagnosed with Asperger's Syndrome

There are a range of childhood disabilities characterised by social, communication and behavioural difficulties including delayed or problematic language development, attachment problems and a lack of reciprocity in social relationships, the absence of imaginative play, and obsessive, rigid compulsive behaviour. There are two major classification systems to describe these disabilities: the first is pervasive developmental disorder, which is the diagnostic label used by doctors according to the ICD-10 (World Health Organisation, 1992) and DSM-IV (American Psychiatric Association, 1994) medical classifications. It contains the subsections of autism, Asperger's syndrome and 'pervasive developmental disorder not otherwise specified'. It is distinguishable from children with speech and language disorders, though many of these children experience similar long-term social and communication problems (Lord and Rutter, 1994).

The second system is the 'autistic spectrum' proposed by Lorna Wing (1995). The autistic spectrum recognises that there is a group of children who experience social, communication and behavioural difficulties and who are *affected differently and to a greater or lesser degree by these problems*. Though two-thirds have an intellectual disability, one-third are of average intelligence and a significant minority (5 per cent) have special cognitive skills in certain areas. The spectrum includes children who have been diagnosed with autism, Asperger's syndrome, atypical autism and serious receptive and expressive language disorders. The spectrum concept is a useful one because it both highlights the common difficulties experienced by these children and families, while taking into account that each child is unique and different, with his or her own cluster of difficulties and strengths.

In recent years, there has been a massive increase in the number of autistic spectrum diagnoses being made. This is, at least, partially due to the broadening of diagnostic criteria to include children with milder forms, as well as greater awareness on the part of the public. It is likely that in previous years, families raised children who were different in this regard without recourse to formal diagnosis. Indeed, I have come across many adults who, in my opinion, fit the criteria for Asperger's syndrome, yet this term has never been used and is never likely to be used. Whether it would have been helpful to them as a child, or would be helpful to them as an adult, is indeed an open question.

Constructive understanding and diagnosis

Parent 1: 'I was delighted when they said "yes, there is a problem with Paul". It explained why I was having problems with him ... At least now he could get the right school.'

Parent 2: 'It didn't come as a surprise to us. It was a relief, even though it was something we didn't want to hear ... There was a honeymoon period after he got a diagnosis, he started the pre-school then and there was tremendous support.'

Parent 3: 'It was an awful shock ... Then you go through the stage of saying "Ah no they're wrong" and you read books about autism and look for other reasons like "he's just a bit slow..."'

> Responses of three parents to receiving the diagnosis that their child was on the autistic spectrum. (Taken from a qualitative study, Sharry, 1999b)

Whereas many parents receive a diagnosis about their child's disability at birth or shortly afterwards, parents of children on the autistic spectrum tend not to receive a diagnosis until the child is four or five or even much later. This is despite the fact that they may have been managing serious behavioural and relationship problems for some years. Though there are problems, it is not obvious as to what is causing them. Indeed, it is the 'invisibility' of the disability that often causes the parents the most problems. As one mother relayed, 'If my child had an obvious mental handicap, people would excuse his behaviour at a restaurant if he suddenly threw his milk on the ground and screamed. But because he looks normal, they think I am doing something wrong and can be very critical.' Parents whose children receive other diagnoses, such as ADHD, often similarly describe this sense of 'invisibility' of the nature of their child's problems, which causes a lot of unnecessary blame.

Some time ago, I saw a notice of a conference for parents of children with 'invisible disorders' such as ADHD, Asperger's syndrome and so on. Rather than insisting that having a debate about the fine details of diagnosis or looking for sub-type for their children, this conference centred on the common experience for these parents and the common needs of their children for special and appropriate education and support.

As illustrated by the quotes above, when a diagnosis finally does come, this can be greeted both with a sense of relief (that this could lead to better understanding and appropriate services) and sadness for the long-term implications for their child.

It is important to note that some parents also have no need for a formal diagnosis of their child's difficulties in order to understand what is at issue and to ensure that their child gets the appropriate services. As two parents in a previous study (Sharry) relayed:

> 'I was well aware that she had special needs ... I never sought a formal diagnosis. She was my child and I would deal with her.' (Mother 1)

'It's funny because I understand very little of what his diagnosis is. I understand very well what his special needs are … If I got a clear diagnosis I might see his limitations which I don't see now, I still think he can do so much more.' (Mother 2)

(Sharry, 1999b)

What is at issue here are the implications of the diagnosis. The parents in the above quotes are attempting to protect their children from the negative consequences of a diagnosis, and to continue to hold an optimistic view of their child's strengths and potential. What counts is not the diagnosis itself, but the broader understanding that puts it in context. As a strengths-based therapist, the aim is to co-create an understanding that may or may not include a diagnosis, but which captures the unique strengths and abilities of a child (as well as the deficits) and links child and family to appropriate supports and services. A core issue is whether autism is perceived as a disability needing services or as a difference needing a different response. Clearly, this question is one that each family and child must answer themselves, and which depends very much on the child's level of functioning (some children have very serious forms of autism, while others are only mildly affected). In addition, there does not need to be an either/or understanding. A child can be *both* different and individual *and* suffer from a disability. Once again, what counts is the personal meaning attributed by child, family and other significant people in the child's life.

Kenneth Hall, the boy whose quote starts this section, believes that the label was helpful to him. He states in his book:

When I was eight I found out about my Asperger Syndrome or AS and since then my life has changed completely. Before that life was very hard for me. I was always depressed. Life was depressing … I always knew I was different, that I wasn't quite like other children … When I heard that I had AS I was very pleased because I had been wondering why everyone else seemed to be acting strangely. So I felt a bit relieved … Things are much better and I understand myself better than I used to. (2001: 14)

He goes on to describe how the label has also has affected other people positively:

People help me and treat me better now. (2001: 15)

What seems to have made the difference in Kenneth's case is the constructive understanding that has been created by the diagnosis. This has not only helped him understand himself and relate to others in a more positive way, but it has also helped his family understand him and deal with him in a better way. He also describes in the book how the diagnosis of AS has also given him access to a supportive professional system. This constructive understanding is best exemplified by a core belief that Kenneth has about AS which he relays in a different part of the book:

When I first heard that I had AS I was sure that God must have a reason for making me different. I am still convinced about this. I also wondered what was God's special mission for me. I was quite determined to find out and I still am. Perhaps writing this book is part of it but I don't know. (2001: 16)

Box 6.1   To diagnose or not to diagnose – that is the question

One day a student asked Ike no Taiga, 'What is the most difficult part of the painting?' Taiga said, 'The part of the paper where nothing is painted is the most difficult.'

Zen parable

From a social constructionist perspective, taking a fixed position against or for diagnoses is not the most helpful stance. A helpful therapeutic stance is to suspend rigid judgments and to create a space of reflection where beliefs and ideas can be examined and their meaning in individual circumstances considered. For this reason, a knowledge of the poles of an argument can provide helpful boundaries for the therapist as they collaborate with the clients to co-create the helpful understandings of what is at stake, while deconstructing the negative implications and beliefs.

Disadvantages

• *Labels emphasise pathology and can be undermining to a client*
For example, a child who finds out that he has a conduct disorder may come to believe that he has a deep underlying problem and feel hopeless about change.

• *Can be limiting and self-fufilling prophecies*
For example, a child who is labeled with attention deficit disorder, may live up to this description and be more likely to behave in that way. In addition, often labels become fixed and have long-term consequences for the identity of the holder in that he can be over-identified with the problem.

• *They are unreliable and inaccurate*
A diagnosis is not an objective assessment. A child is highly likely to receive a different diagnosis from a different clinician (one clinician may propose the child has ADHD, another may believe it is an emotionally-based problem or an attachment disorder); many children receive multiple diagnoses (for example, 30 per cent of children with ADHD also receive diagnosis of oppositional defiant disorder). In addition, many children who present at clinics do not fall into any specific category and thus have clinical problems yet fail to fulfil the criteria for a formal diagnosis.

• *A label is reductive, while children are unique*
Each child and family is unique and a label cannot possibly communicate all the important and meaningful information relevant to the family. Indeed, it does not contain any information on the solution, such as their strengths, skills competencies and resources. Yet a label often blocks our ability to appreciate such positive attributes and causes us to focus on the deficits and problems.

- *Ethical issues – children do not choose their diagnosis*

Generally, in society we are happy with self-labelling. We believe in the right of people to name their own individual qualities and attributes and to define themselves in terms of these, whether they are simple personality attributions, such as being optimistic or pessimistic, or self-diagnoses' such as being an alcoholic. Indeed, in clinical situations it is more ethical to accept a client's self-diagnosis if that is helpful to them. For example, many people are helped by the decision to define themselves as an 'alcoholic' and to believe that alcoholism is primarily a chemical imbalance or a disease. Alternatively, other people exhibiting the same drinking behaviours may find it more helpful to describe themselves as 'heavy drinkers', a habit that they have developed over the years, in reaction to stress, which they now need to change. When people are given the freedom to self-diagnose or at least be collaborators in the process, not only is it more ethical, it is also much more effective. For example, imposing a label of alcoholism or confronting someone with the 'fact' that they are alcoholic is generally a counter-productive therapeutic strategy. In child mental health, the power to diagnose is seen as residing outside the family with a professional, usually a medical doctor. While parents may have some influence to seek a diagnosis, children are rarely consulted and never given the power of self-labelling. Though children are the most affected by a label, they are passive recipients and have the least power in deciding whether it is meaningful and helpful to them.

Advantages

- *Can sometimes provide a helpful understanding*

When presented to them positively, some teenagers diagnosed with Asperger's syndrome can find the label helpful in understanding their different way of communicating with others, and also putting them in touch with the support of others.

- *Can help people gain the support of others*

Clients gain enormous support from meeting others with similar problems and identified with similar labels. Support groups, organised around a label (for example, for parents of children with autism) can reduce isolation, helping people realise that they are not the only one, and increase coping. (Though it is important to note that parents can access this support without having a fixed diagnosis.)

- *Can help reduce blame and build cooperation*

The use of a label like ADHD can provide a helpful explanation to many parents who have been struggling with difficult behaviour in their children, that does not blame them for the problems and which can give some insight and understanding. This new understanding can help them cooperate with treatment plans and therapy.

- *A label can sometimes help parents and others to see children in a more positive light*

Prior to the identification of a specific learning difficulty, some parents can view their children's refusal to do homework or disruptive behaviour in school as 'wilful' or 'deliberately bold' and thus this can inadvertently lead to blaming and punitive response. The naming of the problem can help parents see their children differently, for example as having a disability that they must help them cope with, rather than simply interpreting the behaviour as opposition.

- *Diagnosis gives access to a large body of knowledge*

Diagnoses and labels form a common language for professionals and researchers, which has given rise to a large body of research outlining the problems and experiences of children and families affected by the most prevalent labels and diagnoses. Parents and children can also access this knowledge (via books), and for many this is very helpful to them.

- *Can help families gain resources*

When a child receives a label, this can help the family access much needed extra resources such as special education, or a remedial teacher or even financial help. Many special schools with extra teaching resources require a child to have a formal label before they will be admitted.

Formulation – a strengths-based response to diagnosis

Furious activity is no substitute for understanding.

H.H. Williams

Understanding human needs is half the job of meeting them.

Adlai E. Stevenson

As illustrated in Box 6.1, formal diagnoses and labels can have a number of advantages and disadvantages. What counts is not the label *per se*, but what the label means to the child, to the parents, to the teacher and to the wider network. It is the conclusions that are drawn and the beliefs that are formed which determine much of the impact. For example, a child could conclude that the diagnosis of Asperger's syndrome means that there is something fundamentally wrong with him, or he could see it as a way of explaining how he is different and use it as a way of communicating with other people. From a strengths-based perspective, the aim is to collaborate with families in order to help them create constructive understandings. If a formal label is to be used, then the therapist is interested in helping the family draw the best conclusions, interpreting the diagnosis in the best possible light (as a means to treatment and so on), and to deconstruct the negative beliefs attached to the label, minimising their impact. As framed by narrative therapists, the aim is to 'thin' the plot of the problem-saturated story of the child's life and to 'thicken' the counter-plot of the solution story. The aim is to provide a new story that reclaims the strengths and special abilities of the child and family (Nylund, 2000; White and Epston, 1990).

In this way, the process of formulation and diagnosis is an ongoing dynamic process. New meanings and new understandings are needed at different stages in the journey. It is when labels become fixed in time, reduced in meaning and rigid in definition that they are at their most pernicious. Though the initial intention may have been a constructive one, over time the names we give to problems tend to deteriorate in meaning to have more pathological associations. Sadly, I found recently that the term 'learning difficulty', which had been proposed to replace the more pejorative terms of 'mental retardation' or 'educationally subnormal', has also drifted in pejorative terms in usage among children. I heard in the playground one child tease another, 'Oh, and I bet you have a learning difficulty'.

The strengths-based therapist is interested in placing the *diagnosis in a context of a wider formulation* that includes an appreciation of unique circumstances of the child and family and provides information that is most helpful for them at that stage in their search for understanding and meaning. The formulation is a more elaborate description of the issues at hand that fits the evidence and is meaningful for all parties concerned, providing a constructive understanding that signposts progress or movement towards a solution.

The context in which a professional formulation is made can vary drastically. This can include a child mental health setting where a formal developmental assessment or diagnosis is requested, or an educational psychology setting where an assessment of a child's educational needs is sought by a parent in order to match him with the correct school placement. Formulation can also be used in psychotherapy and counselling settings, for example a summary report co-written with the client for the benefit of the referrer, or a narrative therapy letter co-written with a child, which emphasises his strengths and intentions, that is sent to a teacher or a parent in order to tell a new 'solution-focused' story about the child's life. Professional formulations are also sought in contexts where the child and family are 'reluctant' clients, such as the request to a social worker for a child protection assessment, or an assessment in the criminal justice system.

The following are some of the criteria for creating strengths-based formulations whether they are delivered verbally or in a written report and whether they include formal diagnoses or not:

- *Builds on and includes the clients ideas, understanding and language*
  The best professional formulations are really collaborative understandings that build on and acknowledge the knowledge of the clients. In writing an assessment of a child's difficulties it can useful to incorporate any helpful understandings that the family themselves have generated. For example, when assessing a six-year-old child with behaviour problems, it turned out that many of the problems started at the time of his grandmother's death two years previously. In conversation, the mother said that she felt the bereavement had 'knocked her son off track'. In a written summary sent to the mother and

copied to the school teacher (who had referred the boy), the professional used the mother's metaphor as an explanation for the problems and included in the report a number of suggestions as to how the boy and family could 'get back on track' again, many of which had also been collaboratively generated during the assessment.

- *May or may not include formal diagnosis*
A formal diagnosis is not always necessary in a constructive formulation, even in a formal setting. For many families gaining a constructive understanding without a label (perhaps in a written report) is sufficient to help them understand the issues and to access resources. One mother I worked with, whose child had a range of communication difficulties consistent with Asperger's syndrome, was clear that she did not want any label as she wanted her child to be seen for her strengths and not her weaknesses. In this instance, a detailed report that elaborated the child's special needs and strengths was sufficient to get her a place in a special school that the mother wanted.

  Sadly, there has a emerged a tendency towards production line assessment and diagnosis. Children and families receive a diagnosis such as ADHD, which has life-long implications, after an initial meeting with a professional. In many instances, it would be better to provide an initial formulation and to enter into a collaborative process with the family for further assessment and treatment. Timing is critical and it is important to listen carefully to what the child and family want and to go at their own pace.

- *Highlights the strengths as well as deficits*
A formulation which simply highlights the deficits of the child or the family is not helpful. The formulation should also highlight some of the seeds of the solution, such as the parents' close relationship with one another or the child's ability to play as part of a team in a football match. How qualities are framed or re-framed is also important. For example, we often pathologise mothers as having over-protective or 'enmeshed' relationships with their children. This can be reframed as demonstrating a desire for a very close relationship with her children, or indicating her efforts to protect them. Equally, a father's constant criticism of his children could be reframed as reflecting his desire for them to achieve their potential or his ability to see what they are capable of.

- *Gives meaning to the problem in a way that does not blame the people who are going to solve it*
A formulation that simply criticises the parent's management of the child and thus makes them feel blamed is unlikely to gain their cooperation to come to a parenting group. As a result, it is ineffective because we need the parents' cooperation for any change to occur for the child. Rather, a formulation that highlights their willingness to coming to an assessment and their strengths as parents is much more likely to be successful. Similarly, a formulation that implicitly criticises a teacher's classroom management may undermine her cooperation to a programme.

  Conversely, it can be helpful for a formulation to locate blame for a problem outside a client's immediate system. For example, many narrative therapists construct meanings with clients with anorexia that locate the blame for the problem in the discourses in society which oppress women and dictate to them about body shape. They invite their clients to bind together and take a stance against these oppressive discourses and to reduce their influence on them (Madigan, 1998).

- *Is inclusive and empowering*
  Put simply, we need an inclusive formulation that draws in and empowers all the people who are likely to bring about change whether this is the child, parent, teacher or extended members of the family. For example, if the formulation in a report emphasises the valuable contribution of the grandfather to childcare, this in itself can be used as an invitation to further involve this person in a treatment plan. Perhaps the greatest challenge is to ensure that a formulation is child centred and inclusive of children. Traditionally, many reports and case summaries are designed for exclusively adult circulation (sometimes the parents are not even included in the loop). Rarely is time taken to make the language accessible to children or to use the child's language themselves. As discussed in Chapter 1, however, making ideas simple enough for children to understand, and slowing the therapeutic process to a child's pace, helps ensure that everyone is on board (professionals, parents and children).

- *Gives pathways to the solution and ideas on how to move forward*
  A formulation is useless unless it contains the seeds of the solution or clearly highlights ways forward that the are accessible to the client. Even advocates of formal assessment do not recommend using diagnoses when they are not linked to treatment (Carr, 1999). Diagnoses should be used only when you have something to offer the client. For example, an ADHD label is of no value in itself and is of benefit to the child only when it is a gateway to treatment or resources, such as providing entry to a social skills group or to extra teaching resources at school, or if it allows the parents to have a less 'blaming' and more sensitive understanding of their son (see Box 3.1).

A constructive formulation is an ongoing, evolving work in progress. At its best, it represents the best possible explanation at the time, that is the most empowering and liberating to those most affected (notably the child and the family) and which fits well with the unique circumstances of the family, social and professional expectations. A good formulation changes as circumstances change and as the key players change. Indeed, it is something that may need to be re-constructed and re-formulated as the important evidence changes.

The creation of a constructive understanding is often a long-term journey for parents and children and this is particularly the case with young children with complex developmental delays, such as autistic spectrum difficulties (see the last section), which are not simply named and categorised. Indeed, these children and families are likely to encounter more than one (and often several) diagnoses and professional opinions along this journey. As a collaborative professional, it is important to join with the child and family wherever they are at and to help them make the next step in the path to understanding. This could be served by offering a formal diagnosis and formulation if that is required. It could also mean offering an open formulation and suggesting further assessments or treatments, for example, referring the child for a period of observation to a specialist preschool. It could also mean simply listening to parents and helping them ventilate their feelings and concerns or ensuring they access practical help and treatment, for example in the form of speech therapy or home help. The core issue is to be careful to go at the child and parents pace (which may be different), and to empower them to take charge of the process.

Constructive understanding and formulation – some examples

In Case Example 6.1, a formal label was helpful to the mother as it explained her experience, giving her a helpful understanding, and it gave her son and herself access to resources.

Case Example 6.1 A 'hyper' child

Joe, a four-year-old boy, was brought by his mother to a clinic due to his over-active and impulsive behaviour, which had led him to be excluded from a local preschool. On formal assessment, Joe was found to have significant delays in his development, particularly in his speech and language. His impulsivity and over-active behaviour (as reported by parent and teacher, and observed in the clinic) was also marked and consistent with a potential diagnosis of ADHD. In discussion with the therapist, the mother said she knew that Joey was a 'bit slow and very hyper'. The naming of his problems was a relief to her, as it explained the many difficulties she had in managing him. Exploring the implications of being hyperactive, the therapist realised that the mother did not see 'being hyper' as a life-long condition, as she had experience of a nephew who 'grew out of it'. The therapist added that many young children would make great gains, especially with good parent management and early intervention, in a special preschool. The therapist wrote a formal diagnostic report, highlighting Joey's special needs as well as including information on his family strengths, in particular his dedicated mother. This gave Joey access to a specialist preschool and his mother signed up for a parenting group, which she understood was designed to help her manage Joey's hyperactivity and difficult behaviour.

In Case Example 6.2, a negative interpretation of a diagnosis does not provide the parents with helpful information. When this is understood in the context of a constructive formulation, it becomes more helpful to the parents in solving specific problems.

Case Example 6.2   Sensitive behaviour

Julie was five when she was brought to the child mental health clinic due to her rigid and obsessional behaviour, which could also include difficult to manage behaviour such as biting and screaming in a high-pitched voice for several minutes. The parents took her for several assessments and professional opinions and the consensus among the professionals was that she was on the autistic spectrum. This was very difficult for her parents to hear as they saw autism as a negative long-term diagnosis, predicting only failure for their daughter.

Later, a strengths-based therapist worked with these parents in the following way. The therapist joined with the parents by honouring their refusal to hold a negative view of their daughter and their wish to be positive about her future and their willingness to do what they could to help her. He then established their goal, which was to manage Julie's difficult behaviour (especially the screaming) and to get her access to the right resources. Co-creating a constructive understanding with them, the therapist accepted their right to be agnostic about a fixed diagnosis and explored with them a new understanding of the situation. In relation to the screaming, they came to understand (over time) that Julie was extremely sensitive to change in her environment, particularly new and confusing sounds. They realised that loud sounds, not upsetting to most people, were very upsetting to their daughter. They could observe that much of the difficult behaviour was in reaction to these sounds, such as a door banging or a dog barking in the distance, or hating to be in the presence of a balloon in case it might pop at any minute. This constructive understanding, which flowed from a different interpretation of their child's autistic spectrum diagnosis, helped them take a more compassionate stance to the problem and to come up with realistic strategies to manage it. In addition, it opened the door for them to some useful interventions for Julie, in particular sensory integration therapy, which took into account her special sensory needs.

Even when no formal diagnosis is in question or likely to be used, therapeutic change is often centred on reaching new and more constructive understandings. This is especially the case when working with families and relationships, when often the most significant change is simply a new appreciation or understanding of the intentions and positive qualities of a family member. Consider Case Example 6.3, where a mother undergoes such a change in understanding:

Case Example 6.3   Being perfect

A mother initially attended a parenting group, telling the story of her nine-year-old son's awkwardness and negativity which led to him constantly refusing to do what he was told. Through the course of the therapy, she was invited to look for and encourage the positives in her son. She came to appreciate aspects of his personality that she had not appreciated before. She came to understand him as a sensitive boy who worried about things and who also could be very hard on himself, wanting to do things perfectly. She could identify that she also shared this 'perfectionist' side to her personality. She also began to notice his sensitive side appearing in how he could be kind and thoughtful in ways she had not noticed before. This new understanding helped her take time to be patient with him. She could view his misbehaviour differently, as caused by discouragement and anxiety, and was able to find ways of soothing and encouraging him. Though his difficult behaviour did not disappear, it was not the only thing in her focus and the good times grew in significance. She also came to appreciate a new understanding of her own abilities as a parent. She could appreciate her ability to 'tune in' and understand her son and could let herself off the hook and not blame herself all the time.

Professional misunderstanding

Therapeutic and professional work with clients can run into difficulty when the therapist's understanding of what is at issue differs significantly from that of the client, and particularly when the therapist's understanding inadvertently is critical of the client. What is required here is for the therapist to make a journey to acknowledge their own biases and to deepen their understanding of the client and their life situation in order to reach a more constructive view. Case Examples 6.4A and 6.4B describe this process in relation to a specific case.

Case Example 6.4A Different understandings

As part of an occupational health scheme, a solution-focused therapist was working with a client who presented as very depressed. He was on large doses of medication and had spent several periods in hospital. Currently, he was off sick from work, struggled with completing simple daily tasks and spent a large amount of the day in bed. The therapist followed the classic solution-focused model and established goals, exceptions and small steps the client could take, yet the therapy faltered. The client seemed to get more depressed, saying that nothing worked, and in the third session said he wondered about returning to hospital.

The therapist sought help from a supervisor. In exploring her view of the client and the problem, the therapist realised that she had the idea that client should make progress and that the depression was largely a psychological problem that the client should be able to combat by a variety of solution-focused/cognitive behavioural techniques. The supervisor suggested that the client, however, could have a very different analysis of the problem. To the client the depression could be experienced as a life-long disability from which there could be some periods of respite, but which would be with him constantly. While the therapist may not agree with that view of the problem (because of its pessimistic nature), it could be the worldview through which the client experiences life and a world-view that the therapist should attempt to understand and appreciate. Having conflicting understandings would lead to conflicting expectations and inadvertent 'blaming' if the client did not live up to them.

Instead the supervisor suggested that the therapist go back to the client and 'try harder' to understand and appreciate the client's view, to see the world from his point of view. In the next meeting the therapist began the discussion by saying ' I have been thinking about our work together and I wonder if I have misunderstood you. I wonder if I have not appreciated how difficult things have been for you ...'

Over time, this opened a discussion about the nature of the problem and the client revealed that he did have a largely biological view of the depression, believing that it was not amenable to 'psychological techniques' and that it was experienced as a life-long disability. With the cards on the table, the therapist was able to share his 'different' understanding of the problem (that he saw some evidence of the client being able to combat the depression and keep it under control) not as an imposition but as an 'offer' to the client. This frank discussion cleared the air and allowed the therapy to proceed.

Case Example 6.4B Different understandings and the reflecting team

The 'different' understanding described in the above case could also have been resolved in a collaborative way by using a 'reflecting team' approach (Andersen, 1987, 1992, 1995). Using the approach, and with the client's permission, the supervisor would be invited to attend or observe a session. At a break, the client would be invited to listen to the discussion of the therapist and supervisor who are pondering what is at issue for the client. The supervisor could present the understanding of the problem as a disability which the client was battling with daily without the support of others, and the therapist could present the understanding that the client was also, on a daily basis, finding ways of combating the depression, even though this was often unnoticed.

With the different views offered respectfully, the client evaluates the discussion as to whether either of the views expressed (or perhaps a combination) are helpful to their situation, as well as giving his or her own understanding and feedback. The advantage of a the reflecting team discussion is that it allows for differing views and ideas to be made transparent and offered in an open respectful 'both/and' way, rather than them becoming the subject of an 'either/or' debate between therapist and client. Such an approach is often very helpful when discussing complex childhood diagnoses with a family. The parents can be invited to witness the multidisciplinary team discussing the various perspectives and understandings on the diagnosis, while being collaboratively invited to contribute.

Summary

In this chapter we have explored how the search for understanding is at the heart of professional therapeutic relationships with children and families. We have discussed the collaborative role of the professional as a facilitator of the clients' knowledge as well as being a communicator of their own expertise. We have also discussed the thorny issue of diagnosis and labelling, and suggested formulation as a possible compromise.

From a social constructionist perspective, labels, self-definitions and the language we use to categorise one another are not fixed but rather are in a constant state of evolution. Working as a strengths-based therapist, the aim is to co-create with the child and family a constructive understanding or formulation that is a 'best possible description' of their problem, that is the most empowering and constructive, yet that fits with the evidence of their lives and provides a connection with traditional knowledge and wider social expectations.

In this way, the aim is to co-create a constructive understanding with the client that provides a helpful 'review' of the problem they have arrived with and a 'view' of the solution and goal they seek. Such an understanding can form a bridge between the problem and the solution and in itself can be remarkably helpful.

PART II:

SPECIFIC SOLUTIONS AND APPLICATIONS

---

7   Strength in Numbers – Parenting Groups

In previous chapters, we have focused on seeing children and parents within either individual or family meetings. The focus has been on intervening with the family group. In this chapter we describe a different way of intervening, notably inviting children or parents to join therapeutic groups with other unrelated clients who are coping with similar issues or who have similar goals.

Such therapeutic groups often have a lot of advantages and can be conceived as naturally strengths-based therapeutic interventions. For example, in well-working therapeutic groups clients have not only access to their own strengths and resources, but also to those of the other group members. In groups clients can receive the support and understanding of others who have coped with similar problems or felt the same way about issues, as well as taking on the transforming role of supporting and helping others. This act of helping and influencing others, which is not present in individual work, is enormously beneficial and the person who provides support often benefits as much as the person who receives it. Indeed, it is the simple interchange of support between members that is the 'engine' of a therapeutic group and the single biggest therapeutic factor. Further, groupwork can empower people to bind together to take on outside issues and problems – the whole can become more powerful than the parts – and great change is possible. Establishing a constructive therapeutic group, however, can be a difficult task, requiring careful preparation and skilled facilitation. As well as being crucibles of healing, groups have the potential to do some harm if a critical rather than a constructive culture is established. This chapter briefly describes some of the principles in establishing effective therapeutic groups, illustrating the ideas with two case examples of parenting groups. These ideas are described in much more detail in one of my previous books, *Solution-focused Groupwork* (Sharry, 2001b).

Therapeutic factors of solution-focused groupwork

TABLE 7.1   *Therapeutic factors of groupwork as distinct from individual work*

Group support	Clients can gain huge solace sensing that they are 'not the only one' to have felt a certain way or to have struggled with a certain problem. The simple interchange of support, compassion and understanding from peers – the hallmark of effective therapeutic work – is usually reported as the most valued aspect.
Group learning	Clients can learn a great deal from one another in a therapeutic group, both in gaining new ideas on how other people have coped with problems and from the interpersonal interaction and the feedback group members provide one another. In addition, in psycho-educational groups, the process of learning new ideas can be greatly enhanced with a supportive peer group.
Group optimism	In groups, clients witness other people who are solving or who have solved problems similar to their own and this can give them great hope that such change is also possible in their lives. Groups literally provide a sense of there being 'hope in numbers'.
Opportunity to help others	The opportunity to help others in groupwork gives members a chance to be of value and to contribute meaningfully to the group and thus be valued themselves. It also gives members a distraction from self-absorption in their own problems, and thus can give a new perspective.
Group empowerment	Group members with common experiences bound together in a common purpose can feel empowered to take on outside forces and to address the community and societal issues that they may not have been able to do alone. In addition, by being in a group with complementary resources, they can have much greater impact than as single individuals operating alone.

Groupwork provides a number of therapeutic advantages that are not available in individual work alone, and these are described in Table 7.1. Though there are these extra advantages, it would be naïve to see groupwork as superior to individual work. Groupwork has its limitations and is not appropriate for every client. For example, clients' individual goals and needs may get lost in the collective goals and needs of the group, or clients may be unable to connect with the group members of a particular group (who are from a different background or culture). In addition, the format or 'rules' of group intervention (interpersonal sharing with strangers, taking turns, confidentiality, fixed time and place sessions and so on) may not suit some clients and they may have their needs better met in more individual or family interventions. Unlike groupwork, individual interventions allow for sessions to be tailored exactly to a client's goals and particular requests. The format of delivery can also be flexible and altered to suit the needs of individual clients. For example, the pace of individual sessions can be slowed or increased, content can be altered to exactly what the client needs, and the time and place can be changed (for example, can switch to a home visit at a different time, if that helps).

For these reasons, therapeutic groups are best seen as part of a range of services on offer to a family, not seen as a replacement of other modalities such as individual or family work. Indeed, successful groupwork is often dependent on having parallel access to family or individual work. For example, in order to run a successful children's group, it may be necessary to have several screening/ preparatory family meetings as well as individual meetings with parent and child. Also, during the course of the group (and at follow up) it can be useful to have periodic individual meetings to maximise progress and to ensure that a group is working for an individual family. In this way group and individual interventions are complementary and interdependent rather than exclusive or competitive interventions. Having the option of collaboratively working with the clients to decide which combination most suits them is usually the best way forward.

Principles of solution-focused groupwork

Though there are similarities, the role of the professional in therapeutic group-work is distinct from that of individual work. The particular role of facilitat-ing a therapeutic group and the particular issues of applying individual solution-focused therapy principles to groupwork are explored in great detail in one of my previous books, S*olution-focused Groupwork* (Sharry, 2001b). For the purposes of this chapter we will briefly summarise the principles under two headings:

- The importance of preparation
- The role of leader and facilitator.

The importance of preparation

You are probably familiar with the expression that there are only three things you need to bear in mind when buying a house: location, location and loca-tion. A similar question could be asked about what are the things to bear in mind when running an effective group, and the answer would be preparation, preparation and preparation. So many groups fail or run into difficulty because they haven't been adequately thought through or prepared for. Professionals often think that running a group is a simple as inviting a num-ber of individual clients together at the same time and running the session along similar lines as an individual session. Yet this misses out the careful first steps of planning a group that appeals to your clients, involving them in the decision process and allowing time for the clients and the facilitators to prepare for the group. Case Example 7.1 describes the level of preparation that was necessary to ensure a successful parenting group at a community child and family centre.

Case Example 7.1   Preparing for a parenting group

Staff at a special school were concerned at the lack of parental involvement in the school. As a result Sue, the school counsellor, decided to run a parenting group and sent fliers to the parents about the group, due to start in two weeks. On the first night, very few parents came and they seemed to want different things from the group. As a result, the group never got off the ground and it was abandoned a few weeks later.

The following year, Sue allowed herself several months to prepare and establish the group. She initially consulted with the teachers about what they thought would be useful to cover in a group. She then consulted with the parents, both informally and formally, by sending out a questionnaire for ideas. She also met with the parents' committee and two of the members volunteered to help her facilitate the group. From her consultations, she found that there was support for a group, with the parents having a range of possible goals, including seeking medical information on their child's disabilities, input on language development, help on how to manage behaviour problems and so on. With her co-facilitators, Sue put together a six-week group that focused on different topics being covered each night, centred according to the parents' requests.

Sue and the committee spent the next few weeks promoting the group, sending out fliers to all the parents. Sue also made a particular point of meeting the parents who did not ordinarily reply to letters and whom she or the teaching staff thought could benefit from the group. The teaching staff also promoted the group by word of mouth, as did the parents' committee. As a result, a huge expectation and interest developed in the parenting group and large numbers attended. At the end of the six-week group, an ongoing parents' support group was established that met monthly and which took responsibility to work closely with teachers and to establish future parenting courses in the school as needed.

As described in Sharry (2001b), preparing to run a therapeutic group can be divided into four overlapping stages:

- planning and design;
- engaging and motivating clients;
- selecting and assessing clients; and
- preparing clients for membership.

Planning and design   It is important is to choose collective group goals that fit with the individual goals of your clients. As illustrated in Case Example 7.1, a group with the vague goal of improving their parenting may not fit with clients, as they may perceive it as stigmatising (implying that they are bad parents), but they are more likely to agree to group goals centred on the specific requests they have. Equally, it is important to choose a group method (or style of facilitation) that your clients are comfortable with and which fits with their expectations. For example, some parents may not be comfortable with a formal 'therapy group' format, but are more comfortable with a 'drop in' or informal style, or a group that is based around an educational activity. As in Case Example 7.1, the essential thing is to consult with your clients about what goals they have and what group they want. The more you can involve them in the planning and design, the more likely they are to come on board and the more likely the group is to be successful. Ironically, when we listen carefully and go with our clients' goals and preferences rather than imposing broad 'agency' goals, in the long term we are more likely to make progress towards these 'agency' goals. As in Case Example 7.1, the fact that the initial group was designed around the parents' own goals, facilitated them to become more involved and over time to participate in other groups and to be more involved in their children's education (which was the original goal of the school staff).

Engaging and motivating clients
As described above, if you design your group well to match your target clients' goals, consulting them in the process, you are already on the way to engaging and motivating your clients to attend. It is also important to be able to sell and promote the group. Being a salesperson involves skills that do not come naturally to a therapist, yet unless you are in the fortunate but rare position of having clients banging on your door to attend your group, you must be prepared to get out there and promote the group. This involves circulating positive information to prospective clients and referrer, making home visits and meeting with key referrers. The process works best if other people promote the group for you. Word of mouth from graduates of the group or content referrers is the most powerful promotion and gives the group great credibility. You can build on this by inviting graduates to be facilitators, or to write an endorsement or even to go out and promote the group for you (in many cases these extra roles can personally benefit the graduate as much as the promotion of the group). You can also include some of the target group members in the setting up and planning of the group, as was done in Case Example 7.1.

Selecting and assessing clients
In good preparation, you need to think through the membership of the group to ensure that the group mix will work well and that individual clients won't feel excluded. Essentially, this is about ensuring that clients have similar enough concerns and experiences and are from similar enough backgrounds and cultures so that they can feel accepted and connect with one another. For example, if you run a group that is mainly composed of middle-class, middle-aged couples, a young single parent may feel quite excluded in that group and be at risk of dropping out. Clients generally stay in a group if they feel a connection or identity with one or more of the other group members. In concrete terms, this means making sure someone is not the 'only one' from a significant minority, such as the only father, the only black person, or the only person with a child in care. If this is unavoidable, then you should discuss these issues openly with this client and prepare with them how to deal with it.

Preparing clients for membership   Finally, giving clients time and space to decide about and prepare for a group is generally a good idea. Just as ample preparation benefits the facilitator, so ample preparation benefits the client and helps ensure that the group is a success for them. This preparation can include giving out advance information on the group, revealing some of the teaching content in advance (if a psycho-educational group) and/or preparatory group or individual meetings. The aim of the preparatory meetings is to help clients articulate their personal goals and understand these in relation to the group goals, to ensure that they are well-informed of the group method (and accustomed to it), to anticipate any potential problems (such as not having a childminder for the time of the group, or a worry about not being able to read and so on), and to empower the client to begin the therapeutic process in advance of the group.

The role of leader and facilitator

The terms 'group leaders' and 'group facilitators' capture some of the extra responsibilities that face professionals running therapeutic groups. Professionals need to lead the group in establishing boundaries, such as the finishing and start-ing times, ensuring that rules are kept, chairing and moderating group discussion and ensuring that each group member is heard and gets a fair share of group time. While many of these roles can be delegated to the other group members, and the mark of a mature and well-functioning group is shared leadership, the profes-sional generally needs to be able to take a strong leadership role in the initial stages when rules are being established and at later times if problems in the group occur. For example, if one member became extremely distressed or if there was a personal attack between group members, then the group leader would have a special responsibility to take some control to resolve the situation.

Professionals also act as leaders to therapeutic groups in other subtle ways. How they interact with group members, the attitude they take and what they reveal about themselves all have profound influences on the group culture. For example, if a leader is confrontational or a 'detective of pathology' towards indivi-dual group members, then group members are likely to relate to each other in a similar manner (Yalom, 1995). Alternatively, if the facilitator is supportive towards group members and always seeks to highlight strengths and possibilities, then this will influence group members to act likewise. Potential group facilita-tors should acknowledge and own this influence and make sure they are a 'role model' for the desired group culture.

Group facilitation   Professionals running a therapeutic group also act as facilitators. Their role is to literally facilitate the interpersonal interaction between group members. As stated earlier, it is the interpersonal interaction, such as the interchange of support and the group members listening to and feeding back to one another, that is the 'engine' of a therapeutic group. This is the unique therapeutic factor that gives groupwork its power. Thus it is the special responsi-bility of a group facilitator to engage the ignition of the 'group engine'. Their role is to bring the group members together, facilitate the group conversation and then to 'get out of the way' and let them do the work.

So what is the best way to facilitate a group and to ensure that there is group interaction? This is a pertinent question as group members in the initial stages interact directly with the facilitator rather than with each other in a manner akin to a pupil–teacher relationship.

Encouraging group interaction Facilitators can encourage group interaction by simply asking questions that invite members to talk directly with one another. For example, if one member has shared a difficult problem with the group, the facilitator can suggest that other people offer support by simply commenting 'I'm sure other people in the group can identify with that experience,' and inviting other people to share. The facilitator can later ask those other members how they solved or coped with the problem and thus generate solutions for the original person. Perhaps the simplest way to invoke peer interaction is to open up discussion by asking 'What does anyone else think?' periodically. Often the facilitators' body language and eye contact is significant. If they scan the group and look to others to contribute, then they probably will. Consider the following example, taken from a parenting teenagers group, in which the facilitator draws in other group members, encouraging them to support a group member:

Alice:	And then he swore at me. My own son told me to **** off in public! [Starts to cry]
Therapist:	Oh, that sounds hurtful. I'm sure other people can understand how that must feel. [Therapist scans whole group, inviting others non-verbally to contribute]
Ger:	Yeah, when my teenager swore at me for the first time, I was upset for a week.
Ann:	Yeah, it's so humiliating.
Alice:	And you think you are the only one that this has happened to. That somehow you're to blame.
Ann:	You're definitely not the only one. [Lots of supportive nods from other group members]
Alice:	[Smiles]
Therapist:	It's important to realise you're not the only one.

In the above example the therapist activates the therapeutic power of the group by drawing in the other members to constructively acknowledge and support the first client. The support and understanding of fellow clients struggling with similar issues is of great importance and often more powerful than that of the therapist alone.

Parenting groups

In many settings, it is the parents, rather than the children and adolescents, who are most concerned about the problem and who are most motivated to seek therapeutic help. For example, a 12-year-old boy referred due to disruptive behaviour at home may minimise the problem, only grudgingly agree to come to the family meetings at the clinic and may refuse altogether to attend a group intervention (due to the stigma). This reluctance can be in spite of having highly-motivated parents who are willing to do anything to help their son or to make a difference. In these cases it can be useful to reduce the emphasis on individual work and to consider parent-directed interventions such as parenting groups. Rather than putting all your efforts as a professional into engaging a reluctant adolescent, it can more useful to take the pressure off and to work with the people who are the most motivated with regard to the therapeutic work (and who have a lot of influence) – notably the parents. This is in accordance with the strengths-based principle of working with the resources and strengths that already exist in the family system, rather than working hard to create new ones.

In addition, parenting groups can empower parents into action and help them find more effective ways of influencing their children, as well as provide them with the therapeutic support they deserve in their own right as individuals. Parenting groups should not be seen as being mutually exclusive or a replacement for family work or individual work with the child or adolescent. Indeed, a combination of modalities is often the most effective. Taking the example of the disruptive 12-year-old boy discussed above, as well as offering the parents a ten-week group, it might be useful to invite the boy to infrequent individual or family meetings (perhaps one at the middle and end of the group programme) in order to maximise his cooperation and involvement without over-pressurising him. In many cases I have worked with children and young people who, though initially very reluctant to engage, became curious about the process due to their parents' attendance at a group to the point where they actually asked to attend sessions for themselves.

There are a huge range of types and formats of parenting groups that can be offered from a professional setting. What counts is defining a collective group goal that fits with the goals of your target client group and is appropriate for your professional setting. Sometimes, groups targeted at a wide population are appropriate. For example, as a secondary school guidance counsellor you may offer a parenting group open to all the school parents with the general goal on the brochure of 'helping parents through the joys and challenges of raising a teenager'.

Sometimes specifically targeted groups are appropriate. For example, if you work in a child mental health setting, a parenting group that specifically targets the needs of parents of children with ADHD or Asperger's syndrome may be preferred by these parents, rather than a general parenting group, as it gives them a chance to meet parents with common experiences and facing very similar issues and to receive specialist professional input and information.

The format of parenting groups can also vary a great deal, and as a professional you need to decide what format suits your client group and setting the best. Sometimes, a relatively unstructured or open format works best, particularly in a setting where parents have pre-established relationships and some ongoing contact. For example, facilitating an ongoing monthly support group for parents whose child is attending a special school, you may keep an open agenda. Specific goals could be set each evening, depending on what issues the parents are facing. For example, one parent may be struggling getting their child to bed on time, another may be having difficulty getting the correct benefits or another may be wondering about future educational options. Group time can be divided between addressing these specific goals and supporting the parents concerned.

Sometimes a structured group format can work best, such as a six-week group for parents who have been bereaved or a five-week psycho-educational group for parents who are going through a separation or divorce. In the next section we consider the specific example of a structured parenting group that incorporates cognitive behavioural ideas within a solution-focused framework and which is targeted at parents dealing with difficult behaviour and conflict with their children and adolescents.

Case example – Parents Plus programmes

Behaviour and conduct problems in children, such as tantrums, defiance and aggression, are one of the main reasons that parents seek professional help. In many child mental health settings behavioural parent training, frequently offered in a group format, has been the treatment of choice. The Parents Plus programmes are video-based courses designed to help parents manage behavioural problems and establish good relationships with their children (Sharry, 1999a; Sharry and Fitzpatrick, 1997) and young adolescents (Sharry, 2001a; Sharry and Fitzpatrick, 2001). Focusing on helping parents reflect about and change how they respond to their children's behaviour (particularly encouraging the 'good' and ignoring the 'bad' behaviour), the programmes draw heavily from the behavioural tradition, though they also include ideas on effective communication from the humanistic tradition (Gordon, 1975) and on discipline using choices from the Adlerian tradition (Dinkmeyer and McKay, 1982). The ideas are introduced on video by professionals, illustrated by role-played parenting scenes and backed up by comments from parents about how these ideas have worked at home.

Format of sessions

Below is a sample session plan for a ten-week group using the two versions of the Parents Plus programmes: for parents of children aged five to ten; and for parents of young adolescents.

Session 1

1 Introductory 'getting to know one another' exercises and icebreakers.
2 Groundrule negotiation (for example, confidentiality, respect and so on).
3 Goal setting: what do parents want from the group? Parents are invited to complete goal setting questionnaires, share them in pairs and then share them with the large group.

4 First ideas: group brainstorms on what are the best ways to deal with behaviour problems. Facilitator then introduces the first ideas from the video, namely: one, 'pressing the pause button' and pulling back from excessive rows, and two, going out of your way to notice and attend to positive behaviour in your children (and in yourself as a parent) – to literally catch your child being good

5 Planning: during the following week, parents are encouraged to catch their children being good and also to notice times when things go well for themselves as parents.

Sessions 2–9 The middle sessions follow roughly the same structure:

1 Introduction.
2 Review of week: facilitated discussion of how each client got on during the previous week, attending in particular to exceptions to the problem, or times when they were closer to their goals for the group.
3 New topic: a new skills topic is introduced over the eight weeks as follows:

Parenting children group	Parenting adolescents group
• Play and special time with children	• Pausing to understand teenagers
• Encouragement and praise	• Connecting with your teenager
• Using reward systems effectively	• Getting to know your teenager
• How to set rules and help children keep them	• Empowering teenagers
• How to use active ignoring to reduce misbehaviour	• Communicating effectively: active listening and speaking up
• Using time out and other sanctions	• Managing conflict
• Solution building with children	• Negotiating rules and boundaries
• Bringing it all together – focus on real examples	• Solving problems together

4 Skills practice: in small groups the clients practice the introduced ideas using exercises and role-play with examples from their own lives.
5 Homework/planning: suggested 'homework' is given and in small groups clients plan how they will apply this in their own situation.
6 Conclusion and recap.

Session 10 – final session

1 Review of course material.
2 Review of course goals.
3 Planning for what next: what further support is needed to keep on track?

4   Award ceremony: to mark achievement thus far.
5   Group feedback: each member is given the opportunity to feedback to group and other individuals.

A strengths-based group process

Essentially the Parents Plus programmes are psycho-educational interventions, aiming to provide parents with information and ideas on effective parenting techniques, as well as supporting them to generate their own solutions and ideas. Central to this approach is a collaborative and solution-focused model of group-work (Sharry, 1994; 2001b). Parents are invited to adapt the parenting ideas communicated in the video to their own unique living situation and to identify and build upon their already existing examples of effective parenting. Whatever 'expert' ideas are introduced, clients still need to personalise ideas to their unique situation. The ideas provide a *starting point* for the solution-building process. The input is used to provoke clients into thinking through how the ideas may apply in their own situation, and to generate their own alternatives if they don't. The 'expert' ideas (from cognitive therapy or behaviourism and so on) are placed alongside the ideas generated by the clients in the group discussion with the aim of a finding a solution that fits their unique situation.

This process is described in detail in Chapter 3 of my previous book *Solution-focused Groupwork* (Sharry, 2001b), and generally consists of the following steps:

1   Predicting: encouraging clients to come up with ideas first.
2   Reviewing: reviewing with clients their views in response to presented ideas.
3   Finding fit: helping clients choose the ideas that fit for them.
4   Planning: helping clients plan how to adapt the ideas at home.

Let us consider Case Example 7.2, which illustrates the process in action.

Case Example 7.2   Pausing at the right time

Using the Parents Plus Adolescents Programme, the facilitator was introducing the first topic – 'pressing the pause button' – to a group of ten parents. This focused on the conflict resolution principle of not reacting angrily in conflict situations and instead pausing to step back from rows and disputes before they escalate. The facilitator proceeded in the following way:

Predicting

Before showing the video footage, the facilitator encouraged the parents to come up with their own ideas with the following questions:

Therapist: What is the best way to deal with conflict from teenagers?

Parent 1: If I knew that I wouldn't be here. [Laughter from the group]

Therapist: [Smiling] Yes, it is hard to manage ... but thinking about it now, what do you think is the best way?

Parent 2: Well, you can't let it get to you.

Therapist: Yes.

Parent 3: You have to remain calm.

Therapist: Ah, you have to remain calm. That certainly helps. In the video, we are going to look at how important it is to remain calm when dealing with conflict or, as it says on the video, to 'press the pause button'.

Reviewing

The relevant section of video was shown, which included parents and young people talking about how a calm approach worked best, as well as a role-played scene. The scene showed a mother initially confronting her son in an angry exchange over money going missing, before realising what was happening and then taking a deep breath to pause, saying ' I am too angry to deal with this, we will talk about this later'.

Therapist: So what do you think of this video piece? Do you think pressing the pause button would work?

Parent 3: I think it would. You have to remain calm, there is no use shouting and screaming.

Parent 2: Yeah, though it is hard, being calm is best.

Therapist: So though it's by no means easy, its best to try and remain calm.

Finding fit

The therapist now goes on to explore the idea in more depth with the group, helping them think through how it might apply in their individual situations. One of the parents raises a valid objection based on a difficult experience. Notice how the therapist listens empathically, offering support to the parent as they try to constructively understand what happened.

Therapist: Does everyone think 'pressing the pause button' would work, or does anyone disagree?

Parent 4: I don't think it would work. I tried it with my 14-year-old daughter and it didn't work.

Therapist: What happened?

Parent 4: Well, she came in late one evening; we got into a row. So I stopped it and sent her to her room. Then when I went to her room later, I discovered she had tried to kill herself by cutting her wrists.

At this point the therapist is a little shocked, as is the rest of the group, but proceeds in the following way to invite group support:

Therapist: Gosh, I am sorry to hear that. That sounds really scary to deal with.

Parent 4: It was.

Therapist: And I'm sure other people in the group can appreciate how difficult that must have been. [Therapist scans the other group members, inviting them to come in]

Parent 2: That sounds really difficult. I just don't know how I would deal with that.

Parent 5: It happened to me as well. [Therapist turns attention to Parent 5, inviting her to continue]

Parent 5: My daughter took some tablets a while ago. It was the most devastating thing. I felt it was my fault.

The group go on to discuss the fear of suicide and how to deal with this. At a later point the therapist reflects:

Therapist: So you have to be really careful in how you back off from conflict with a teenager; you have to make sure they are OK.

Parent 4: I think my daughter was so wound up at me because of the row, that is why she did it. I think she needed a bit of space before I got into discussing why she was out so late. I needed to pause earlier with her.

Planning

Having acknowledged the parent's experience, the therapist now helps the parent identify what she has learnt from what happened and how she wants to more forward.

Therapist: Ah, I see what you mean, you would have preferred to pause earlier. Your daughter needed a bit of space first.

Parent 4: If I was doing it again, I would not jump down her throat. I would listen first, see how she is and then deal with why she was out so late.

Therapist: You would listen and give her a bit of space before dealing with the problem.

Given the severity of the problem, the above case was difficult for the facilitator to deal with. Correctly, when challenged the facilitator did not impose a solution, but simply listened empathically, inviting the other people to offer support. By giving the parent some space, she was able to think through how she wanted to respond to her daughter. Coincidentally, the parent's idea of giving space and listening first to her daughter mirrored the facilitator's approach towards her in the group. It was also important for the facilitator to 'press the pause button' and to take time to listen to what was going on in the group.

Summary

Groupwork is naturally a strengths-based intervention, putting clients in touch with the support and resources of each other as well as their own. In this chapter we have described some the importance of preparation in establishing effective groups and highlighted the dual skills that the group therapist needs to possess, namely being able to lead and direct a group as well as being able to step back and facilitate group members interacting with one another. We have also considered the particular case of facilitating parenting groups, and illustrated some of these ideas with the example of the Parents Plus Programme. Central to this is a solution-focused group process that aims to harness the power of groups by inviting members to provide each other with support and encouragement as they work on specific parenting goals. In this way, parents have access not only to their own strengths and resources, but also to those of the other group members as well as the ideas contained in the course material itself.

8 Groupwork with Children and Adolescents

In the previous chapter we described some of the general principles of establishing and facilitating therapeutic groups, illustrating the ideas with a series of case examples from parenting groups. In this chapter we consider how these principles can be applied to the particular cases of establishing and facilitating therapeutic groups with children and adolescents.

Groupwork with children and adolescents is particularly useful in settings such as schools, colleges, after-school services or community youth centres, where as a facilitator you have a 'captive audience' and a big enough 'pool of referrals' from which to create a therapeutic group. In community settings, such as family centres and child mental health settings, it is possible to establish therapeutic groups, though these groups require more active parental involvement (for example, to take the children to and from the group outside of the normal school routine). Groupwork with children and adolescents has a number of advantages over individual work, facilitating the clients to learn from one another and to establish important friendships and connections. This is particularly the case when the presenting problem is inherent in the child or adolescent's peer group, such as drug use or bullying. In Chapter 1 we discussed how influential relationships with friends and the child's peer group become, the older the child gets. Whatever the parental or teacher input, a crucial factor in children's mental health or wellbeing is whether they are able to make friends and how their peer group at school treat them. In addition, adolescents are likely to gain much of their information about sex, drugs and alcohol from their friends, and it is members of the peer group that provide the most influential role models. For this reason, it is therapeutic groupwork that intervenes directly with children and adolescents' peer groups that can be the most effective way to deal with problems (either preventatively or remedially) such as bullying and drug taking. Successful therapeutic groupwork can influence the peer group culture to make it more respectful, supportive and based on accurate information. See Case Example 8.1 for a description of a solution-focused groupwork approach to dealing with bullying in schools, adapted from the innovative work of Sue Young (2001).

Case Example 8.1   A support group approach to dealing with bullying in schools

Adapted from (Young, 2001)

Rather than simply doing individual work with the identified victim (which may inadvertently reinforce their victim status) or directly confronting the identified bully (which may increase defensiveness and push the problem underground), this approach centres on creating a supportive peer group for the victim (which may include some of the children named as bullies) to overcome the problem. The approach is solution-focused in that it does not focus on the cause or blame people for the problem, but on eliciting everyone's cooperation, including the bullies', in establishing a solution. The approach consists of three stages

- interview with the 'victim';
- the support group meeting; and
- follow-up meetings.

Interview with 'victim'

Carefully taking time to establish an alliance built on the child's strengths, the counsellor clarifies the reason for the meeting (for example, that a parent or teacher is worried about them, if the child, as is usual, has not self-reported the bullying). The counsellor then identifies the following:

- Who is making the child unhappy or who are they finding it difficult to deal with? (There is no need to explore in detail what happens.)
- Who else is present when the problems happen? (People who witness the bullying or who act as 'bystanders' are a feature of school bullying and represent a group who are important to include in the support group.)
- Who are child's friends or who would he or she like to have as friends? (Often the child includes children already named as bystanders or even bullies. In some instances, bully-victim relationships can be the result of friendships that have run into trouble.)

Finally, the counsellor collaboratively identifies children from the above-named groups who might help and support the child in overcoming the problems and making him or her happier at school. As Sue Young (2001: 89) describes, the ideal is to create a support group of five to seven children and if possible to 'include all the children who are causing the child difficulties, plus a couple of bystanders and any friends or potential friends'.

Support group meeting

The counsellor welcomes all the children and explains the purpose of the meeting. 'My job is to help children if they are not happy in the school. I invite you here to today to help N [the identified child].' The counsellor then helps children empathise by inviting them to share about times that they have been unhappy in school (the children often raise other bullying incidents), and finishes the discussion with a concluding comment like 'It certainly is tough being unhappy; that's why I was hoping you could all help N'.

The children are then invited to make suggestions as to how they can help and the counsellor reinforces these, asking the children to elaborate with questions like 'How will you do that?' or 'How would that help?' or 'Do you think that would be easy?' The counsellor does not make the children promise to do anything, but simply notes down the suggestions, welcoming and complimenting them (unless they are unacceptable) and then finishes the meeting with the arrangement of a follow-up meeting.

Follow up meetings

The counsellor first meets with the identified child, identifying what progress has been made and reinforcing their contribution. Generally, they report progress particularly in the relationships with the children in the support group.

At a separate time, the counsellor reviews progress with the support group. The focus is on identifying progress and helping the children name their individual and collective contributions. As Sue Young (2001: 91) indicates, it is not unusual for the children identified as bullies to remain quiet during the initial meetings of the support group. Often, they have simply backed off from the child and this is in itself a positive result, and thus can be included in the compliments. If necessary, the support group can be reconvened, though generally one or two short meetings is all that is sufficient to make a difference.

Over time, convening these non-blame, solution-focused support groups can have a positive impact on a school's culture with respect to bullying. Once children see that they are not centred on punishment or blame but on responsibility and helping, more and more children can seek help in this way, including those who have previously been identified as bullies or bystanders.

Groups with children and adolescents – specific issues

Though many of the principles (discussed in the previous chapter and elsewhere (Sharry, 2001b)) for establishing and facilitating groups are generic, applying equally well to adult and younger populations, there are a number of specific issues raised by groupwork with developmentally dependent children and adolescents that you need to bear in mind as a facilitator. These are listed in Box 8.1.

Box 8.1   Groups with children and adolescents – specific issues

- Group goals.
- Structure and activity.
- Parental involvement.
- Group rules and discipline.

Group goals

Though there are exceptions, generally children and adolescents are initially 'visitors' when attending a therapeutic group (see Chapter 3). It is the adults in their lives, namely parents and teachers, who think the group is a good idea and often the children and adolescents are mandated to attend. The groups are usually centred on adult goals, such as social skills groups, anger management groups, anti-bullying groups, groups to prevent drug use and so on.

From a solution-focused perspective, the power of groupwork can be undermined when over-identified with negatively formulated problems. For example, an 'anger management' group for young offenders expects the participants to be angry, defining them as having this problem. If the group culture becomes focused on anger and delinquency, and group members gain esteem according to their level of anger or offending, then the group can actually become counterproductive and train the participants in more serious versions of the original problems. From a solution-focused perspective, the aim is to work hard to form a group identity that is positive and focused on the participants' goals. This might mean meeting each of the potential participants and working hard to discover what they want from a group, aiming to answer the simple question 'What will they be doing differently, when the problem (for example, anger) is gone? For many clients this future will have little to do with the problem and will involve ordinary daily living activities, such as enjoying school, getting a part-time job, making friends, doing interesting leisure or sports, getting on better with parents and so on. It is more useful to make the group centred on these simple goals. For example, as well as including input on communications skills, you can make sure that the group includes interesting recreational activities and affords opportunities for making friends.

Structure and activity

When running children's groups, it is important to include games and activities which allow children to express themselves non-verbally as well as reflective exercises and discussions that emphasise verbal communication. Depending on their developmental level, children can find cognitive exercises difficult to complete and these need to balanced by expressive exercises including painting, sand play and sculpting as well as activities such as role-play, puppet play or drama. In addition, children's groups are 'faster moving' than those of adults and require many different changes of activity and task. Though equally valuable, group discussions may be shorter with children and require a new exercise or change of activity at the end. Children may tire of an activity and group facilitators need to be armed with several options depending on the mood and energy of the group. Though flexibility is crucial, routine and structure are important in helping children's groups run smoothly. For example, the group could always start with a 'getting to know you' exercise, have a snack break near the end, include some 'high-energy' physical games in the middle and end with a more relaxing reflective exercise.

Groups with adolescents are also characterised by a balance between activities and discussion, and though these need to be adapted to an older age group, many of the same principles apply. For teenagers, the social and fun aspect of the group is often the most attractive reason for attendance, and this can be included as an explicit goal within the group or used as a reward for the 'hard work' undertaken by the group members. For example, it is useful to include a fun activity at the end of a group, such as being able to play pool or use a computer game or whatever else is appealing. In addition, it can be powerful to organise a recreational trip in lieu of a group session, and to involve group members in the planning of this. This can act as a powerful reward to the group, especially if it is linked to the completion of the group task or to mark progress made towards their goals.

Parental involvement

Children   Though legally all that is necessary for children to attend a group is their parents' consent, therapeutically it is generally necessary to have the parents' active support and involvement, particularly if the group is to have a wider positive impact on the children's lives. For example, running a social skills group may be a useful format to help eight-year-old children learn better ways of dealing with their anger, but the work is undermined if the parents who care for the children on a daily basis are not fully supportive of the intervention, or do not witness it as having value for their children and their family as a whole. For example, many parents will faithfully bring their children to a therapeutic group in the hope that it will make a difference, yet will disclose that they see little evidence of change in the home.

How you can involve parents and the nature of that involvement depends very much on the context in which you find yourself working as a professional. For example, as a school counsellor running a children's group it can be difficult to involve parents (just as many teachers find it hard to involve parents in their children's education) because the group is perceived as an extra part of the school curriculum. Whereas in a child mental health setting, it can be easier to involve parents (and indeed they often request it) as they generally bring their children to and from the group. A parallel parents group is often a successful way of capitalising on parent involvement and maximising positive outcome. For example, running a parent management group in parallel to a social skills group for children can be an excellent way of improving outcome for children with behaviour problems. Or running simultaneous parent and children groups for recently separated families can be a way of ensuring that both parties get adequate support and information.

Even an informal parents' group can be extremely helpful. This was brought home to me after a social skills group for children on the autistic spectrum, run a number of years ago. The parents used to gather in the waiting room as they waited to collect their children. Over the weeks, many of them began to talk and share and this became a valued aspect of coming to clinic. It is easy to take steps to capitalise on this informal process. For example, rather than letting the parents simply wait in the waiting room, it can be useful to give them a dedicated room with tea and coffee, and to allocate some therapist time (10 or 15 minutes) to meet this group to provide feedback and information and to facilitate conversation.

Adolescents   While older teenagers can decide to attend a therapeutic group without the involvement or knowledge of their parents (and this work mirrors many of the aspects of working with adults), parental permission, and in some cases active participation, is necessary for groupwork with children and younger adolescents. The exact age that a young person can decide to engage in a thera-peutic service without their parents' knowledge depends on the professional con-text. For example, some community youth counselling services allow for teenagers as young as 15 to attend a therapeutic group without necessarily involv-ing their parents, whereas an adolescent psychiatric service may insist on parental involvement for all referrals where the child is under 18 (or even older).

In addition, teenagers are at a stage of life when they are separating from their parents. It is perfectly appropriate, and indeed desirable, for them to be seeking independence and privacy from their parents and this should be reflected in the level of parental involvement in the group. It can be a useful part of the group for-mation for the facilitator to spend some time negotiating with the adolescents about confidentiality and the level of parental involvement. For example, if a report has to be made, the teenagers can be invited to take charge of this process and to decide (within reason) what should be included and what should remain confidential. Indeed, much of the substantial therapeutic work with teenagers is achieved via negotiation and helping them articulate their point of view, whilst appreciating wider issues and the feelings of others, with the view of reaching and keeping an agreement.

Group rules and discipline

Children   When facilitating children's groups, you are quite likely to encounter discipline problems on a more frequent basis than when working with children individually. Indeed, many children's groups can become derailed by the disruptive behaviour of one or two children, and therapists can find themselves spending all their time managing behaviour rather than attending to the group task. For this reason, it is important for therapists to think through in advance their 'discipline strategies' and how these can be used to the benefit of all the children concerned. This is not just an unpleasant chore that is necessary to ensure a focus on the group task, but is something useful to the children in gen-eral. In some children's groups, such as social skills groups for children with behaviour problems, helping children understand, appreciate and keep the group rules is the primary group task. For example, in a group for children with ADHD, helping children attend and listen to one another, concentrate on the group activities and not being disruptive in the task, aside from ensuring a smooth-running group, is likely to be of great benefit to the children individually and collectively. Some strategies that are worth considering are:

- Establish and agree group rules (listening, only one person speaking at a time, sitting in one's chair).
- Be clear and focused when asking children to do things and when reminding them of the rules.
- Attend to positive behaviours. Actively praise and reward children who keep to the rules. For example, select the child who is sitting down in his seat listening to carry out a group task. It can also be useful to have rewards allocated at the end of a group, such as stars or points which lead to a prize.
- Ignore minor breaches, attending to the positive behaviour of the children.
- Structure the group setting in a way that promotes the rules. For example, ensure that the room is not distracting and the seats are far enough apart so as to give children space.
- Think through how you will deal with a child who is continually disruptive. For example, you might operate a 'time out' system, whereby the child has to sit in another part of the room (or in a separate place) for a few minutes until they are able to rejoin constructively in the group activities. If they are continually disruptive, you may ask the parent to take the child out of the group for a few minutes.
- Recruit the parents' support in discipline strategies. For example, parents could run a corresponding reward chart in the home, or if a child is disruptive the parent could support by ensuring to talk things through with the child at home.

Adolescents   Similar to working with younger children, group facilitators should expect challenges to group rules when working with adolescents. These challenges often reflect the developmental stage of adolescents as one of seeking independence and attempting to work out their own views in relation to the adult world. While a group facilitator should have clear limits (no aggression and bullying and so on) and a range of discipline consequences (time out from group, 'extra homework') for serious breaches, the challenges themselves provide many therapeutic opportunities. Indeed, negotiation and debate about group rules often proves to be one of the more fruitful aspects of the therapeutic work with adolescents. This can include preventative discussions at the beginning about the group values they want to see, such as respect for one another, confidentiality and 'reparative' discussions after a problem has occurred. For example, after an incident of verbal abuse between two teenagers in a group, a facilitator could invite people to express feelings and to reflect about what happened, with the aim of encouraging an apology or a resolution. Helping adolescents communicate more effectively in the 'here and now' of the group can be a very valuable component.

In addition, negotiating not only the group rules but also the content of the session can be very useful when working with adolescents. For example, when facilitating a drugs awareness group, the therapist could give participants choices about possible guest speakers (for example, a reformed drug user, a police officer and so on.) and then empower them to contact the speaker and arrange the meeting. Such negotiations help teenagers take responsibility for the group and to more fully participate.

Case Example 8.2 illustrates groupwork in practice with children, and Case Example 8.3 groupwork with adolescents.

Case Example 8.2   The Dinosaur Club

In a primary school in a deprived area, the teachers were concerned about the increasing levels of behaviour problems in a small group of children leading to significant classroom management problems, and thus sought the help of the local child mental health clinic. Rather than targeting the children identified with the problems (and thus increasing stigma), a psychotherapist and a psychologist from the clinic combined resources with the school staff to run a preventative group programme based in the school to include all the children in first class (aged six to seven years old).

The intervention was based on the Dinosaur Programme, developed by Webster-Stratton in America (Webster-Stratton and Hammond, 1997) that aims to teach social skills to young children aged five to eight years old, based on cognitive-behavioural ideas, using creative means such as video, games, puppets and fantasy play. Topics of the programme include:

- making good friends;
- understanding feelings;
- solving difficult problems;
- managing anger; and
- succeeding in school.

The children were divided into two groups of 15, twice a week for a one-hour group session. Each group had two leaders, a therapist from the clinic and a teacher, and the sessions mirrored 'circle time' which was already successfully practised in the schools. The children called the group the Dinosaur Club and understood it as about learning to get on with everyone and to solve problems. All parents were informed of the group and were invited to attend information mornings at the beginning and the end. In addition, notes and homework from the children's group were sent home each week, and parents encouraged to adapt some of the ideas at home (such as reward systems). A typical session was as follows:

1 *Introductory game*
   For example, 'Oranges and Apples': each child is designated as an orange or an apple. A child in the middle calls out either 'orange',

meaning all the oranges have to change seats, or 'apple', meaning all the apples have to change, or 'fruit bowl', meaning everyone changes. The child left in the middle takes a turn. This is a high-energy game that provides a good start to the group. Quieter games are also appropriate depending on the needs of the group.

2 *Review of week*
This involves a short discussion with the children on how they have applied the ideas thus far learnt at the Dinosaur Club, at home or at school. Each child is invited to share news.

3 *New ideas*
New ideas are introduced with pictures and cards or using a video from the Dinosaur Programme that includes snippets of videos taken from everyday life in a school, illustrating children coping and not coping with situations. The children watch the video and discuss the ideas.

4 *Role play or practice of ideas using puppets*
The facilitators introduce role play with puppets, who act out problem situations; for example, one puppet grabs a toy off another and gets into a fight. The children are asked for suggestions on what the puppets are feeling and asked for solutions: how can the puppet get the toy without fighting? The puppets then replay the scene acting out the children's solution ideas. At later stages in the group the children role-play themselves in problem situations, trying out new positive ways of resolving things.

5 *Game to explain ideas*
A game is introduced that helps explain the ideas. For example, children will pick feelings out of a hat and then have to put on a face that corresponds to the feeling. Other children have to guess which feeling. Alternatively, children pick problem situations from a hat and then give possible solutions.

6 *Story time*
A story based on the ideas covered can be read out to the group. This can include stories on how children learn to get on or get rid of the temper monster (Silver, 1999). Stories are a good way of quietening the energy near the end of a group.

7 *Relaxation exercise*
This can include the children acting out being 'turtles' and withdrawing into their shells when they are feeling very angry, or it can be based on a guided relaxation where the children are asked to close their eyes and imagine themselves in a safe, happy place.

8 *Rewards*
Dina the dinosaur puppet appears at the end of each session and provides 'ticks' to children who had behaved well, or who have made progress, or who thought up good ideas in the group. A special effort is made to include children who might have special difficulties.

At the end of each week, the school principal would visit the class to reinforce the ideas being taught and to provide small rewards, such as pencils or copybooks, to the children who received sufficient ticks.

Case Example 8.3   The Chill Out Club

In a school for adolescents with emotional behavioural problems, several children were referred to the school psychologist due to behaviour problems at home and in the classroom. The psychologist decided that a group intervention might be a useful way to intervene and gained support for this from school staff. He met with the referred adolescents individually and with their families to see if they were willing to join a group and to see what goals they had for membership. The psychologist felt that six of the seven referred adolescents were suitable to attend. He felt that the seventh did not have a positive view of the group and could not articulate a positive goal for membership. The group was run during the school day for one and a half hours over ten weeks. Parents were involved in the group and a condition of attendance was three family meetings before, during and at the end of the group.

The first session focused on establishing the group rules (respect for one another, turn taking, taking part and so on) and agreeing a contract with the participants (that if they kept the rules and worked constructively each session, they would be entitled to a snack and 20 minutes' free time at the end, playing pool or computer games). The first session also focused on establishing their personal goals for the group. These ranged from 'having fun' or 'taking a break from class' to 'learning to get on better with parents and classmates'. Their parents' and teachers' goals for them to manage their temper or to be less disruptive in class were also acknowledged. Finally, in the first session they brainstormed a good name for the group and the adolescents came up with the Chill Out Club, which creatively reflected both the goal to relax and enjoy the group and the goal to manage temper. Subsequent sessions used the following format:

1 *Review of progress*
  The facilitator gave a recap of what was covered in the last session, particularly noting contributions from each of the group members. (In later sessions the young people were invited to provide this summary of events themselves.) The adolescents were then invited to share about progress they had made towards their goals in the previous week and to report any news or 'differences'. Enough time was allocated to ensure that each person had an opportunity to speak.
2 *New topic*
  Each week some new ideas were introduced to the group by the facilitators. Videos of popular soap operas and films were often used to do this. For example, the facilitators would show snippets of videos from a popular film that highlighted issues such as conflict, loyalty, friendship and so on. These provoked heated debate and discussion. In later sessions, the adolescents selected videos to be shown.
3 *Problem solving/specific issues*
  A space was allowed for discussion of specific issues raised by individual group members. The facilitators would guide the group in problem solving.

4 *Planning*

A summary was made of the issues covered in the sessions and the group members were invited to share plans for next week.

5 *Recreation*

A recreational time which included a snack and access to a variety of games (pool and computer games) took place at the end of the session.

Summary

In this chapter we have considered some of the particular issues that are raised in designing and facilitating groups with children and adolescents. Such groups work best when they are centred on the goals of the children and adolescents as well as those of their parents and teachers, when they are well-structured with clear boundaries and rules, and when they involve activities and exercises (and not just verbal input) targeted at the age and interests of the participants, ensuring that the groups are enjoyable and recreational as well as hard work. We have illustrated the ideas with outlines of three different groups, notably an anti-bullying support group, the Dinosaur Club for six and seven year old children, and the Chill Out Club for adolescents.

9 Pausing at Solutions – Strengths-based Video Feedback

John Sharry, Grainne Hampson and Mary Fanning

A friend's eye is the best mirror.

Irish expression

Teaching holds a mirror to the soul. If I am willing to look in that mirror, and not run from what I see, I have a chance to gain self-knowledge.

Parker Palmer

From the client's point of view we are holding up a mirror of his or her current experiencing. The feelings and personal meanings seem sharper when seen through the eyes of another, when they are reflected.

C.R. Rogers (1990: 128) on psychotherapy

The metaphor of a mirror has often been used to describe a functioning human relationship. Psychoanalysts such as Winnicott have argued that in the course of healthy development the parent acts as a mirror to the infant child, reflecting their feelings and emotions. When the child looks in the face of a responsive parent they see themselves reflected in the parent's facial expression and gestures. This reflection provides them with a sense of themselves and they begin to learn who they are (Winnicott, 1974). In a similar way, the professional relationships that psychotherapists and teachers have with their clients have been likened to mirroring ones. Within the relationship the teacher or therapist provides the learner or client with a mirror containing a self-image that facilitates self-reflection and learning. Therapists (or teachers) aim to respond in a way that helps the clients understand themselves better. As Rogers states:

> For my clients these responses are, at their best, a clear mirror image of the meanings and perceptions that make up his or her world of the moment – an image that is clarifying and insight producing. (1990: 129)

---

[1]Grainne Hampson and Mary Fanning are speech and language therapists at the Department of Child and Family Psychiatry at the Mater Hospital Dublin.

The metaphor of a mirror is also a useful way to describe the approach of a strengths-based practitioner. There is an important difference, however: whereas Rogers, coming from a modernist perspective, believed there was in fact a true reality to be reflected in the therapeutic mirror, that the therapist's aim was to be an accurate mirror in order to illuminate the client's 'real' feelings and thoughts, from a social constructionist perspective there are many different 'images' that could be reflected back to the client, each of them relatively true and *fitting with* the clients experience and sense of reality. When you listen as a therapist, it is not an 'objective' science of uncovering another's feeling. You can make many different therapeutic responses, all of which can be interpreted positively by clients and give them a sense of being understood. (Indeed, the reverse can happen, whereby you use a 'classic' listening response and the client inadvertently feels misunderstood or disrespected).

From a strengths-based perspective, the aim is to hold up a constructive mirror to clients that presents a self-image which includes strengths, resources, potentials and possibilities. The aim is to provide an 'image' that inspires clients and which garners their resources to take action. This is not about simple positive thinking or about simply putting a positive gloss on a bad situation. The mirror must provide an image that fits with the evidence and client's experience and should encompass the light as well as the dark, trauma as well as survival and problems as well as solutions. The overall aim is to reflect the situation with a self-image that is most likely to promote change and progress towards the client's goal for coming to therapy.

This chapter describes how we can provide a constructive mirror to clients using the technology of video feedback. By reviewing a videotaped parent–child interaction, in particular pausing at times when the interaction is going well or at exceptional times when the solution the parent seeks is actually occurring, parents are facilitated to witness a constructive mirror of themselves and their children. By pausing at and replaying these exceptional times they can be expanded in detail and significance and clients can witness themselves being successful with their goals.

The use of video feedback as a teaching tool is not new and it has been used in individual and group therapy since the technology became accessible and widely available (Yalom, 1995). Video recording has also been employed as a research method in the analysis of the therapeutic process. For example, Hill showed clients videotapes of their sessions and asked them to discuss and evaluate the process. Ironically, many of the clients reported that they found these review sessions more useful than the original therapy (Hill, 1989 as cited in Garfield and Bergin 1994). Thus the research study inadvertently gives an endorsement of the use of video as a direct therapeutic tool.

In recent times, there has been increasing realisation of the power of strengths-based learning and use of video recordings as a means to focus on 'snippets' that reflect strengths and successes, rather than ones that reflect weaknesses and problems. The strengths-based orientation characterises most of the new parent training approaches that use video feedback as a core component, such as the Hanen Program (Manolson, 1992), a psycho-educational group programme to empower parents to promote language development in their young children with language delays; or Mellow Parenting (Puckering et al., 1996), a group-based parent support and training programme; or the Marte Meo approach (Aarts, 2000), an individual programme tailored to specific client goals. This strengths-based orientation also characterises the approach of the Parents Plus Early Years programme.

Parents Plus Early Years programme

As discussed in Chapter 7, the original Parents Plus programmes for children and for adolescents (Sharry and Fitzpatrick, 1997) use videotapes of role-played parenting interactions along with interviewed comments from parents, young people and professionals to facilitate this learning and therapeutic process. Parents are invited to review and analyse the videotapes and to identify skills that could be useful to them. Though this process was effective, parents could some-times feel dis-identified from the video examples and comments of 'other people' and thus feel that the illustrated ideas would not exactly work in their situation. For this reason, in the recent development of the Early Years programme targeted at parents of children from one to six years old, we have been keen to incorporate the parents' own videotapes in the therapeutic process and thus allow parents to self-model and learn from their own examples of successful parenting. We were also keen to maintain the benefits of a group format for parents that would capitalise on shared learning and support. Thus a 12-week programme was evolved that combined six individual sessions with six group sessions.

Parents and children complete the Early Years programme for a variety of reasons. This can include childhood problems such as developmental delay, over-activity, difficult to manage behaviour and emotional problems. It can also include parental problems such as depression or stress and so on. Some of the children have formal diagnoses, such as ADHD or Autistic spectrum disorder, though in the majority of cases no formal label is used (due to the child's young age). The programme is also targeted as a preventative measure at parents and children with no identified problems who are keen to enhance and build upon their parenting skills. As the programme focuses on helping parents discover satis-factory ways of relating to and managing their children, whatever problems they are experiencing, the programme has broad applicability.

Individual sessions

Setting   Parent and child attend together for the individual session, either in the neutral setting of the playroom at the clinic or in the home, depending on the needs of the family.

Making the video   The therapist then videos a short interaction between the parent and child. Generally the therapist videos a play interaction between parent and child as this is the basis of communication, but depending on the specific goals of the parent other scenes and situations can be videoed. For example:

- If the parent wants to know how to improve his child's language, the videoed scene could be parent and child in a free-play situation with parent attempting to maximise the child's language expression.
- If the parent is concerned about the child's constant opposition, the scene could be a free-play one, followed by a parent-led activity such as tidying up the toys before moving on to reading.
- If the parent wants to know how to help their child concentrate, then the scene could be one of free play, where the child has to stick to the choice of play object or activity.
- If the parent wants to know how to help her children share or play well together, the scene could include two children around a common flash-point, such as a shared meal or play activity.
- If the parent is keen to establish a morning routine with his children, a visit could be arranged to video the different part of the morning routine in the home.

While following the programme's goals of establishing a responsive parenting style, the specific goals of the parent for their child and situation are paramount and should be incorporated into the session.

Reviewing the video   Once the videotape is made, the parent and therapist make a space to review the tape. This can be done either straight after the videoing, after the pause of a short break and/or at the next individual session, depending on the needs of the family and the familiarity of the therapist with video analysis. It is generally a good idea to carry out some review after the video session to ensure that the parent is given some space to reflect about the experience and to generate some ideas to take away. (It can be ideal during the review for a co-therapist or other family member to interact with/entertain the child, so as to give the parent freedom to watch and review the video, though sometimes in busy circumstances this is not possible and parent and child watch the tape together.)

The tape is then watched and reviewed collaboratively by parent and therapist. The tape is watched through and the client is asked for their thoughts and reflections with questions such as:

- What do you think of what you just saw?
- What struck you as important?

They can also be invited to think constructively about what is going on with questions such as:

- What do you think went well in the interaction?
- How did you manage to connect with your child just now?

Providing feedback   The therapist then provides his or her own feedback and analysis, rewinding the tape to pause at key moments. Operating from a strengths-based paradigm, the therapist is looking for exceptions to the problematic interactions and particular skills demonstrated by parent and child as well as specific examples of where the parent is achieving or beginning to achieve his or her goals. Simple concrete feedback with the video paused at the right point works best. For example:

- I notice that here when you simply repeated what your son said, he looked up at you and said the word again ... This is helping him learn a new word and express himself.
- Here you made sure to make eye contact with your child before asking him to tidy up in a calm, polite voice ... And then he complies ... I think the fact you made eye contact and used a calm, polite voice helped him comply.

Group sessions

The groups can work best when they are targeted at certain client groups, such as parents of children with developmental delays or on the autistic spectrum or parents of children with behaviour problems or over-activity. Equally, there are advantages to having mixed groups and this decision really depends on the context in which the group is formed – for example, on how it is provided and who provides it.

Depending on the collective goals of the group members, a syllabus for the group sessions is developed. This can include sessions on promoting children's language and development, managing behaviour problems, helping children concentrate and learn, getting children to cooperate or play with siblings and so on. In conjunction to a teaching tape that includes taped examples from parents who attended previous groups (and who gave permission for their tapes to be used), the video snippets made with the parents during the individual sessions can used as the basis of the 'teaching' during the group. The facilitators select video snippets from the various tapes that reflect the specific group topic and which illustrate the ideas and skills in question. It can be a powerful learning experience for parents to have their own tapes reviewed in the group. Not only is it very reinforcing to have their successes validated and reinforced by the group, it can be very affirming for parents to see that they have some expertise (via their tapes) to offer the other members of the group. This is one of the key therapeutic factors of solution-focused groupwork (Sharry, 2001b).

In addition, parents can be invited to make their own selections from the individual videotapes that they want to share and review in the group. They can be invited to select pieces that they felt went well or pieces about which they want some feedback and ideas from the group. The latter can be particularly useful in later sessions when group members have developed a sense of trust between one another.

Making the parents' own videotape, the basis of the group sessions helps build cohesion and confidence in the group as parents can see each other in action and this can facilitate sharing and open discussion.

Parenting model

There is a parenting model inherent in the programme that influences the ideas covered in the group sessions as well as the focus of the video analysis and feedback. This model is based on well-researched ideas on what are the best interactions to promote child development and to manage and avoid behaviour problems. The model draws on many established approaches and systems that attempt to promote supportive patterns of communication between parents and young children, notably:

- The work of Maria Aarts in the Marte Meo Programme (Aarts, 2000).
- Manolson and others in the Hanen Programme, which teaches how to positively promote children's language and development (Manolson, 1992).
- The work of Forehand and McMahon who developed the Parent/Child Game as a systematic individual intervention to reduce behavioural problems in young children (Forehand and McMahon, 1981).
- 'Emotion coaching' and the recent work of John Gottman on helping parents connect with and support their children's emotional development (Gottman, 1997).
- The Mellow Parenting group intervention programme for parents of young children (Puckering et al., 1996).

Essentially the approach aims to help parents become responsive to their children's and their own needs. Parents are encouraged to 'tune into' their children, anticipating their feelings and wishes, to find ways to 'connect with' and enjoy their children and to become self-aware of their own reactions and responses (and thus be able to choose them). Concretely, parents are invited to positively attend to and reward their children, to develop a cooperative assertive style of parenting and to manage their own reactions in calm consistent manner. This responsive style of parenting maximises the child's ability to learn and develop (whatever his or her problems), and allows parents to anticipate, avoid and manage behaviour problems as well as building a positive, well-attached relationship between parent and child.

Collaborative Style

As stated in Chapters 2 and 3, collaboration is an important characteristic of a strengths-based professional. Collaboration is also critical in the work of the therapist in the Parents Plus Programmes. Therapist and parent work together in analysing the videos and in deciding what are the important points to note. The parent brings their own knowledge of their child and their unique parenting style and the therapist brings the knowledge of the parenting model inherent in the programme (see above). In addition, the therapist is transparent about the ideas during the group sessions and parents are invited to debate and adapt them to their own unique situations. Finally, the process is also collaborative during the filming. In some instances the therapist can intervene and act as coach to the parent as she interacts with her child.

Case Example 9.1 is a good illustration of working as a collaborative coach with a parent. Rather than simply filming, the therapist intervened and supported the parent through managing the tantrum. This was probably preferable to letting the tantrum run its course in the unsatisfactory manner usually experienced by the child.

In other instances the therapist can collaborate by demonstrating certain skills to a parent. For example, before videoing the parent and child, a speech and language therapist may work with the child directly, with the parent observing, and demonstrate some of the key skills in promoting a child's language development. Whether to intervene, either directly or indirectly, depends on what the parent wants, what would be the most helpful, and the particular skills and knowledge of the therapist.

Case Example 9.1   Video feedback in action – 'Coaching a parent to ignore a minor tantrum'

Jamie was a four-year-old boy who was referred due to tantrums and difficult behaviour. During the individual sessions, the therapist made videotapes of the mother playing with Jamie and his little sister Kate (she was included as it was during sibling play that many of the problems occurred).

Most of the work focused on providing feedback to the mother on how she was providing positive attention to both children, helping them play in parallel. During session two, a minor tantrum occurred. Jamie began to grab a toy from his sister, without asking. The mother said 'Don't grab,' and gave the toy back to the sister. Jamie protested angrily and the mother argued with him in a loud voice. Jamie became more angry and raised his hand in a threatening way.

The therapist at this point (while filming) intervened, suggesting to the mother that she pull away from Jamie and turn her attention to Katie. Jamie continued to protest a bit and the therapist encouraged the mother to remain relaxed and to play with Katie. He suggested that the mother say simply 'Jamie is angry right now; when he calms down he can come back in and play'. After a minute, Jamie slowly moved back towards his mother. The therapist said 'I think Jamie is ready to come back now, maybe show him what he can play with.' The mother then turned to Jamie and asked 'Come and play with the LEGO?' He sat close to his mother as she helped him get started.

During the video review, the mother was fascinated to see how the ignoring approach could work. She described how she normally would argue or shout with him and how this would make things worse. The therapist highlighted the different skills involved in ignoring, such as remaining calm, turning completely away and crucially returning positive attention – which were all illustrated in the video snippet. Rather than being 'taught', the mother could see herself on tape (with a little bit of coaching) carrying out the skills.

Advantages of strengths-based video feedback

Using video in this way can enhance the therapeutic process in a number of different ways:

- allowing exceptions to be highlighted and expanded;
- giving immediate and concrete feedback;
- using videos to encourage reflection;
- self-modelling; and
- expanding the witness group.

Allowing exceptions to be highlighted and expanded

Many parents are trapped in a problem focus and find it hard to recall times when they were coping or when they were successfully parenting their child. By closely scrutinising a videotaped parenting situation, such as play or a mealtime, these instances can be noticed and highlighted and given extra attention and analysis. With skilled observation, even within the most problematic interaction, exceptions to the problem can be observed. For example, even with very active children you will be able to find times when they concentrate a little more or when they heed their parents' instructions (see Case Example 9.2). Without the video these 'exceptions' can easily be forgotten and unnoticed. By using pause and replay, the exception can be expanded in time and receive thorough review and analysis. In Case Example 9.2, though the exception lasted only three to five seconds in real time, the review of the incident (with much pausing and replay) lasted 20 minutes and proved to be an important moment of insight.

Case Example 9.2   Video feedback in action – 'Slowing down'

Simon was a hyperactive and developmentally delayed three-year-old boy. His mother felt overwhelmed by his problems and described in despair how she could 'never' get him to sit still or attend to a task. As a result she felt very helpless. Her goal was to find some way of getting Simon to slow down.

In the first videotaped interaction, the child was indeed very active and demanding and for the majority of the tape the mother responded in an agitated, rushed state. In order to manage Simon she tended to give a lot of instructions and commands, all of which seemed to go over Simon's head and were not effective.

On close scrutiny, however, there were a couple of incidents where the mother slowed down and was successful. In one incident, she sat back for a moment and watched her child. She noticed that he wanted a car from the box and simply said 'You want a car'. The child turned, looked at her and repeated 'Car'. The mother helped him get a car from the box and the child took it gladly and played with it.

During the feedback the therapist paused the tape at this incident and reviewed it with the mother. He pointed out that this was a time when she slowed down and named what Simon was interested in. As a result, her son did listen to her (he looked up) and she was able to help him concentrate and play with the car (albeit briefly!).

As the incident was so concrete and immediate, it struck a chord with the mother and it proved a pivotal moment of insight for the mother. During subsequent video sessions she reduced her commands and followed more of Simon's actions and initiatives. As a result she noticed an improvement in Simon's concentration and she was able to make enjoyable, shared connections with him. Crucially, she began to feel able to influence her son and be re-empowered as a parent. When asked to explain the change she saw in her own words, she said 'I need to slow down with him more; if I get rushed when he is hyper, he gets even more hyper. He needs me to go slow with him.'

Giving immediate and concrete feedback

A picture speaks a thousand words

Rather than relying on verbally-expressed memory, video review can re-enact 'exceptions', allowing clients to witness the rich concrete detail that would be impossible to remember. Clients can witness important details such as the body language and facial expressions of themselves and their children, which would be impossible to convey in a verbal description. Indeed, watching and learning from videos does not require literacy.

One of the surprising benefits I have discovered within this way of working is the positive influence that it can have on young children, even those at very early stages in their language development. The children are as interested in themselves on video as are the parents, and are equally influenced. If you replay a positive time to a parent and child, for example a happy play interaction, this can reinforce this positive behaviour for the child and make it more likely for them to repeat it, especially if they are encouraged and rewarded during the watching. The first time I learnt this lesson was with one mother and her three-year-old son, who had very delayed language and was referred because of oppositional behaviour at home. On reviewing the tape, the son sat on his mother's lap and expressed delight at seeing himself play with his mother. The following week the mother reported that the son constantly watched the tape at home and wanted to show it to all the extended family. The mother was convinced that the repeated playing of the tape was helping her son, acting as a reinforcement for him to behave well. She further added that she thought it was 'great for everyone in the family to see him in a different light, playing so attentively'.

It can be an excellent idea to make an 'edited highlights tape' for children to take home, which invariably they will watch over and over again. It can become like a positive motif for how the family want to behave together.

Using videos to encourage reflection

Therapy is primarily a process of reflection. It requires someone to 'step out of' or back from an immediate problem and to reflect about themselves and others in that situation. The fact that you watch a video as part an audience as opposed to being a participant in the drama encourages this process of reflection. The act of watching necessarily places some distance between the viewer and the watched events and thus invites opinion, comment and reflection. Watching a video generally encourages the process of self-reflection.

Self-modelling

When I first used videotapes to coach parents, I often used tapes of other parents (role-played or actual) demonstrating parenting skills (for example, Sharry and Fitzpatrick, 2001). While this could be helpful to parents, it had a number of disadvantages. Parents could easily feel dis-identified from the tapes, for example, saying 'It would never work with my child', or 'My child/situation is too different'. Sometimes the tapes could leave a parent undermined in that they would think 'I could never have the courage to behave that way'. (Ironically, sometimes these tapes worked best when the parents were critical of them, in that they were empowered to think what they could do differently and better than the parents in the role plays!)

Using video examples from the parents' own interactions with their children eliminates this dis-identification (see Case Example 9.3). Parents are given an opportunity to learn from and model their own solutions. They literally become their own teacher and role-model. Rather than exclusively learning from 'experts' or other people communicating with children, the parents are invited to self-model and to learn from their own expertise, thus building on their own strengths and confidence.

Expanding the witness group

The fact that a video recording has been made allows for the possibility of other people reviewing it and thus for the ideas to be further enhanced and reinforced. This is the principle of the group sessions in the Parents Plus Programme, where parents receive powerful validation and reinforcement in the group review of their tapes.

The videotape can also be used with other members of the family who cannot attend the groups, such as partners or grandparents. By including such people in the 'video review process' they can be recruited as supporters for the parents and children. For example, I once worked with a mother who felt her own mother (who was very involved in childcare) was very undermining of her. They would disagree over discipline and the grandmother would blame the mother for being too soft (and thus causing the son's problems). The grandmother did not want to be videoed herself, but she did come to some of her daughter's video review sessions. By the facilitator highlighting some of the mother's successes on tape, particularly when she was able to calmly insist on her son keeping rules, the grandmother became more positive about her daughter's ability. In addition, the grandmother was positively influenced by the positive parenting techniques of the course (as demonstrated by her daughter on videotape!) and tried many of these out herself. In this way, the video allowed a second significant family member to be included.

Case Example 9.3   Video feedback in action – 'Going at the child's pace'

Tim was a three-year-old boy with severe speech and language delay (he used single words on occasion) and a question about whether he was on the autistic spectrum. His parents were very concerned about his development and wanted to know how they could help his language develop.

Working with the father and Tim, the therapist made a videotape of a free-play situation. In the play the father was warm and enthusiastic, but his language was over complicated for Tim. He used a lot of four- and five-word sentences and would ask a lot questions which Tim could not understand.

On close scrutiny of the tape, the therapist noticed a time when Tim dropped a block (that they were playing with) and burst out laughing. The father matched the laugh (tone and facial expression), getting face-to-face with Tim. Tim looked up at his father and smiled. 'Fell' his father said pointing at the block. 'Fell' Tim repeated, also pointing at the block.

The therapist picked this incident out for review, highlighting how the father was successful in connecting with his son by matching his laugh and facial expression and being face to face. Building on this connection, he then helped Tim speak by commenting on something Tim was interested in (the block) and using very simple one-word language ('fell').

The father was fascinated by this incident and was empowered to feel that he had a possible role in promoting his son's language. The tape segment was used as a teaching example in the group, which further reinforced his confidence.

Summary

In this chapter, we have described how video-based feedback can be incorporated into a strengths-based way of working with parents and children. By replaying videos of parent–child interactions, but mainly focusing on what is working well and the times parent and child are relating in a preferred way, we can help parents build on their own skills and strengths.

This process is truly strengths-based as clients learn from observing themselves and their children about what works for them. They can come to appreciate their own way of doing things and become their own 'role models'. The use of video has a number of other advantages in that it is immediate, it can be replayed many times, it provides richer detail than memory alone, and the act of watching encourages clients to reflect about and see themselves differently.

10 Defeating Temper – A Case Study

As discussed in previous chapters, a strengths-based response to problems involves first treading carefully to find a constructive alliance with all the significant people in the system including the child, the parents and others. Then it is important to elaborate client goals and to co-create a strengths-based understanding of the situation that can act as a bridge between the problem and a solution. When clients become stuck in problem definitions and attributions of blame, however, it can be hard to shift the conversation to strengths and goals, and progress can easily become stifled. In this chapter we outline a useful procedure called 'externalising the problem' that accepts the client's focus on the problem, while inviting a different conversation that can change how they see the problem. The ideas are explored in relation to an extended case study about a boy with behaviour problems.

Externalising the problem

Love the sinner but hate the sin.

St Augustine

As discussed in Chapter 6, diagnoses such as ADHD or oppositional defiant disorder should be very judiciously used as they easily become 'stuck' to or internalised by children and thus negatively affect their self-esteem and even compromise their relationships with their parents. From a strengths-based perspective it is useful to help children and families *externalise* the problem that afflicts them. Rather than seeing the problem as an internal attribute or quality of the child, it can be seen as an external problem that child and family are united in outwitting and defending against. This process of externalising problems and their labels is central to narrative therapy, originally proposed by White and Epston (1990) and developed by many others (Freeman and Combs, 1996; Freeman et al., 1997; Monk et al., 1997; Nylund, 2000).

Externalising the problem is a very useful therapeutic approach when clients feel over-identified with the problem (whether this is a mother who feels she is a 'bad parent' or a child with a formal diagnosis of ADHD), which leads to them to feeling blamed, defensive or stuck with the problem. It is particularly useful when working with more than one client, for example families and children, where there is blame and counter-blame for the problem, leading to high conflict and little cooperation. Essentially, externalising the problem is about shifting from a frame where a person is identified as the problem, to a frame where the person is identified as more than the problem. Rather than being seen as intrinsic to their nature, the problem is located as being separate from them. Within this new frame it is easier to collaborate with clients and work with their agendas. It is the difference between confronting a person because they are an alcoholic and working with them to eliminate an alcohol problem. The approach works well with families or couples who are in dispute over an issue, for example a child involuntarily brought to therapy because he is 'aggressive or disturbed'. Labelled and described in this way, the child is likely to be defensive and uncooperative and 'resist' treatment. By externalising the problem he can be seen in a more positive light, for example he can be seen as a child with many strengths coping with a debilitating behaviour problem that affects the whole family. Within this new frame he is more likely to be cooperative and ally with his parents and the therapist to defeat or reduce the influence of the problem.

There are a number of different formats for the process, such as the SMART approach developed by Nylund (2000), particularly when applied to working with children diagnosed with ADHD. The format below is adapted from the original work of Michael White (1997), which essentially divides the therapeutic process into two stages. The first stage is the process of externalising the problem, which aims to separate the problem from the person to loosen its hold on the client's life. The second stage is about building the solution, in particular building a new compelling story of the client's life, which centres on their goals, strengths and exceptions to the problem. As you might expect, the metaphor of the story is very important in narrative therapy. As Freeman et al. (1997) might put it, the aim is to 'thin' the dominant plot of the problem story and to 'thicken' the counter plot of the solution.

Stages of externalising the problem

Problem-free talk   As discussed in Chapter 2, engaging in problem-free talk that emphasises what is going well in the clients' lives, as distinct from the problems and failures that affect them, is a useful way of establishing a therapeutic alliance and beginning the process of solution building. As problem-free talk allows a therapist to connect with the client as a person who is more than the problem, it is also a very important 'pre-step' of externalising the problem. By engaging in conversation that has nothing to do with the problem but which is about the clients' strengths, talents, resources, hobbies and interests, therapists can begin to loosen the dominance of the problem and take a step not to define the client in terms of the problem and thus begin to explore a different identity for the client in the room.

Naming of problem as external   The second stage in the process is to ensure that when the problem which brought the family to therapy is discussed, it is done in a way that locates the problem as outside the family members' identity. The strategy is to invite a slightly subtle change in language; for example, instead of saying that the child is explosive or aggressive, you can say that the child is affected by temper or behaviour. The aim is to avoid blaming stances and to reach a point where no one is seen as exclusively owning or being identified with it. Rather than the parent blaming the child for being aggressive or the child blaming the parent for being critical and strict, parent and child can ally against the rows and arguments that spill into and take over their lives. A crucial part of the process is to invite the child and family to name the problem and thus make it external. Usually a child-centred name is best, as it often introduces a lightness to what is otherwise a fraught conflictual situation. For example, White and Epston (1990) describe a case with a six-year-old boy with a soiling problem who names the problem as 'Sneaky Pooh', which accurately described the situation from his frame of reference.

Generally, this process of naming the problem as external is introduced by the therapist asking a series of questions. Nylund (2000: 73) suggests the following questions in the particular case of ADHD:

- ADHD is the doctor's name for the problem. What name would you give it?
- Families have found it helpful to view the problem as something outside the child. It helps to bring some new ideas on the problem and can pave a way for solutions. Is it OK if we experiment with talking about ADHD in this way?
- So has ADHD been running the show? Since when? How much of the time?
- When did ADHD show up in your life?
- Which part of your body does ADHD show up in first?
- Would you like to call the problem ADHD or some other name?

Exploring the effects of and evaluating the problem   During this stage, the therapist invites the child and family to explore the impact of the problem in their lives. This gives them the opportunity to tell their story of how the problem has damaged and limited their lives. With the problem named as external, this facilitates a sharing of experience, rather than a defensive debate. For example, a child is more able to listen to how 'Temper' has upset his mother and curtailed her life, rather than if it was exclusively seen as his actions against her. Equally, a mother is more able to hear the upset her child is in as a result of Temper taking over. The effects of the problem can be explored with questions such as:

Questions for child

- What effect does Temper (or ADHD) have on you in the classroom? How does it interfere with your learning?
- What things does Temper make you do?
- How does Temper make you feel?
- How does Temper trick you into doing things your don't want to?
- What does Temper say to you about yourself?
- How does Temper affect you at home?

Questions for parents

- What effect does Temper have on you as parents? How does it make you feel?
- How does Temper make you respond?

- Who in the family is affected most/least by Temper?
- How does Temper affect the whole family?

For other questions, see Nylund (2000).

Taking a position   The final stage of the externalising process is to invite the child and the family to take a position on the problem, that is, to make a judgement about whether they want the problem in their lives as well as inviting them to make a decision to take action against it. This is generally a crucial stage in the process, especially for children. Whereas most parents eagerly make a judgement that they want to diminish the influence of ADHD or Temper in their family's lives, children are often not consulted nor invited to make their own evaluation and judgement.

Though a child's cooperation is crucial to solving behaviour problems, in many of the treatments, such as medication, parent training or classroom management strategies, they are often viewed as passive recipients. The treatment is 'done to them' rather than them being viewed as agents of change. It can be very powerful, however, to take time to consult with children about the problems and then invite them to take a position. Put simply, this means asking children questions such as:

- Given all we have discussed about how Temper has messed up your family's life (list examples that the child has generated in the last section), do you think Temper is a good thing or a bad thing?
- Would you like to stop Temper from messing up your life?

Once the child answers 'yes' to the above question, he or she has become a customer to the process. You now have created an alliance with the child and parents (presumably who also answer 'yes' to the question) and are working on the same goal. If the child says 'no' – and it can happen – it usually means that the therapist did not go through the process at the child's pace nor make it meaningful to them. Generally, this means having to renegotiate an agreed problem and thus repeating the above steps.

Following an affirmative to the above question, it can be helpful to ask the child to justify their judgement with questions such as:

- Why do you not want Temper in your life?
- Why do you want to get rid of or reduce the times Temper is bothering you and your family?

Getting the child and family to answer the above questions further reinforces their decision and garners motivation for change.

Stages of solution-building

Once the problem has been named and externalised and the child and parents have decided that it is a problem and something to work to reduce or eliminate, the scene is now set for solution building. The purpose of solution building is to build a picture of the preferred future for the family and to link this to exceptions, strengths and resources that the parents and children already have access to. In narrative terms, it is about co-authoring the counter-plot of the solution to the dominant plot of the problem and thus helping the child and family weave a different and preferred story for their lives. As the child and family are now customers to the process, solution building can follow the stages of a traditional solution-focused session. As these principles are outlined in detail in Chapter 2, we will only briefly reprise them here.

Goal setting   First, the child and family are invited to describe a compelling and detailed picture of the preferred future. The question becomes 'What will things be like when Temper is gone?' This is often best explored via the Miracle Question (see Chapter 2 or the case study below).

Exceptions and strengths   Second, they are invited to reflect on the times that elements of the preferred future are already taking place in their lives. Guiding questions are:

- When are you able to outwit Temper?
- What happens on the days when Temper does not bother you?
- How do you keep Temper at bay on the good days?

Progress and next steps   Third, using scaling questions, they are invited to appreciate progress already made while determining possible next steps. In this way a bridge can be made from the 'now' to the preferred future. Sample questions include:

- On a scale of one to ten, where ten is Temper completely gone (and the miracle completely present) and one is the worst things have been, where would you say you are now?
- What tells you that you have come that far?
- What would move you one point further on?

Case study

Referral information

Rob is an eight-year-old boy (the third of four children) referred to a child mental health clinic because of serious behavioural problems at home and in school. These have included defiance, disruption and aggression. He can also be very verbally abusive to his mother, calling her insulting names in public. At times she has used physical discipline, but this has ended up in a fight. His mother, a single parent, is very hurt by his behaviour, especially the abuse, is very stressed by the level of defiance and aggression and worries that there is something seriously wrong with her son. She dreads going to school because of the constant negative reports she receives, and is fearful for his future education.

Engaging the family

The therapist telephoned the mother in order to make an initial connection with her and to consult with her about how to proceed. She described how, on a previous visit to a child mental health clinic, Rob had been very disruptive when she talked about the problems and the session had to be abandoned. As a result, the therapist suggested that she come alone to the first appointment so that he could hear her side of the story and they could plan how to engage Rob.

During the meeting, the mother described her long history of difficulty with Rob and how she really wanted some help in managing. The therapist empathised and offered different therapeutic options such as a parenting group, further individual parenting meetings or family meetings with Rob. The mother selected family meetings as she was very keen for the therapist to meet Rob. They discussed how they could engage Rob to take part in the meetings, and the therapist suggested that they make the session child-centred and positive, focused on trying to reach goals rather than on problems. In particular, he described the process of externalising the problem, which the mother thought was interesting and wanted to try out.

In the above engagement, the therapist attempts to be collaborative by not making assumptions about who should come to the first meeting and how they should be contacted. Instead, he discusses these issues openly with the mother, who is the initiator of the referral (and thus the person who is most likely to see the appointment as possibly useful) and attempts to make a collaborative decision. Having a preliminary meeting with family members who are keen for professional involvement (usually the parents) and to think through how to involve those who are unsure about the process (usually the children) is an excellent way to plan the therapy session. Indeed, such initial meetings often give parents an opportunity to tell their own story and ventilate their own feelings in a way that may not be appropriate with the child present. It also gives the therapist a chance to make an independent 'adult' connection with the parents before engaging on a child-centred session.

Meeting with Rob

Rob came to the meeting accompanied by his mother. He was clearly reluctant to attend, and this was confirmed by his mother who said she had to do a lot of persuading to get him to come. Therefore the first part of the meeting was dominated by the therapist taking time to put Rob at his ease and attempting to establish an alliance with him. The therapist acknowledged with Rob how difficult it was to come to the meeting and agreed some rules with him: that no-one was going to scold or blame Rob here; and that he didn't have to answer any questions that upset him. The therapist took time to explain to Rob about the clinic and gave him a tour of the video room. They also agreed that there would be a snack at the end of the meeting.

Problem-free talk   The therapist spent the first few minutes talking to Rob about his interests and what he was good at. He learnt that Rob was a keen footballer, that he played football at the school and that his favourite team was Manchester United. Rob began to open up and chat about his interests.

Naming the problem as external   The therapist judged that there was now sufficient rapport to return to the goal of the meeting.

Therapist: So, Rob, what do you hope might happen by coming down here?
Rob: Dunno.
Therapist: Well, what has brought you down here?
Rob: [Looks down] Behaviour.
Therapist: What sort of behaviour?
Rob: I get angry.
Therapist: I see ... Can anger be a bit of a problem?
Rob: Yeah.
Therapist: So it can be hard to keep anger away sometimes?
Rob: Yeah.
Therapist: What do you call that problem, when anger comes in and takes over?
Rob: Dunno ... Temper.
Therapist: Ah ... Temper is a good name for it.

In his use of language, the therapist is separating the child from the problem. Rather than exploring 'why Rob gets angry' and implicitly locating the problem within Rob, the therapist asks 'Can it be hard to keep anger away? , thus beginning to co-construct the problem as separate acting in on the child.

Evaluating the effects of the problem   The therapist moves on to explore the effects of Temper on Rob's life.

Therapist: How does Temper affect you? What happens when Temper comes in and takes over?
Rob: I dunno ... I get angry ...
Therapist: So it makes you angry?
Rob: I hit someone.
Therapist: So when Temper takes over, it can cause you to hit out? ... And what happens to you then?
Rob: I get into to trouble ... I get kept in, in school.

The therapist slowly explores how Temper affects Rob's life, particularly his schooling and family. Rob is able to name how he gets into a lot of trouble in school as a result and often is restricted from playing sports. A critical moment is later, during an exploration of how Temper affects his family.

Therapist: What else does Temper make you do?
Rob: I get into a fight with my Mum.
Therapist: What happens?
Rob: I shout at her or kick her. [Looks nervously to Mum]
Therapist: Oh ... that doesn't sound good ... How do you feel when that happens?

Rob:	I feel bad.
Therapist:	So you feel bad when Temper comes and takes over, making you hit out at your Mum. [Rob nods] ... How does your Mum feel about it?
Rob:	She feels sad. [Rob looks down, a little sad too]
Therapist:	[Empathetically] So you feel bad and your Mum feels sad ... [Both Rob and Mum look at one another, both are a little emotional] ... Sounds like an awful thing, this Temper. [Rob and Mum nod]
Therapist:	So what do you think of the fact that Temper comes in and makes you hit out and get into trouble and can make you feel bad and your Mum feel sad?
Rob:	I don't like it.
Therapist:	And what does your Mum think?
Rob:	She hates it.
Therapist:	She doesn't like it either ... What does your Dad think?
Rob:	He really hates it ... especially when I am cheeky. [Rob smiles at his Mum and she returns this]

The above sequence is a critical moment in the therapy. By the problem being externalised as Temper, Rob is able to begin to understand how it 'makes his mother feel sad'. His mother, in turn, is a witness to hear Rob articulate how he is also upset by the effects of Temper. In this way they can make an emotional connection. This is a moment where they are not fighting with one another, but beginning to support one another and to ally together against the externalised problem. In the next sequence, the therapist attempts to reinforce this alliance by inviting Rob to make a judgement and to decide whether he wants temper in his life. It is likely that this is the first time that he has been consulted and invited to make this decision, rather than it being assumed or made for him.

Taking a position

Therapist:	So, Rob, given all you have said about Temper and how it affects you at home and at school [Therapist summarises all the examples Rob gave] ... do you think Temper is a good thing or a bad thing in your life?
Rob:	A bad thing.
Therapist:	Why do you say it is a bad thing?
Rob:	Well, because I get into trouble and it upsets my Mum.
Therapist:	And would you like to get rid of Temper? Or at least make sure it doesn't take over all the time?
Rob:	Yes, I would.
Therapist:	Why do you want to get rid of Temper?
Rob:	Because it gets me into trouble ...
[The therapist goes on to help Rob articulate other reasons ...]	

This is a crucial moment in the session. Rob is asked to take a position on the problem that is at the crux of why he has been referred to therapy. It is a moment that should not be rushed, but explored in extensive detail. In Rob's case extra questions can be asked, such as 'Who else in the family would agree with his decision?', 'Would his mum or dad agree with the decision?' and 'Why would they want to get rid of Temper also?'. The aim is to help Rob clarify and justify his own decision as well as negotiate with his parents a shared decision. In Rob's case, his decision to 'get rid of Temper' builds on all the thinking and reflecting that he has done before. If an alliance had not been established and the problem sufficiently externalised, Rob may have not made the decision to 'get rid of Temper', as the question may have been experienced as a personal attack, that he was to blame. By taking time to *slowly* go through the arguments and to elicit Rob's thoughts, he is helped to think through issues in a 'blame-free way', to take a different position and to access the support of his family.

The decision now forms the turning point in the session. With the problem clearly negotiated and agreed by all parties, now it is time to ask Rob and his family for a detailed picture of their preferred future. This is a good time for the miracle question.

A useful way to slow down a session at crucial moments to ensure that important insights and descriptions are not missed and given extra attention, is for the therapist to take notes. Simply say 'That sounds really important, let me write it down.' As the therapist slowly writes down the key insights in the child's or parent's words, repeating them out loud as he writes, this allows space for further thought and reflection. It also gives extra weight to the family's own ideas and is thus a big reinforcer in helping them feel that they are being taken seriously, valued and recognised as collaborators. The fact that the therapist repeats out loud the child's words as he writes them down not only adds extra weight to what the child is saying, it also reassures everyone that the therapist is, in fact, writing what is being said, rather than making other 'professional judgements or comments'. The notes can then be used as the basis of case notes or a report and given to the family as a summary of the session.

Solution building

Therapist: I want to ask you a really interesting question. It can be a hard question because it requires lots of thinking, but I know you can do it. And most children find it really fun … .

Rob: [Sits up interested] OK.

Therapist: Supposing when you leave here today, a miracle takes place tonight that means that the problem – Temper – is completely gone, not half gone but completely gone, from you life. But, of course, you don't know the miracle has taken place because you were asleep [Therapist pauses to see if Rob is following]. So what would be the first thing you would notice in the morning that would tell you the miracle has happened?

Rob: [Thinks] I would get up and get dressed quickly.

Therapist: You would get dressed quickly? [Mum smiles]

Therapist: Your Mum is smiling.

Rob: She likes it when I get dressed quickly … when she doesn't have to keep calling me.

Therapist: Ah, I see … What else would your mum notice about you that would tell her that a miracle had taken place?

Rob:	Well, I would be happy.
Therapist:	How would she would know you were happy
Rob:	I would be smiling ... [Rob puts on a big smile]
Therapist:	So you would be smiling ... a bit like the way you are now?
Rob:	Yeah.
Therapist:	And what would your mum be doing?
Rob:	She would be happy and smiling too ... [Mum matches his smile and they share a joke]
Therapist:	So you would be happy and smiling the way the two of you are now.

Later, the therapist explores how school would go when the miracle has taken place.

Therapist:	What would you notice in school when the miracle has taken place?
Rob:	Well, I wouldn't be fighting.
Therapist:	You wouldn't be fighting ... What would you being doing instead?
Rob:	Dunno ... Getting on with everyone.
Therapist:	What happens when you get on with everyone?
Rob:	I share.
Therapist:	You share ...
Rob:	If a boy asked me for a pencil, I'd give it to him.
Therapist:	Ah ... that is a great example, if a boy asked you for a pencil you would give it to him ... that would mean you were getting on with him ...
Rob:	Yeah.
Therapist:	What way would you give it to him? ... [Therapist reframes question as Rob looks a little confused] I mean, would you give it to him in a grumpy way or in a happy way ...
Rob:	A happy way.
Mum:	With a smile.
Rob:	[laughs] Yeah, with a smile.

In the above sequence, the therapist is taking pains to elicit a detailed response from Rob about the miracle. The more individual and concrete the details of the solution description, the more meaningful and compelling this is to the family. For example, instead of Rob saying that he would share when the miracle takes place, it is more effective for him to elaborate the example of giving a pencil in a happy manner. The latter description is richer and more elaborate. It allows the counter-plot of the solution to be thickened and witnessed. Equally, the elaboration of how Mum and Rob would be happier in the morning by a detailed description of the shared smile and then it being enacted in the session makes the experience all the more powerful. The therapist's role is important. Rather than assuming that he knows what each of these things mean, the therapist dons the role of a respectful inquirer, ensuring to note down the child's descriptions and ideas.

Exceptions ... when the miracle is already happening

Therapist: So let me ask you another interesting question ... When in the last week do you think you have been closest to the miracle happening?

Rob: Last Friday, when I got a star in school.

Therapist: What did you get the star for?

Rob: For doing well in class in the spelling test and drawing.

Therapist: Well done ... And Mum, did you know that it was a good day for Rob and that he got a star?

Mum: Yeah, yeah, I noticed he was happy, he came rushing out to tell me. He was working on his spelling all week.

Therapist: Right, so he was working hard ... and was Friday a good day for other reasons?

Rob: Yeah, no homework! [Mum and Rob laugh]

Therapist: And were things also good at home?

Rob: Yeah ...

Therapist: What was good?

Rob: I helped mum clean up ...

Therapist: Wow ... is that right? He cleaned up?

Mum: I think he might have ... He can be very helpful when he is in good form. I think because he had a good day at school he took that home with him.

Therapist: I see, so you noticed that he was in better form ...

Mum: Yeah, I could see because he was getting on with his sister ... they weren't fighting.

Therapist: How did you do that, Rob? How did you get on with your sister?

The remainder of the session was spent elaborating the exception with Rob. At the end the therapist wrote with Rob a summary of the session that highlighted Rob's goal to defeat Temper and that listed all the skills he used to keep Temper at bay and all the supports he had to do this.

Follow-up meetings   Rob attended three follow-up meetings with his mother. The sessions focused on elaborating the progress he had made towards his goals. Though there were ups and downs in his behaviour, overall the mother and Rob felt they were making progress. The critical change seemed to be a better understanding between Rob and his mother. They were working together rather than against one another as they both tried to defeat Temper.

Summary

In this chapter we have described the technique of externalising the problem. This approach works well when parents and children feel blamed or defensive about the problem. It provides a way of talking about the problem that promotes responsibility in a blame-free way and which can help parents and children move from conflict to ally with one another against a problem in pursuit of a shared goal. We illustrated the ideas with an extended case study about an eight-year-old boy referred due to behaviour problems.

PART III:

SOME CHALLENGING CONTEXTS

---

11 Working with Suicidal Adolescents[1]

John Sharry, Melissa Darmody and Brendan Madden

Mr and Mrs Walsh have been concerned about their 14-year-old daughter Tina. Over the last year she has become very moody and difficult. Her school grades have suffered and she has been getting into trouble all the time. Matters came to a head when, after a row over staying out late, Tina stormed up to her room and was found later to have cut her wrists. Her parents, very distressed about this, took her to casualty. The doctors, after dealing with her injuries, referred her to the local child and family clinic.

William, a 15-year-old boy, has come to the attention of the school counsellor. He has become increasingly withdrawn and isolated in the class. His parents have just separated and he is known to be very upset about this. He opened up to his English teacher and said that he felt hopeless and 'just wanted to die'.

Self-harm and suicide are amongst the most challenging and frightening problems that you can encounter as a professional in the course of your work. The risk of clients harming themselves can debilitate you from acting creatively and collaboratively and make your actions defensive, focused solely on risk assessment rather than therapeutic change. Yet it is precisely a creative and collaborative response, such as that engendered by a strengths-based approach, that is the most likely to facilitate change and re-empower clients to take back charge of their lives. This chapter describes some principles of a strengths-based approach to working with suicidal clients that can be used in conjunction with traditional

---

[1]This chapter is an adapted version of an article published in *The British Journal of Guidance and Counselling* (Sharry, Darmody and Madden, 2002) http://www.tandf.co.uk. Melissa Darmody and Brendan Madden are co-founders of the Brief Therapy Group in Dublin.

approaches and which focus on establishing safety as well as assessing risk. Working from this model, the clinician shifts to identifying client strengths and coping skills, to collaborating with the client to establish meaningful goals and to helping the client envision a positive future. Arguably, such an approach can increase collaboration between therapist and client and lead to a more client-centred safety plan.

Depression and suicide

Depression is an every-person's illness and it is one of the more common reasons for people to come to the therapist's office or to seek the help of a professional. Depression as a diagnosis is really a 'semi-formal' term as the word exists in the vernacular and people commonly frame their problems as being connected to 'being depressed' or 'feeling low'. People are more likely to present at the therapists office saying they are depressed, rather than saying they have an anxiety disorder.

With children and young people, the problem of depression is generally less explicit and many of them are referred on account of other problems, such as moodiness, conduct problems or disruptive behaviour in the classroom. The naming of the problem as 'depression' can have some benefits to the young person in question. For example, it can elicit more support from parents and teachers who can reframe the child's actions as understandable in the context of certain life events, rather than being simply disruptive or oppositional.

Self-harm and suicide are serious problems that affect large numbers of people in the Western world. Particularly alarming are the recent increases in suicide and suicide attempts by young people and teenagers, especially young men (Cantor, 2000). There are specific differences in the rates of suicide and attempted suicide between young men and women. Young women are more likely to attempt suicide, but less likely to be successful and more likely to seek the support of family friends and mental health services. Young men are more likely to choose lethal means, less likely to seek support and thus much more likely to complete suicide (Carr, 1999). Depression and suicide are highly correlated in that studies have shown that between 29 per cent and 88 per cent of people who committed suicide were depressed, and about half of all people with a diagnosis of depression report having suicidal ideation (Lonnqvist, 2000). However, it is important to note that not all young people who attempt suicide report being depressed. Other factors such as drug and alcohol use, risk taking and impulsive behaviour are all very significant contributors to a decision to make a suicide attempt. Though for some young people a suicide attempt is a one-off event, studies have shown that 50 per cent are likely to repeat an attempt within the following 12 months, and some of these are successful (Carr, 1999).

Though a significant number of people at risk of suicide do not seek professional help – especially young men (Pfeffer, 2000) – some studies have shown that over half of those who attempt suicide are already in contact with mental health services (Hawkes et al., 1998). This puts an onus on mental health professionals to find therapeutic ways of reducing the risk of the many suicidal and depressed clients who come to the attention of services, while also finding creative ways of reaching out to the significant groups of young people who are at risk and who avoid professional contact.

Traditionally, the professional response has consisted of risk assessment and management, followed by treatment interventions such as medication or psycho-therapy (Carr, 1999; Hawton and van Heeringen, 2000). Alarmingly, there has been little empirical research to suggest that either medication or psychotherapy-based interventions, in their current format, are effective in reducing the risk of suicide when compared to a non-treatment control group (Heard, 2000; Verkes and Cowen, 2000). (This is partly due to the ethical and practical difficulties in conducting such research.) Cognitive and problem-solving therapies, however, that focus on helping the young person and their family solve practical and rela-tionship problems show the most promise (Hazell, 2000).

In addition, many of the techniques used by practitioners, such as entering into a no-suicide contract with clients during treatment, are not as effective as com-monly believed. For example, in a postal survey of clinicians examining the rates of suicidal attempts following treatment, Kroll (2000) found that 41 per cent of respondents had treated people who committed or made a serious attempt *after* entering into a no-suicide contract with the clinician. While this data tells us nothing of the efficacy of contracting relative to not contracting, it does indicate that no clinician should take excessive comfort from the fact that a suicidal person agrees to a contract for safety. Indeed, it suggests that we should continue to be search-ing for more effective ways of working with this high-risk client group.

A strengths-based approach to suicide risk

In recent years, many practitioners have been exploring how solution-focused therapy can apply to work with clients who are suicidal or who have a history of self-harm (Calcott and MacKenzie, 2001; Hawkes et al., 1998; Softas-Nall and Francis (1998a). In particular, the authors have explored how solution-focused ideas, particularly scaling questions, can be used to enhance traditional approaches to suicide risk assessment in order to establish a safety plan with clients and their families. Though there is a growing body of research for solution-focused therapy in general (George et al., 1999), there is as yet no empirical evidence for the effectiveness of the approach with suicidal clients. There is, however, some evidence that the strengths-based orientation which solution-focused therapy engenders may be a fruitful one. For example, Malone (2000) studied 84 depressed individuals, many with a prior history of suicide attempts. Depressed individuals who had *no* history of suicide attempts had greater survival and coping beliefs, more moral objections to suicide, and more reasons for living. While being far from definitive, these results suggest that rather than exclusively carrying out risk assessment, clinicians should also spend time doing the things that might prevent depressed individuals from attempting suicide, such as high-lighting their coping skills, exploring their reasons for living, and helping them envision a more hopeful and optimistic future.

In addition, there have been a number of suicide prevention programmes in the US that have raised awareness about suicide amongst teenagers and which have focused on helping teenagers identify the warning signs in themselves and others, as well as teaching them how to access help and support. Follow-up empirical studies, however, have not shown a decrease in suicidal behaviour and alarmingly there has been some evidence that risk has been increased (Schaffer and Gould, 2000). One hypothesis is that this is due to the usual problem-focused nature of the interventions, which may increase the appeal to teenagers. Indeed, many studies have shown that there is an increase in suicides when a prominent figure in youth culture (such as a pop or movie star) commits suicide and this is well publicised in the media (Schmidtke and Schaller, 2000). For this reason, it is likely that prevention programmes that focus on wellness and health, teaching young people social and coping skills, are likely to be more successful. Indeed, some studies suggest that these health-focused interventions are the most promising in reducing suicidal intention among teenagers, though further evaluation is needed (Klingman and Hochdorf, 1993). This underpinning wellness philosophy resonates with the strengths and goal focus of solution-focused therapy and is where a contribution can be made.

Solution-focused therapy is not unique in engendering a strengths-based collaborative approach to working with suicidal clients and the ideas strongly resonate with other brief interventions, particularly those from the cognitive behavioural tradition. For example, the SNAP programme (Miller et al., 1992), a cognitive-behavioural intervention for adolescent suicide attempters and their families, has much in common with solution-focused therapy in that it focuses on establishing practical goals, encouraging strengths-based communication between family members and using scaling questions to assess risk and to establish safety plans.

Some people have expressed caution about using a strengths-based approach with suicidal clients, especially given the implicit lack of emphasis on risk assessment. Indeed, a strict application of strengths-based techniques without taking into account the dangers that clients could be in would be an unethical way of practicing, as clearly there will be times when the therapist has to take unilateral action to ensure a client's safety (such as informing other family members or the family doctor, or arranging an involuntary in-patient stay). However, there are also dangers from being excessively problem or risk focused in that this can close down the possibility of therapy. Clients will simply not talk to you if they feel that you are going to react in a specific way without consulting or listening to them first. For example, many people will not disclose just how depressed or hopeless they feel for fear someone will 'lock them up'. Ironically, it is these clients, who are without a person with whom they can supportively communicate, who are at the most risk of harming themselves.

In their model combining the benefits of the solution-focused therapy model with the caution of risk assessment, Hawkes et al. (1998) have recommended using the standard solution-focused therapeutic interview as the starting point of engagement with the client. Safety can be explored using some of the model's techniques, notably scaling questions (as we shall see later). If concerns still exist about safety, for the therapist or the client, then the therapy stops and a management plan is negotiated. The overriding concern is the safety of the client.

Three strengths-based interventions

In the remainder of this chapter we describe three strengths-based interventions, notably:

- listening for strengths
- moving from problems to goals
- using scaling questions

These have a particular relevance to working with young people and their families when there is a concern around suicide. We conclude the chapter with the important area of how suicide risk can be assessed and managed from a strengths-based perspective, particularly using scaling questions.

Listening for strengths

Young people who have attempted suicide can experience a lot of blame and anger from those around them. Their family and friends can be upset and angry at what has happened, and the young people themselves can feel guilty at what they have done and fear that they must be 'losing it' or going mad. The suicide attempt is often experienced as a shameful event for the family and the parents can often feel blamed that there must be something 'wrong with their family' or with their relationship with their son or daughter for the attempt to have happened. In addition, they can feel guilty that they did not protect their child and be anxious and hypervigilant about there being a repeat attempt. Many parents have described the situation immediately after a suicide attempt as being like 'walking on eggshells' as the parents fear saying or doing anything that might provoke another attempt.

When faced with the above web of blame and guilt, the therapist must find a way of not adding to these negative feelings but of establishing an alliance with each family member. Often initial individual interviews with the parents and then the young person before embarking on a family meeting can be the best way forward. A gentle, strengths-based, multi-partial listening style can also help facilitate this.

How this is done is often very subtle, depending a lot on both the verbal and non-verbal communication the therapist employs. Consider the differing impacts of the two possible opening questions to a young person and to their parents in a post-suicide attempt interview.

- *to young person*

  Therapist: What made you do what you did?
  OR
  Therapist: You must have had a pretty good reason for doing what you did?

- *To parent*

> *Therapist*: What has being happening in the family just prior to what Tom did?
>
> OR
>
> *Therapist*: I'm sure you have been coping with quite a lot since what happened with Tom?

In both cases, the first questions can inadvertently communicate a judgement or make the clients feel defensive. In the case of the young person, he may be surrounded by family and friends asking him this question who implicitly blame him for what happened. By the therapist asking the same question, he may feel that the therapist blames him also. In the case of the parent, the first question may reinforce a parent who already feels guilty and powerless. The second opening statements are more empathetic, disarming, and non-judgemental. It is difficult for the clients to disagree with them and they implicitly assume a positive strengths-based view of the clients, for example that the young person acts reasonably and with good cause, and that the parent takes action to cope with difficult events. In this way strengths-based listening has begun and both young person and parent are gently invited to tell more of their stories.

How we listen and communicate with the young person and their family after the suicide attempt helps construct how the event is understood by them and thus their expectations and actions as they go forward. For example, the event could be understood by the young person as 'a further example of the hopelessness he feels' or as 'a turning point in his life when things changed positively for him'. Or the parents could perceive the attempt as the beginning of a downward slide to even more serious problems, or they could view the event as a 'lucky escape' which gave them an opportunity to get closer to their son/daughter and to make a difference in the future.

While therapists cannot control how parent and child communicate with each other and come to understand what has happened, they are highly influential and co-authors with the family of the process. Helping the family communicate supportively with one another and create a strengths-based and possibility focused understanding of what has happened, *which fits with all the evidence and the unique experience of the family*, is likely to be the best protective factor going forward. This means 'bracketing' our negative expectations and predictions about the family (many of which can flow from professional theories about the problem) and genuinely seeking to understand the family in a different and more constructive light. It also means actively searching with the family for signs of change and hope, and helping them to use the difficult event of the suicide attempt as an opportunity to learn from one another and constructively to move forward.

Consider the following example of this strengths-based listening with a teenage mother who has had suicidal thoughts and a near-fatal attempt:

> *Therapist:* How did you pull back at the last moment [from the suicide attempt]?

Client: [Thinks] Well, I thought of my children.

Therapist: I see, what did you think about them?

Client: I thought of how alone they would be if I killed myself, of how much they need me.

Therapist: Sounds like you have a lot of love for them ... that you really want to be there for them.

Client: Yes. [A little tearful]

Therapist: What does that say about you as a person ... that you want to be there for your children ... even despite the pain you feel yourself?

Client: [Pause] ... It means that I want to be the best mother I can be for them.

Therapist: I can really see that.

The shift to a strengths-based conversation starts with the therapist thinking positively about the clients and their actions and beginning to reflect this back to them. For example, when faced by a family who have come to therapy because of a suicide attempt, rather than seeing them simply as having 'dysfunctional communication patterns', the therapist can reflect about the courage and organisation it took to come to therapy and state:

> *Therapist:* You're the type of family that doesn't sweep problems under the carpet, but faces them bravely and takes steps to sort them out ... I think it also shows a great willingness to change and learn, the fact that you all got here today.

Or rather than reflecting about the action of a suicide attempt, the therapist can reflect back to the client the underlying motivation that underpins it, stating, for example:

> *Therapist:* I'm struck by how desperately you must want things to change for the better, given that you were prepared to consider ending your life.

The focus on strengths, skills and resources is not about simple 'positive thinking' or about denying or minimising the problem. A strengths-based approach is not a problem or pain phobic. Clients need to feel that their problems and difficulties are taken seriously, that their suffering is acknowledged and that they are not blamed for the problem. A good strengths-based therapist communicates this empathic understanding, while also communicating a belief in the strengths of the client and in the possibility that they can influence things for the better. Therapy should both provide the client with compassion and understanding about their difficulties as well as encouragement and inspiration that things could be made better.

Moving from problems to goals

Suicidal thoughts and suicide attempts are serious problems, but they are not goals. Suicide is more of a means to an end rather the end or goal in itself. Clients who see suicide as an option desperately want things to be different in their lives, whether this is ending the hurt they feel or ensuring that other people take notice. Though it is a drastic course of action, they feel hopeless and believe that suicide is the only way to achieve these goals. The aim of therapy is to uncover with the client the positive goals and intentions that underpin their suicidal actions and to explore with them how they can achieve these by other means. For example, if clients say that they wish to die, the therapist becomes interested in what they hope to be different by this. The question becomes 'How do you hope that being dead will help or be different for you?' Consider the following more elaborate example:

Therapist:	Things must have been really difficult for you, for you to consider harming yourself ... You must really want things to be different in your life?
Client:	Yeah, I want an end to the pain I'm feeling.
Therapist:	I see, you don't want to feel this pain anymore, you'd prefer to feel a bit ...?
Client:	... a bit better.
Therapist:	Ah ha, how are things for you when they are better?
Client:	Well, I wouldn't wake up with this dark cloud over me ... I'd wake up and feel lighter.
Therapist:	So when things are better, you wake up in the morning feeling lighter ... maybe rather than a dark cloud there would be ...
Client:	Sunshine.
Therapist:	Ah ... so you would like more sunshine in your life?
Client:	Yeah, that is it.
Therapist:	[Curious] Tell me then, what would you be doing differently if there was more sunshine in your life?
Client:	Hum ... I guess I would be able to go back to work, it has been a while since I went to work ... feeling so down and all.
Therapist:	What else?
Client:	Well, I guess I would not feel like ending it. I would feel like there was something to live for.
Therapist:	Like?
Client:	That people cared, you know? I would know that people cared; it just seems that they don't anymore.
Therapist:	So it is pretty important for you to know people care ... When was the last time you had that feeling?

The therapist attempts to help the client articulate clear, positive goals, defined in terms of things the client wants rather than what he or she doesn't want. For example, it is not sufficient to know that the client does not want to be depressed anymore; the therapist wants to know what will be present in his or her life when the depression is gone – what will the client be feeling or doing when the depression is gone? The more concrete and detailed the goal is, the better. The aim is to help the client envision a future where the problem has been eliminated and to describe this in detail. A useful way to do this is with imaginative questions such as the miracle question (Berg, 1991; de Shazer, 1988), which has been discussed in Chapter 2.

Goals for the therapy   As well as uncovering the positive goals that underpin clients' suicidal intentions, the solution-focused therapist is interested in establishing an agreed goal for the therapy with the client. The question is not 'What problem brings you to therapy?' but 'What would you like to achieve by coming to therapy?' Or, as Iveson (2000) frames it, 'What is your best hope for these meetings? Establishing goals with children and parents is a tricky business as they often have goals that appear directly in conflict, and this is especially the case when dealing with a serious and frightening problem like suicide, though the discovery of an agreed goal marks a critical step towards change. Consider the following sequence, taken from a family session with a teenager who had attempted suicide:

Therapist: [Addressing whole family] So what would you hope to get out of coming to these meetings?
Father: We're here for Tina.
Therapist: You're here for your daughter.
Father: I don't want anything bad to happen to her ... I want to help her.
Therapist: You want her to be safe and well ... and you want to find a way of helping her.
Father: Yeah.
Therapist: What do you think of what your Dad is saying?
Tina: [Shrugs] Dunno!
Therapist: [Addressing Tina] What would you hope for coming down to this meeting?
Tina: I just wish everyone would stop making a fuss and leave me alone.
Therapist: Yes ... you'd like some space?
Tina: Yeah, I wish they'd trust me again.
Therapist: You'd like your parents to trust you and give you some space?
Therapist: What do you think? [Addressing the mother] What would you like to happen?
Mother: I'd just like to get the old Tina back.
Therapist: What do you like about the old Tina?
Mother: Well, she'd smile a lot more.
Therapist: I see, you'd like to see a lot more smiles.

When the client sees suicide as the goal   Establishing goals with clients often isn't easy and it can be especially challenging with clients who initially describe 'suicide as the goal'. While as a professional you can't ethically agree with such a goal, arguing with, confronting or trying to persuade clients to have a different goal is usually an ineffective way forward. It can be more fruitful to explore with them what life would be like after the suicide has happened and thereby begin to discover goals and distinguish the suicidal act as simply one means of many. Consider the two following sample questions that can often work well when they are put as a challenge to teenagers who are initially resistant to envisioning alternatives:

Therapist: I've got an unusual question now ... but I'm not sure you'd be able to or want to answer it.

Client: Go on, try me.

Therapist: OK. Supposing you've done it and gone through with the suicide ... and suppose your spirit survives and is hovering above looking down, what would be different?

OR

Therapist: Suppose that after you die you find yourself at the pearly gates. You are greeted courteously by an angel who informs you that you have been granted a second chance. When you return to earth you find that all your problems are gone and your life is very satisfactory. How would life be for you then? (Calcott and MacKenzie, 2001)

In other instances an honest revelation of the professional's goals for the work can sometimes create the circumstances where you can negotiate a realistic goal (that doesn't involve suicide). Consider the following example where the client, who is in an inpatient ward, feels very hopeless and sees no other way out but suicide:

Therapist: So what are your best hopes for these meetings?

Client: I dunno, I don't see any other way out. I just can't bear the pain anymore.

Therapist: Things sound really hard for you at the moment.

Client: Yeah, I just want to end it all. And that is what I'm going to do when I leave here. They can't keep me in forever.

Therapist: You're pretty serious about trying to kill yourself?

Client: And I don't think coming to meet you can change my mind.

Therapist: You're not sure yet what we can achieve in these meetings. [Pause] Can I make a proposal to you?

Client: OK.

Therapist: I'm sorry that you are in so much pain, so much so that you feel like ending your life. And I'd like to be of help to you, but I don't want to see you killing yourself. Would you be interested in talking with me about how things could be different, how you could end the pain without ending your life? You can then decide if it is helpful to you. Even if we don't come up with anything new, you can still go back to your old option, but I think we might be able to find something helpful. Would you like to give this a try?

The aim is to invite clients into conversation about alternative perspectives on the problems they are facing and to open up the possibility of a future where life is better for them, with suicide sidelined as a potential method of moving forward.

Using scaling questions

As discussed in Chapter 2, scaling questions provide powerful and versatile ways of measuring change and breaking goals down to small achievable steps. They are particularly helpful in working with suicidal teenagers and their families in identifying what they want from one another and in establishing a client-centred safety plan. The question simply becomes 'On a scale of one to ten, where ten is you feeling happy and safe and one is the worst you felt, where would you put yourself now?' The power of the question is not in the answer, but in the important follow-up questions that can elicit concrete positives and examples of change. For example, suppose a teenage girl, who had attempted suicide, rated herself at three on the scale (where ten was 'feeling happy and safe'), the therapist can ask questions such as 'What has got you to three on the scale?', 'What is different being at three rather than two?', 'Who in your family helped you to get here?'

In addition, scaling questions can help identify times when thing were better for the teenager. For example, the therapist could ask 'In the last two weeks, what is the highest point you have reached on the scale?' Once again it is the follow-up questions which are the most fruitful: suppose she answered that she was 'at a six' during the weekend, the therapist could explore how the family could help in the following way:

Therapist: What was happening when you were at a six? What were things like in your family then? What were you doing differently? What were your parents doing differently? What did you feel about those times?

In addition, the therapist could ask the parents corresponding questions:

Therapist: What do you remember about the time when things were six in the family? What did you notice about your daughter then? What was she doing differently? What were you doing differently?

Even if a client scores very low on the scale, follow-up questions can be used to elicit what next steps need to be taken. For example, if the client states they are at one on the scale – the lowest point they have ever felt – the therapist can respond:

Therapist: I'm sorry to hear things are so low for you at the moment ... Supposing things were to be a little better for you, say you were to move one point (or half a point) forward on the scale ... what would that be like? What would you first notice that would tell you that things were beginning to improve?

Assessing safety using scaling questions

As distinct from working with other clients we have a responsibility, when working with suicidal clients, to assess the suicide risk and to take action if clients are in danger. Some therapists have explored how solution-focused therapy can complement more traditional forms of risk assessment by using scaling questions to collaboratively establish with clients the level of risk and the safety action needed (Calcott and MacKenzie, 2001; Softas-Nall and Francis, 1998b; Hawkes et al., 1998). Useful questions are:

Therapist: On a scale of one to ten, how confident are you that you will be able to get through the weekend without attempting to harm yourself, where one means you feel you have no chance and ten means you are totally confident? What makes you that confident? What needs to happen to make you more confident … to move one point forward on the scale?

Therapist: Suppose over the weekend your mood drops two points on the scale, what will you do to ensure you get back on track? What would help to get you back up to six on the scale?

Where appropriate, other family members should be involved in safety discussions, and often they can provide great resources in helping the client to be safe. Questions can be addressed to them such as:

Therapist: On the same scale, how confident are you that your son will be safe this weekend? What makes you that confident? What needs to happen to make you more confident … to move one point forward on the scale?

In order to work safely in a therapeutic contract, clients ideally should be able to give some sort of guarantee that they will not harm themselves between sessions. If this is not the case, therapists may need to consider other options. Consider the following example:

Therapist: On a scale of one to ten, when ten is you can 100 per cent guarantee me you will be able to keep yourself safe until we meet again and one is after our meeting you think you are definitely going to end things, where would you say you are now?

Client: Two.

Therapist: What would help you feel more confident that you would be able to be safe until next week?

Client: Don't know, I guess I just feel so out of control again. I had been doing really well, but recently it is just scary … Maybe I have to go back into the hospital. I hate to say this, but it would be the only place I would feel safe at the moment. If I am on my own, I just couldn't promise anything.

Therapist: It sounds pretty scary at the moment. should we call your GP and see if he can arrange for you to go in hospital?

In the above example, though the therapist has to take action (that is, contacting the GP) to ensure the safety of the client, this is done in as collaborative a way as possible to preserve the client's sense of self-efficacy in deciding the resources needed to protect himself or herself. If the client was not able to cooperate and demonstrated a high level of risk, then the therapist would have to consider taking unilateral action (for example, in extreme cases arranging for the client be detained involuntarily). It can be acknowledged with the client that you cannot simply do nothing if they intend to harm themselves, that you have a duty of care to protect them and do what you can to preserve life. As Hawkes et al. (1998) state, this is the point where therapy should stop and case management should begin, though this should be done in as a respectful and collaborative way as possible.

Conclusion

Traditionally, professional responses to suicidal and self-harming clients have consisted of risk assessment and case management. In recent times there has been a growing interest in exploring more collaborative and strengths-based approaches to working with this client group. In this chapter we have outlined how the principles of focusing on strengths, reframing problems as goals and using scaling questions can be applied to working with clients who are suicidal and/or at risk of harming themselves. The approach can be best conceived as enhancing and complementing traditional approaches and not a replacement for solid risk assessment and management. The aim of therapy is to move away from an exclusive focus on the problem and to help clients envision a positive future where suicide is not an option.

12 Working with Child Abuse and Neglect[1]

Declan Coogan and John Sharry

After his parents separated, Tom, a 15-year-old boy, moved in with his father, Mike. They argued every night. Tom dropped out of school and went missing for long periods during the evening, and his parents thought he was using drugs. As a result, the family were referred to an adolescent mental health service. During one of the sessions, they described a fight that had taken place between them and Tom accused his father of treating him roughly and of 'pushing him down the stairs'.

Anyone working with children and families faces the challenges of dealing constructively with the issues of child abuse and neglect. Depending on your professional context, difficult questions are likely to emerge. For example, when a parent hints at the use of physical discipline during a therapeutic conversation, should the therapist ask more direct questions about what happened? Or when a parent describes her own regret about mistreating her child to a family worker, what, if anything, does the worker need to tell the child protection services? Or working as a child protection worker, what is the best way to conduct an assessment of risk in a way that keeps the parents and family engaged?

Child abuse legislation and procedural guidelines offer little assistance when it comes to answering in concrete terms these difficult questions that arise when working with children and families. Further, cases of child abuse and neglect evoke strong feelings and reactions from people in general and professionals in particular which can divert workers from responding creatively and thoughtfully. When confronted by a father reporting physical discipline towards his 'out of control' teenage son, the worker could have conflicting feelings of anger towards the father for his use of violence, and/or of exasperation with his son for his persistent provocation of his father. The worker may experience an immediate impulse to take the part of the victim and condemn the perpetrator of violence. But such an approach may increase the father's defensiveness, reduce engagement and close down the possibility of therapeutic change. On the other hand, the worker may feel uncomfortable about pursuing any further the suggestion of physical abuse for fear that it could damage the therapeutic relationship with the father. It could appear that keeping silent on potential controversial issues is a better way to build a

---

[1]Declan Coogan is a senior social worker at the Department of Child and Family Psychiatry, Mater Hospital Dublin.

therapeutic relationship. But there is a real danger that such an approach could be collusive and give tacit support to the father's rough treatment of his son. The two approaches of condemnation or collusion are fraught with danger.

From a strengths-based perspective, the aim is to avoid the twin pitfalls of *collusion*, whereby the worker avoids conversation about possible abuse thereby increasing risk, or *condemnation,* where the worker rushes to blame and judge, which leads to a therapeutic cul-de-sac. Instead, the aim is to arrive at a the 'middle way' of *collaboration* with parents and other professionals in order to protect children and to increase safety.

Towards collaboration, not collusion or condemnation

Throughout this book we have emphasised the importance of establishing a collaborative partnership with families as the necessary platform for making therapeutic progress towards solutions. This is especially the case in situations of child abuse and neglect. Even though we may need to take strong protective action, such as formally reporting child abuse or acting to remove a child into foster care, these actions are best done in ways that involve some degree of collaboration with parents and with children (see Box 12.1). We do not serve a child's interest if we remove him or her into care in a way that alienates the parents so that any ongoing relationship with the child is damaged, causing them to either break off all constructive contact or to try and sabotage or undermine the child's placement. Most of the abused children that I have worked with tell me they want two things: they want the abuse to stop and they want some ongoing, more positive relationship with their parents (including the parent who has abused them). Thus, even in extreme cases, it is important that we work hard to listen to the needs of children and to work hard to collaborate with their parents. Successful child protection, like successful therapy, depends on establishing a collaborative partnership between parents and professionals.

How this partnership is established is largely determined by the professional context of the worker. A different response is called for by a child protection social worker doing an initial assessment to formally investigate an allegation of child abuse, rather than a psychotherapist in a mental health clinic responding to child protection concerns that have emerged in the course of the therapy. Drawing on a strengths-based perspective, let us consider some general principles that apply across these contexts and which correspond to the over-arching principles outlined in Chapter 2.

Box 12.1   Collaboration for child protection

- Being honest and open about child protection responsibilities.
- Joining respectfully to invite responsibility.
- Focusing on strengths, resources and safety.
- Focusing on goals and positive intentions.

Being honest and open about child protection responsibilities

Dangerous practice occurs when professionals are not prepared to acknowledge their responsibility to protect children, nor to openly discuss and negotiate difficult issues or concerns with parents. Describing the experience of child protection social workers who adopted a solution-focused approach to casework, Trish Walsh emphasises the importance of relationship building and the need for clarity and honesty about the legal context within which a practitioner works (Walsh, 1997). When conducting an initial assessment, the worker can begin with an explanation of how the worker will direct the interview, how he or she relates to a team and/or the referrer and the meaning of confidentiality. In fact, most parents respect such an honest and upfront approach.

For example, a child protection worker may begin an assessment as follows:

My role is to work with parents to ensure their children are safe and free from harm. Out of respect for parents, I always try to be honest and upfront about concerns and problems and I hope you can be honest and upfront with me. In the course of the interview I want to explore not only problems but also strengths and what you are doing right as parents. My hope is always to work constructively with parents and to put together a plan to support them in the care of their children. I will report back what we discuss today to my team leader and together we will try to make the best decision as to how to proceed. Does that sound OK to you?

Even where there is no suggestion of child protection concerns, there needs to be an honest recognition of these dynamics in the therapeutic relationship from the outset. Working with children and families, whether in a therapeutic or statutory agency, inherently involves a relationship in which a degree of worker authority and responsibility cannot be denied. There needs to be an honest recognition from the outset that the worker and the client may have to consider the need to involve the statutory services. As Turnell and Edwards point out:

> Professionals, whether charged with statutory obligations or not, have a responsibility to children in actual or possible situations of abuse and neglect to make judgements regarding their safety. This could be construed as 'social control' but we would rather view it simply as responsible professional practice. (Turnell and Edwards, 1999; 164).

In practical terms, this can simply mean having a child protection policy/leaflet that is made available to parents that states the positive goals of child safety and welfare as well as including principles for working with parents (for example, that they will be informed of any concerns and consulted with about referral to other agencies). When running a parenting or children's group, it can be helpful to discuss child protection and confidentiality in advance so that parents can be aware from the start of how you intend to proceed. The essential point is to frame child protection as a shared responsibility between parents and professionals.

Joining respectfully to invite responsibility

Though it is tempting to condemn or immediately confront parents about parenting concerns, it is worth taking time to understand the situation constructively from their point of view. In the situation of physical punishment, it is worth considering that anyone who looks after children rarely feels completely happy with the use of physical punishment, and when it is used it is often as a last resort. Rather than immediately criticising, workers can join with clients in their uncomfortable feelings about what happened and begin with them a search for effective alternatives to slapping and physical discipline. Consider the following dialogue in response to a parent who reports that she has hit her child in a 'fit of rage':

Worker: Things must have been very difficult for you for you to get to the point of hitting out like that.

Mother: They were. He was driving me crazy and he was deliberately misbehaving. I felt humiliated because it was in public.

Worker: It is really hard when a child misbehaves in public like that, it can feel so personal.

Mother: Yes, exactly ... I hit him because it was the only thing I could do to stop him.

Worker: You wanted him to stop.

Mother: Yes. [Pause] I know it is not right to hit him...but I didn't see another way.

Worker: You feel a little unsure about hitting ...

Mother: Yeah, I felt really bad about it ... I know it does not help him in the long term.

Worker: I see what you mean. [Pause] Would you be interested in looking at other ways of managing a difficult situation like that?

Mother: Yes, I would.

By appreciating in a compassionate way the circumstances that led to the mother hitting out, this gave 'space' in the therapeutic conversation for the mother to reflect and 'confront herself' and take responsibility for her actions. Thus an alliance emerged between the worker and the mother, focused on the search for effective alternatives to physical discipline.

Parents can also be invited to become collaborators by ensuring that they are consulted about and given many choices about the process of the child protection assessment. For example, as a child protection worker, it can be useful to take time to discuss with the parent how to set up the initial assessment, asking questions such as:

- I need to meet with you to discuss a concern that has been reported. Would you like to come into the office to discuss this or would you prefer me to visit you at home?
- When would be a convenient time for me to visit or for you to come into the office?

Equally, when making a formal child protection referral from a non-statutory agency it is useful to involve the parents as fully as possible in the process. Consider the following explanation to a parent:

- I need to also report what has happened to the child protection agency. But I would like to give you the option of contacting the agency first yourself, or you may prefer to contact them after I send the report. Equally, I would like to discuss with you what I put in the report. Perhaps we could decide together what should go in. As well as the concerns, I want to make sure to put in how you are coping and your plans to ensure that your children will be safe.

Even in cases of confirmed serious abuse it is still worth finding ways to respectfully join with a client in a way that promotes responsibility. Working with men who have perpetrated sexual violence towards women and children, Alan Jenkins (1990) argues that it is ineffective to argue with or confront these abusive men about their violence as this can lead to denial and evasion and thus reinforce their lack of responsibility for their actions. For example, asking the question 'Why did you sexually abuse your child?' can lead a person to deny that they did, or to give an explanation that blamed the child or other circumstances and thus not result in the client taking responsibility for their actions. As Jenkins argues, the onus is on the therapist to construct dialogues that invite responsibility on the part of clients. More subtle strengths-based approaches are often more effective in this regard, such as highlighting and acknowledging any small steps the client has taken towards responsibility, and appreciating the courage and strength this involved. For example, Jenkins suggests the following questions in the first session:

- Are you sure that you can handle talking about your violence?
- It isn't easy – it takes a lot of courage to face up to the fact that you really hurt someone you love.
- Many men deeply regret hurting their loved ones and want to stop it, but most of them find it too difficult to face up to what they have done – to look it in the eye so that they can do something about it – let alone come and see a counsellor. (1990: 66)

The above approach emphasises joining with the 'part' of the client that wishes to take responsibility and that desires change. The therapist is respectfully inviting the client to assume the courage to take responsibility for their actions. Even if the client denies his own responsibility in actions already taken, the therapist can persist and focus on the fact that, even if he was coerced or sent to therapy, some degree of cooperation was necessary on his part.

> Come on – a lot of men wouldn't come within one mile of this place, no matter how much they were told or threatened by others – let alone talk about their violence. I've heard of men who sit out in their cars unable to pluck up the courage to enter the building. It must have taken a lot of courage to walk through the door … How did you succeed here today? (Jenkins, 1990: 67)

Focusing on strengths, resources and safety

When parents feel that they are failing to look after their children and that others believe they are incompetent, hearing that there is something they are doing well can make a real difference and unlock their potential for change. As a child protection worker, it is often useful to begin an initial meeting with a family with an exploration of what is going right, rather than immediately focusing on concerns and problems, as illustrated in Case Example 12.1.

Case Example 12.1   Getting to the school play

A child protection worker was tasked with following up a teacher's report that a single mother had failed on a number of occasions to collect her seven-year-old son from school. There was concern that this was related to the mother's deteriorating drug use. Before meeting the mother, the worker took time to talk further to the teacher, to seek out examples of what was also going right in this family. The teacher said that the son was relatively bright and doing well in school. He also said that, despite the problems, the mother did come to the school play in the previous term and her son, who had a leading part, was delighted with this and 'spoke of nothing else in the classroom'.

In beginning the session, the worker chose to talk about the strengths-based information first with the mother, complimenting her on the fact that her son was doing well and asking her about the school play, sharing the teacher's observation about how delighted the son was that his mother came to the play. The mother spoke of how much she wanted to be at the play, and how proud it made her feel to see her son in an important part. This initial strengths-based conversation put the mother at her ease and helped her open up when the worker addressed the concerns regarding her failing to collect her son at other times. The mother later reported that she was pleased to see that the teacher could also see some of the good things she was trying to do for her son, and not just all the bad things. Going forward, this helped to create a better working alliance between the mother and the school.

A central feature of the strengths-based approach to child protection is to orient work around creating safety rather than simply reducing risk. As well as carrying out a risk assessment, it can be fruitful to carry out a safety assessment and to explore with the parents signs of safety that exist within the family system, either currently or in the past, or that could exist potentially in the future. When working with families with complex problems it can be helpful to persist in the search for exceptions and small successes that the parents can be held accountable for. This is the key to real empowerment. As Berg and Kelly note:

> ... taking advantage of these little successes, however small, and getting them to repeat those successes, rather than [the worker] taking over the tasks themselves. Insisting that the clients use knowledge and skills they already have leads to true empowerment. (2000: 228)

Consider Case Example 12.2, where an assessment of safety and exceptions, in particular a step-by-step exploration of how the parents succeeded in getting their children to school, helped transform the therapeutic alliance and create the basis for more constructive work.

Case Example 12.2   Getting to school

Helen and Sean were the parents of a 16-year-old son, a 13-year-old daughter and an 11-year-old son. The family had intermittent contact with the local child protection service through the years. A more recent referral to the local police and to the child protection service expressed concerns about both parents' misuse of alcohol, and there were suggestions of domestic violence and child neglect. During the follow-up social work home visit, family difficulties and risk factors were considered. The social worker then signalled a change in the focus of the meeting:

Worker: We've spoken for a while, Helen and Sean, about the recent problems you've had. We've talked about the drinking, the fighting, and about what the children have seen and heard. But if it's OK with you, I'd like to change direction a little and talk about some of the things you do well as parents. Is that OK?

[Both parents nodded in agreement]

Worker: Tell me about school – I've heard that the children get to school every day. Given the chance, most children will do anything they can to stay out of school. Can you tell me how you get them to get to school every day?

Sean: Well, they like school, their friends are there.

Worker: Yes. It's good to hear they enjoy school and have friends there. But tell me, is there anything you do to make sure they're ready for school?

Helen: Yes. I set the alarm every morning and I get up and get them their breakfast. It's not easy, you know what I mean?

Worker: Sure. Is there anything else you do?

Helen: I make sure they have their school uniforms clean, I like them looking well. You know, clean shoes, clean shirt, clean noses and all that.

Worker: Anything else?

Helen: I don't know ... I ask them about their homework and I went to a meeting in the school last week.

Worker: Really? What happened there?

Helen: Nothing much. They're doing OK at school but Ann is having trouble with Maths.

Worker: So what did you do then?

Helen: I asked the teacher about getting some help for her. He said something about a resource teacher. Then I came home and told them what the teachers said about them being very good.

Worker: So you made sure to praise them, that was a good idea ... It seems to me you're doing a lot well in helping your children succeed at school.

Helen: Really?

Worker: You make sure your children get to school in the mornings and you show an interest by asking about their school and homework and by going to meetings. That's really great stuff.

Helen: I try my best.

The parents then described some other exceptions to problems in their lives. Sean was putting in a full day's work each day after a long time on unemployment benefit, and Helen was attending a local Alcoholics Anonymous group meeting. These exceptions and changes were all carefully noted and reinforced by the worker. At subsequent meetings, the parents reported further positive change and the work moved to a more cooperative stage.

As well as looking at individual family strengths, it is also useful to highlight the community resources that families may currently or potentially access. Many of the families referred to child protection services live in deprived areas and are marginalised and isolated within their communities. The child protection concerns have arisen in the context of poverty, lack of support and appropriate services. For example, a contributing factor in a mother's physical abuse of her children could be the fact that she is caring for the children all day long without a break or support. A placement for her children in a preschool, with access for the mother to a family resource centre, could make a vital difference. A strengths-based worker is mindful of these issues and seeks to use their professional authority to increase families' access to extra services, such as additional financial and welfare payments, educational placements, family support services, community addiction counselling services and so on.

Focusing on goals and positive intentions

Negotiating client-centred meaningful goals is the central feature of a strengths-based approach. In the context of child protection, this can appear to be fraught with difficulty as parents and professionals can appear to have divergent and conflicting goals. However, unless an agreed goal can be negotiated it is almost impossible to make therapeutic progress. Even a limited goal determined by the context of a child protection responsibility can be a useful place to start. For example, an initial therapeutic alliance may be formed with parents through a search for an answer to the following question: 'What do we – you as parents and I as a child protection worker – need to be in a position to say to the Case Conference (or the Court) that will mean that your children stay in your care?'

In the search for a goal it is often a question of 'digging deeper' or 'listening harder' to discover underpinning positive intentions and common ground between parental and professional goals. For example, Turnell and Edwards (1999) suggest making a distinction between physically abusive behaviour and the positive intentions that may underpin it. They suggest that the parent's use of physical discipline can be considered as a means to an end, rather than as an absolute goal in itself, enabling the worker and the parent to focus on what the parent hopes to achieve in these situations. Let us consider this process in action in Case Example 12.3.

Case Example 12.3   What do you hope to achieve?

After his parents separated, Tom, a 15-year-old boy, moved in with his father, Mike. They argued every night. Tom dropped out of school and went missing for long periods during the evening, and his parents thought he was using drugs. As a result the family were referred to an adolescent mental health service. During one of the sessions, they described a fight that had taken place between them and Tom accused his father of treating him roughly and of 'pushing him down the stairs'.

At this point the worker was faced with a dilemma of how to proceed. He knew he had to address the issue of possible physical abuse, but wanted to do this in a way that would open therapeutic possibility and increase safety. As a result, the worker first took time to appreciate how difficult the situation was before seeking to understand positive intentions underpinning the behaviour:

Worker: You must feel really under pressure when you lash out like that.

Father: Yeah, I just feel that there's nothing that works. He never listens to me, doesn't do a thing I say. We're always fighting. And sometimes I just snap. I just lash out at him...

Worker: At the time when you pulled Tom out of bed and pushed him, Mike, what do you think you were you hoping would happen?

Father: I dunno ... maybe I wanted to get through to him ... but nothing works.

Worker: So you want to get through to Tom, that's what you're really hoping for; is that what it's about ?

Father: Yes, I guess.

Worker: If you got through to him, what would happen, what would be different?

Father: Well, he'd know that it's not all about power trips! That's not why I'm always asking about school, about who he's with and what he's doing. And he thinks I don't know, but I do know that he goes drinking sometimes. And maybe he's using drugs. And if he's drinking and using drugs, you don't know what else could happen, you know, street fighting, the police and all that. He always tells me he's fine and looks after himself but you don't know ...

Worker: So when you're fighting with Tom, what you're trying to do is to make sure that he is safe?

Father: Yes. That's what it boils down to.

Worker: Mmm, that is interesting ... I'm wondering what you and Tom can do to make sure that Tom is looking after himself and keeping himself safe?

The conversation now became focused on an exploration of what would convince the father that his son was safe and how he would know this and they listed things like letting the father know where he was, 'checking in' before he went out, using his mobile phone to ring him and so on.

Later in the session, the worker returned to the issue of the physical fight and generated alternatives to violence, such as taking a break during arguments and discussing difficult issues at a later time when they are calmer. The worker also stated that he needed to make a report to the child protection services about what happened. The father was initially unhappy about this, but came to accept this when the worker agreed to involve him in the drafting of the report and to include descriptions of his positive intentions for his son, his willingness to engage in therapy and the positive plans for going forward.

With the agreement of child protection services, the report became the basis of ongoing work with the family. At a later stage, the worker was able to write an updated report to child protection services that described the progress that had been made. As a result the case was closed.

In Case Example 12.3, as well as using the father's positive intentions and goals for his son as a guide for the therapy, the worker also used the statutory responsibility to report the incident to child protection services as an opportunity to help structure the work, in particular providing a helpful outside agency to witness and monitor progress and change.

A goal-focused, strengths-based way of working has much to contribute to interventions with clients who have been court mandated due to abusive behaviour. The Plumas Project in America (Lee et al., 2003) developed a solution-focused group intervention for clients convicted of violence towards their partners. Rather than confronting the clients about their violent behaviour (which could evoke defensiveness and resistance), the approach centres on helping them articulate a personally meaningful goal in concrete terms that they are willing to work on for the course of the treatment. This is one of the screening criteria: the clients are only allowed to attend and complete the programme if they are willing to articulate and commit to such a goal. Whether the goals identified are directly related to changing violent behaviour (such as goals to communicate better with a partner, or to spend better parenting time with children), or whether the goals are only indirectly related (such as attending a literacy programme or having more confidence about speaking in a group), the project found that such a goal-focused approach not only transformed the therapeutic alliance, but also led to a reduction in outside violence. In a six-year follow-up study, reoffending rates for 90 clients who completed the programme amounted to 16.7 per cent (Lee et al., 2003). These results are very impressive when compared to recidivism rates at five-year follow-up for traditional treatments, which are as high as 40 per cent (Shepard, 1992).

Difficult decisions – sometimes the best solution involves care

A strengths-based approach to child protection does not offer a recipe for success in every case where the children are at risk. There are many situations where professionals may have to face the uncomfortable truth that the children's needs would be better served if they did not continue to live with their parents. While child protection guidelines in most countries provide criteria for the assessment of 'good enough parenting' and procedures for arranging alternative care for children, what counts is not only choosing the correct procedures but also *how* the worker implements them. As Berg and Kelly state:

> The single most important factor may be how one follows the guidelines. When a worker collaborates with the parents and includes them in every step of the decision making process, they experience the entire process as respectful of them and humane to the children. (2000: 227)

Maintaining such a collaborative and respectful approach to working with parents when a decision is taken to remove children from their care can be challenging as a professional. It can seem natural to criticise a parent for not trying hard enough or for not doing enough to care for their children, particularly when the worker has invested a lot of commitment in trying to keep the family together. However, children's needs are generally best served when difficult child protection decisions are carried out with as much collaboration and involvement as possible from the parents. Such a collaborative approach is generally in the children's best interest, both in the short term (reducing the trauma of the immediate transition and reducing the likelihood of parents undermining the placement) and also in the long term (in increasing the chance of parents remaining constructively involved in their children's lives, whether they return to their care or not). Consider Case Example 12.4, which is a continuation of Case Example 12.2, though in the difficult situation where the initial gains made by the parents are not sustained and foster care is considered.

Case Example 12.4 Preparing for foster care

Though there were some initial improvements in the work with Helen and Sean, over time serious child protection concerns re-emerged. There were a number of domestic violence incidents and Sean had left the family home following a court hearing. Helen had continued to misuse alcohol and had broken agreements with the child protection worker and the family support worker. She had also left the younger children alone at home a number of times. The local Child Protection Conference felt it necessary to place the children in long-term foster care (with foster parents whom the children had previously stayed with for respite). The child protection manager feared that Helen might sabotage the placement of the children by criticising and undermining the foster parents. As a result, the social worker worked hard to continue to collaborate with Helen. While acknowledging the positive changes that Helen had made and the commitment she had to doing her best for her children, the worker discussed frankly with Helen the current difficulties and the need for the children to come into care. This was very difficult for Helen to accept, who became angry at the initial suggestions, but the worker stayed with her, acknowledging how difficult this could be, and continuing to express his belief in the importance of Helen as mother to the children. Though this was very hard for Helen, over several meetings the worker was able to slowly involve Helen in the preparation of her children coming into care.

Worker: What do you think is the best way to help your children prepare for going to the foster parents so that they will know that you still love them and that you want the best for them?

Helen: I want to tell them myself. And I want to be here when they go. I want to say goodbye to them ... but it will be so hard.

Worker: I understand how hard it could be ... What do you think might make it easier for them and for you?

Helen: I'm not sure. We'll do something nice the day before. We'll talk about it a lot and I'll stay away from the drink. And we can make plans for phone calls and for when they can come and see me. And if I call them soon after they get there. It's good they're going to [foster-family named]. We know them a while and I get on well with Joan. I like her. The kids know that.

Worker: You're right, that'll be very important to the kids and it'll help them settle there. You've always done your best to get on with the foster family when the children were in respite care before, though I know it took a lot of courage on your part. You didn't take sides when the children complained about house rules in their foster home.

In the above dialogue, as well as involving Helen in the planning, the worker also highlighted the positive steps that Helen had already taken in her relationships with her children and the respite foster carers. At a later stage, the worker also explored with Helen the signs that might suggest there could be increased contact between Helen and her children and what might indicate the possibility of family re-union.

Using this collaborative approach, the worker maintained an alliance with Helen that considered both her needs and the needs of her children.

Such work seemed to bear fruit after the children made the move to foster care. Helen did not undermine the placement but supported the foster parents and their care of her children when it came to matters of discipline and house rules. The children continued to have constructive contact with their mother, including regular weekend overnight visits. In addition, Helen facilitated them continuing to attend the same local schools and to maintain the same friendships and contact with the extended family.

Child protection – a shared responsibility between professionals

Though child protection legislation and guidelines in most countries nominate specific statutory agencies that are responsible for investigating and intervening in suspected cases of child abuse and neglect, these guidelines also make it clear that successful child protection relies on inter-agency cooperation and is, in fact, a shared responsibility between all professionals who work with children, adolescents and families (Department of Health and Children, 1999). Thus all professionals who work with children have a responsibility to promote their welfare and ensure their safety and to take protective action when children are at risk (even if this is simply a referral to child protection services).

Throughout this chapter we have emphasised that child protection works best when it is conceived as being a shared responsibility with parents. Equally, successful child protection depends on collaboration between the many professionals who work with children. Dangerous practice occurs when professionals engage in avoiding responsibility, blaming other agencies for problems, and work in an isolated way. The values of collaboration, the search for common goals and genuine partnership need to inform the relationships not just between workers and clients, but also between workers from different agencies. Just as it is important to acknowledge mutual responsibilities, respectfully join, establish goals and to focus on strengths with parents so it is equally important to adopt the same attitudes towards our colleagues. As Turnell and Edwards note:

> The child's safety is best served by collaboration, respect and cooperation among all parties involved in child protection ... In fact it can be downright dangerous if different professionals involved with the same family alienate themselves from one another, sending the family mixed messages and compromising children's safety. (1999: 198)

Summary

A strengths-based approach has much to contribute to the process of constructive engagement of families when there are concerns of child abuse and neglect. In this chapter we have attempted to highlight a therapeutic pathway that avoids the twin pitfalls of inadvertently colluding with or condemning parents when faced with child abuse and instead builds a collaborative working alliance with them focused on an agreed goal of ensuring their children's welfare and safety. We have described the importance of joining respectfully with parents, while being honest and open about child protection responsibilities, acknowledging the context within which the worker operates. We have also described the power of reorienting practice so it is driven by agreed goals and focused on strengths, resources and safety, rather than exclusively problems, deficits and risk assessment. We have argued that such a collaborative respectful approach is helpful even in difficult situations, such as arranging alternative care arrangements for children, as well as a model for informing how professionals can work collaboratively as part of a team to promote the safety of children.

Epilogue

Life should be more about holding questions than finding answers. The act of seeking an answer comes from a wish to make life, which is basically fluid, into something more certain and fixed. This often leads to rigidity, closed-mindedness, and intolerance. On the other hand, holding a question – exploring its many facets over time – puts us in touch with the mystery of life. Holding questions accustoms us to the ungraspable nature of life and enables us to understand things from a range of perspectives.

Thubten Chodron on Buddhism

So we have come to the end of this book, and in doing so I recall what I said in the preface, that writing a book about human affairs is a precarious venture. Any time that we propose a theory or answer a question, we exclude other possible theories and other possible answers. A written theory or description never captures the complexity of the human experience or the mystery of interpersonal encounters that occur in the helping relationship. It is important that we never satisfy ourselves with answers and keep asking questions. Each time I meet a client, I endeavour to put to one side all my fixed answers and to start with a simple open question: How can I be of best help to this person who has come to see me?

You may have noticed that throughout the book I have enjoyed telling stories. Stories often reveal deeper truths and are far more inspirational than prose or theoretical debate. As a result I would like to introduce a final, somewhat paradoxical story, which for me personifies a central aspect of the strengths-based approach to helping people. Many children, adolescents and families start therapy focused on their limitations and deficits with a vague sense of what they want to achieve but often feeling hopeless about making progress. They can be burdened by feelings of failure and blame. Like the eagle in the story below, they are often out of touch with their strengths and resources and the possibilities that could be open to them. A strengths-based approach to therapy is about helping the client awaken to the potentials and strengths that are within their reach and to move to a more transformational and ideal view of self. Drawing on the story's metaphor, the role of a strengths-based professional is to help clients realise the 'eagles' they already are, and to believe that they can fly high in the skies like the 'king of all the birds'.

A man found an eagle's egg and put it in a nest of a barnyard hen. The eaglet hatched with the brood of chicks and grew up with them. All his life the eagle did what the barnyard chicks did, thinking he was a barnyard chicken. He scratched the earth for worms and insects. He clucked and cackled. And he would thrash his wings and fly a few feet into the air. Years passed and the eagle grew old. One day he saw a magnificent bird above him in the cloudless sky. It glided in graceful majesty among the powerful wind currents, with scarcely a beat on his strong golden wings. The eagle looked up in awe. 'Who's that?' he asked.

'That's the eagle, the king of the birds,' said his neighbour.

'Wow' replied the eagle 'I wish I could fly like him, how I wish I was an eagle … but unfortunately I am only a barnyard chicken.

Adapted from the book *Awareness* by Anthony de Mello (1997)

References

Aarts, M. (2000) *Marte Meo: Basic Manual.* Harderwijk, Aarts Productions.

American Psychiatric Association (1994) *Diagnostic and Statistical Manual, fourth edition.* Washington: American Psychiatric Association.

Andersen, T. (1987) 'The reflecting team: dialogue and meta-dialogue in clinical work', *Family Process*, 26 (4), 415–28.

Andersen, T. (1992) 'Reflections on reflecting with families', in S.S. McNamee and K. Gergen, J. (eds), *Therapy as Social Construction.* London: Sage.

Andersen, T. (1995) 'Reflecting processes; acts of informing and forming', in S. Friedman (ed.), *The Reflecting Team in Action: Collaborative Practice in Family Therapy.* New York, NY: Guilford.

Anholt, C. and Lawrence, A. (1994) *What Makes Me Happy.* London: Walker.

Annis, H.M. and Chan, D. (1983) 'The differential treatment model: Empirical evidence from a personality typology of adult offenders', *Criminal Justice and Behavior*, 10 (2), 159–73.

Assay, T.P. and Lambert, M.J. (1999) 'The empirical case for the common factors in therapy: Quantitative findings', in M.L. Hubble, B.L. Duncan and S.D. Miller (eds), *The Heart and Soul of Change: What works in therapy.* Washington, DC: American Psychological Association. pp. 33–56.

Atkins, D. and Christensen, A. (2001) 'Is professional training worth the bother? *Australian Psychologist*, 36 (2), 122–30.

Axline, V.M. (1971) *Dibs – In Search of Self: Personality Development in Play Therapy.* London: Pelican.

Bachelor, A. (1991) 'Comparison and relationship to outcome of diverse dimensions of the helping alliance as seen by client and therapist', *Psychotherapy*, 28, 534–49.

Bachelor, A. and Hovarth, A. (1999) 'The therapeutic relationship', in M.L. Hubble, B.L. Duncan and S.D. Miller (eds), *The Heart and Soul of Change: What works in therapy.* Washington, DC: American Psychological Association. pp. 113–78.

Bandler, R. and Grinder, J. (1979) *Frogs into Princes.* Moab, UT: Real People.

Barkley, R.A. (2000) *Taking Charge of ADHD.* New York, NY: Guilford.

Beck, A. (1976) *Cognitive Therapy and Emotional Disorders.* New York, NY: International Universities Press.

Berg, I.K. (1991) *Family Preservation: A brief therapy workbook.* London: Brief Therapy.

Berg, I.K. (1994) *Family-based Services: A solution-focused approach.* New York, NY: Norton.

Berg, I.K. and Kelly, S. (2000) *Building Solutions in Child Protective Services.* New York, NY: Norton.

Berg, I.K. and Miller, S.D. (1992) *Working with the Problem Drinker: A solution-focused approach.* New York, NY: Norton.

Bergin, A.E. and Garfield, S. (1994) 'Overview, trends and future issues', in A. Bergin and S. Garfield (eds), *Handbook of Psychotherapy and Behaviour Change*, 4th edn. New York, NY: Wiley. pp. 821–30.

Beyebach, M., Morejon, A.R., Palenzuela, D.L. and Rodriguez-Arias, J.L. (1996) 'Research on the process of solution-focused therapy', in S.D. Miller, M.A. Hubble and B.L. Duncan (eds), *Handbook of Solution Focused Brief Therapy.* San Francisco, CA: Jossey-Bass.

Blomquist, G. and Blomquist, P. (1990) *Zachary's New Home: A story for foster and adopted children.* Washington, DC: Magination.

Boldt, L.G. (1997) *Zen Soup: Tasty morsels of wisdom from great minds East and West.* New York, NY: Penguin.

Butler, G. (1999) 'Formulating Meanings: Integration from the perspective of a cognitive therapist'. Paper presented at the Joint One Day Conference of the Royal College of Psychiatrists and the British Psychological Society on the Integrative Developments in Psychotherapy, 9 October.

Calcott, A. and MacKenzie, J. (2001). 'Solution-focused approaches with people who have self-harmed'. CPNA Conference, March.

Cantor, C.H. (2000). 'Suicide in the western world', in K. Hawton and K. van Heeringen (eds), *The International Handbook of Suicide and Attempted Suicide.* Chichester: Wiley. pp. 9–29.

Carr, A. (1999) *Handbook of Clinical Psychology: A contextual approach.* London: Routledge.

Cohen, P., Cohen, J., Kasen, S., Velez, C., Hartmark, C., Johnson, J., Rojas, M., Brook, J. and Streuning, E. (1993) 'An epidemiological study of disorders in late childhood and adolescence – 1. Age and gender-specific prevelaence', *Journal of Child Psychology and Psychiatry*, 34 (6), 851–67.

de Mello, A. (1997) *Awareness.* New York, NY: Fount.

de Shazer, S. (1988) *Clues: Investigating solutions in brief therapy.* New York, NY: Norton.

de Shazer, S. (1991) *Putting Difference to Work* 1st edn. New York, NY: Norton.

de Shazer, S. (1994) *Words Were Originally Magic* 1st edn. New York, NY: Norton.

Department of Health and Children (1999) *Children First – National Guidelines for the Protection and Welfare of Children.* Dublin: Government Publications Office.

Dinkmeyer, D. and McKay, D.G. (1982) *STEP: Systematic Training for Effective Parenting.* New York: Random House.

Ellis, A. (1998) 'How rational emotive therapy belongs to the constructivist camp', in M. Hoyt (ed.), *The Handbook of Constructive Therapies.* San Francisco, CA: Jossey-Bass.

Forehand, R.L. and McMahon, R.J. (1981) *Helping the Noncompliant Child: A clinician's guide to parent training.* New York, NY: Guilford.

Freeman, J. and Combs, G. (1996) *Narrative Therapy: The social construction of preferred realities.* New York, NY: Norton.

Freeman, J., Epston, D. and Lobovits, D. (1997) *Playful Approaches to Serious Problems: Narrative therapy with children and families.* New York, NY: Norton.

Furman, B. and Ahola, T. (1992) *Solution Talk: Hosting Therapeutic Conversations.* New York: Norton.

Garfield, S. and Bergin, A. (1994) *Handbook of Psychotherapy and Behaviour Change,* 4th edn. New York, NY: Wiley.

Garland, S. (1995) *Going to Playschool.* London: Puffin.

Geldard, K. and Geldard, D. (1997) *Counselling Children: A practical introduction.* London: Sage.

George, E. (1998) 'Solution-focused therapy training'. Seminar, Maynooth, Ireland.

George, E., Iveson, C. and Ratner, H. (1990). *Problem to Solution: Brief therapy with individuals and families.* London: Brief Therapy.

George, E., Iveson, C. and Ratner, H. (1999) *Problem to Solution: Brief therapy with individuals and families,* 2nd edn. London: Brief Therapy.

Gergen, K.J. (1999) *An Invitation to Social Construction.* London: Sage.

Gergen, K.J. and McNamee, S. (eds) (1992) *Therapy as Social Construction.* London: Sage.

Gordon, T. (1975) *PET: Parent Effectiveness Training.* New York: Penguin.

Gottman, J. (1997) *The Heart of Parenting: How to raise an emotionally intelligent child.* London: Bloomsbury.

Grieves, L. (1998) 'From beginning to start: The Vancouver anti-anorexia/anti-bulimia league', in S. Madigan and I. Law (eds), *Praxis: Situating discourse, feminism and politics in narrative therapies.* Vancouver: Yaletown Family Therapy.

Grinder, J. and Bandler, R. (1981) *Trance-formations: Neuro-linguistic programming.* Moab, UT: Real People.

Gurman, A.S. (1977) 'The patient's perception of the therapeutic relationship', in A.S. Gurman and A.M. Razin (eds), *Effective Psychotherapy.* New York: Pergamon.

Haggerty, R.J., Sherrod, L.R., Garmezy, N. and Rutter, M. (1997) *Stress, Risk, and Resilience in Children and Adolescents: Processes, mechanisms, and interventions.* Cambridge: Cambridge University Press.

Haley, J. (1963) *Strategies of Psychotherapy.* New York, NY: Grune and Stratton.

Haley, J. (1973) *Uncommon Therapy: The psychiatric techniques of Milton H. Erickson MD.* New York, NY: Norton.

Hall, K. (2001) *Asperger Syndrome, the Universe and Everything.* London: Jessica Kingsley.

Hammond, S.A. (1998) *The Thin Book of Appreciative Inquiry*, 2nd edn., TX: The Thin Book.

Hawkes, D., Marsh, T.I. and Wilgosh, R. (1998). *Solution Focused Therapy: A handbook for health care professionals.* Oxford and Boston, MA: Butterworth-Heinemann.

Hawton, K. and van Heeringen, K. (2000) *The International Handbook of Suicide and Attempted Suicide.* Chichester: Wiley.

Hazell, P. (2000) 'Treatment strategies for adolescent suicide attempters', in K. Hawton and K. van Heeringen (eds), *The International Handbook of Suicide and Attempted Suicide.* Chichester: Wiley.

Heard, H.L. (2000) 'Psychotherapeutic approaches to suicidal ideation and behaviour', in K. Hawton and K. van Heeringen (eds), *The International Handbook of Suicide and Attempted Suicide.* Chichester: Wiley. pp. 9–29.

Heegaard, M. (1988) *When Someone Very Special Dies: Children can learn to cope with grief.* Chapmanville, WV: Woodland.

Heegaard, M. (1992) *When Mom and Dad Separate: Children can learn to cope with grief from divorce.* Chapmanville, WV: Woodland.

Henggeler, S.W., Melton, G.B. and Smith, L.A. (1992) 'Family preservation using multi-systemic therapy: An effective alternative to incarcerating serious juvenile offenders', *Journal of Consulting and Clinical Psychology*, 60 (6), 953–61.

Henggeler, S.W., Schoenwald, S.K. and Pickrel, S.G. (1995) 'Multisystemic therapy: Bridging the gap between university- and community-based treatment', *Journal of Consulting and Clinical Psychology*, 63 (5), 709–17.

Hill, C.E. (1989) *Therapist Techniques and Client Outcomes: Eight cases of brief psychotherapy.* Newbury Park, CA: Sage.

Hoyt, M.F. (1998) *The Handbook of Constructive Therapies: Innovative approaches from leading practitioners*, 1st edn. San Francisco, CA: Jossey-Bass.

Hubble, M.L., Duncan, B.L., and Miller, S.D. (1999) *The Heart and Soul of Change: What works in therapy.* Washington, DC: American Psychological Association.

Hughes, S. (1993) *Giving.* London: Walker.

Hurley, J. (1989) 'Afiliativeness and outcome in interpersonal groups: member and leader perspectives', *Psychotherapy*, 26 (4), 520–23.

Iveson, C. (2000) 'Solutions for Everyone: Brief therapy in clinical practice and beyond'. Brief Therapy Group Conference, Dublin.

Jenkins, A. (1990) *Invitations to Responsibility: The therapeutic engagement of men who are violent and abusive.* Adelaide: Dulwich Centre.

Jones, E. (1993) *Family Systems Therapy: Developments in the Milan-systemic therapies.* Chichester: Wiley.

Kazdin, A. (1997) 'Practitioner Review: psychosocial treatments for conduct disorder in children', *Journal of Child Psychology and Psychiatry*, 38 (2), 161–78.

Klein, M. (1957) *Envy and Gratitude.* London: Tavistock.

Klingman, A. and Hochdorf, Z. (1993) 'Coping with distress and self-harm: the impact of a primary prevention program among adolescents', *Journal of Adolescence*, 16 (2), 121–40.

Kraft, A. and Landreth, G. (1998) *Parents as Therapeutic Partners*. London: Jason Aronson.

Kroll, J. (2000) 'Use of no-suicide contracts by psychiatrists in Minnesota', *American Journal of Psychiatry*, 157 (10), 1684–6.

Krupnick, J.L., Sotsky, S.M., Simmens, S., Moyher, J., Elkin, I., Watkins, J. and Pilkonis, P.A. (1996) 'The role of the therapeutic alliance in psychotherapy and pharmacotherapy outcome: Findings in the National Institute of Mental Health Treatment of Depression Collaborative Research Project', *Journal of Consulting and Clinical Psychology*, 64 (3), 532–9.

Lambert, M.J. and Bergin, A. (1994) 'The effectiveness of psychotherapy', in S. Garfield and A. Bergin (eds), *Handbook of Psychotherapy and Behaviour Change*. New York, NY: Wiley.

Lee, M.Y., Sebold, J. and Uken, A. (2003) *Solution-focused Treatment with Domestic Violence Offenders: Accountability for change*. Oxford: Oxford University Press.

Lieberman, M.A., Yalom, I.D. and Miles, M.B. (1973) *Encounter Groups: First facts*. New York, NY: Basic Books.

Lonnqvist, J.K. (2000) 'Psychiatric aspects of suicidal behaviour: Depression', in K. Hawton and K. van Heeringen (eds), *The International Handbook of Suicide and Attempted Suicide*. Chichester: Wiley.

Lord, C. and Rutter, M. (1994) 'Autism and pervasive development disorders', in M. Rutter, E. Taylor and L. Hersor (eds), *Child and Adolescent Psychiatry: Modern Approaches*. Oxford: Blackward.

Madigan, S. (1998) *A Narrative Approach to Anorexia*, 1st edn. San Francisco, CA: Jossey-Bass.

Mallinckrodt, B. (1996) 'Change in working alliance, social support, and psychological symptoms in brief therapy', *Journal of Counseling Psychology*, 43 (4), 448–55.

Malone, K.M., Oquends, M., Haas, G., Ellis, S., Li, S. and Mann, J. (2000) 'Protective factors against suicide acts in a major depression: Reasons for living', *American Journal of Psychiatry*, 157 (7), 1084–8.

Manolson, A. (1992) *It Takes Two to Talk: The Hanen program for parents of children with language delays*. Toronto: The Hanen Centre.

McGolderick, M., Heiman, M. and Carter, B. (1993) 'The changing family life cycle – a perspective on normalcy', in F. Walsh (ed.), *Normal Family Processes*, 2nd edn. New York and London: Guilford.

Miller, S., Rotheram-Borus, M.J., Piacentini, J., Graae, F. and Castro-Blanco, D. (1992) 'SNAP: a brief cognitive-behavioral family therapy manual for adolescent suicide attempters and their families', Columbia, OH: Columia University.

Miller, S.D., Duncan, B.L. and Hubble, M.A. (1997) *Escape from Babel: Toward a unifying language for psychotherapy practice*. New York, NY: Norton.

Miller, W.R., and Hester, R.K. (1989) 'Treating alcohol problems: toward an informed eclecticism', in R.K. Hester and W.R. Miller (eds), *Handbook of alcoholism treatment approaches*. New York, NY: Pergamon.

Miller, W.R. and Rollnick, S. (1991) *Motivational Interviewing: Preparing people to change addictive behaviour*. New York, NY: Guilford.

Mills, J. and Chesworth, M. (1992) *Little Tree: A story for children with serious medical problems*. Washington, DC: Magination.

Mohl, D.C. (1995) 'Negative outcome in psychotherapy: a critical review', *Clinical Psychology*, 2, 1–27.

Monk, G., Winslade, J., Crocket, K. and Epston, D. (1997) *Narrative Therapy in Practice: The archaeology of hope*. San Francisco, CA: Jossey-Bass.

Nylund, D. (2000) *Treating Huckleberry Finn: A new narrative approach to working with children with ADD/ADHD*. San Francisco, CA: Jossey-Bass.

O'Connell, B. (1998) *Solution-focused Therapy*. London: Sage.

O'Hanlon, W. (1998) 'Possibility therapy: an inclusive, collaborative, solution-based model of psychotherapy', in M. Hoyt (ed.), *The Handbook of Constructive Therapies*. San Francisco, CA: Jossey-Bass.

O'Hanlon, W.H. and Weiner-Davies, M. (1989) *In Search of Solutions: A new direction in psychotherapy*. New York, NY: Norton.

Orlinsky, D.E., Grawe, K. and Park, B.K. (1994) 'Process and outcome in psychotherapy – noch enimal', in A.E. Bergin and S.L. Garfield (eds), *Handbook of Psychotherapy and Behavior Change*, 4th edn. New York, NY: Wiley.

Patty, W.L. and Johnson, L.S. (1963) *Personality and Adjustment*. New York, NY: McGraw Hill.

Perversi, M. and Brooks, R. (1998) *Henry's Bed*. London: Puffin.

Pfeffer, C.R. (2000) 'Suicidal behaviour in children: an emphasis on developmental influences', in K. Hawton and K. van Heeringen (eds), *The International Handbook of Suicide and Attempted Suicide*. Chichester: Wiley.

Prochaska, J.O., DiClemente, C.C. and Norcross, J.C. (1992) 'In search of how people change: Applications to addictive behaviors', *American Psychologist*, 47 (9), 1102–14.

Prochaska, J.O., Norcross, J.C. and DiClemente, C.C. (1994) *Changing for Good*. New York, NY: Morrow.

Prosser, J. (2001) 'Solution Focused Therapy'. Paper presented at Solutions with Children Conference, Brief Therapy Practice. 11 May.

Puckering, C., Evans, J., Maddox, H., Mills, M. and Cox, A.D. (1996) 'Taking control: a single case of mellow parenting', *Clinical Child Psychology and Psychiatry*, 1 (4), 539–50.

Ray, W.A. and Keeney, B. (1993) *Resource Focused Therapy*. London: Karnac.

Rogers, C. (1951) *Client Centered Therapy*. Boston, MA: Houghton Mifflin.

Rogers, C.R. (1961) *On Becoming a Person: A therapist's view of psychotherapy*. London: Constable.

Rogers, C.R. (1986) 'Client-centred therapy', in I.L. Kutash and A. Wolf (eds), *Psychotherapist's Casebook*. San Francisco, CA: Jossey-Bass. pp. 197–208.

Rogers, C.R. (1990) 'Reflection of feelings and transference', in H. Kirschenbaun and V.L. Henderson (eds), *The Carl Rogers Reader*. London: Constable.

Ryan, T. and Walker, R. (1993) *Life Story Work*. London: British Agencies for Fostering and Adoption.

Saleeby, D. (1996) 'The strengths perspective in social work practice: extensions and cautions', *Social Work*, 41 (3), 296–305.

Sanchez-Craig, M. (1980) 'Random assignment to abstinence or controlled drinking in a cognitive-behavioral programme: Effects on drinking behavior', *Addictive Behaviour*, 5, 35–9.

Schaefer, C.E. and O'Connor, K.J. (1983) *The Handbook of Play Therapy*. New York, NY:Wiley.

Schaffer, D. and Gould, M. (2000) 'Suicide prevention in schools', in K. Hawton and K. van Heeringen (eds), *The International Handbook of Suicide and Attempted Suicide*. Chichester: Wiley.

Schmidtke, A. and Schaller, S. (2000) 'The role of mass media in suicide prevention', in K. Hawton and K. van Heeringen (eds), *The International Handbook of Suicide and Attempted Suicide*. Chichester: Wiley.

Selekman, M.D. (1997) *Solution-focused Therapy with Children: Harnessing Family Strengths for Systemic Change*. New York: Guilford Press.

Sharry, J. 1994 'Solution focused parent training', in B. O'Connell (ed.), *Solution Focused Therapy in Practice*. London: Sage.

Sharry, J. (1999a) *Bringing up Responsible Children*. Dublin: Veritas.

Sharry, J. (1999b) 'A study of the coping strategies and resourcefulness of parents with an able child on the autistic spectrum', *Irish Journal of Social Work Research*, 2 (1), 87–101.

Sharry, J. (2001a) *Bringing up Responsible Teenagers*. Dublin: Veritas.

Sharry, J. (2001b) *Solution Focused Groupwork*. London: Sage.

Sharry, J., Darmody, M. and Madden, B. (2002) 'A solution-focused approach to working with clients who are suicidal', *The British Journal of Guidance and Counselling: Symposium on Suicide*, 30 (4), 383–99.

Sharry, J. and Fitzpatrick, C. (1997) *Parents Plus Progamme: A video-based guide to managing and solving discipline problems in children aged 4–11*. Dublin: Parents Plus.

Sharry, J. and Fitzpatrick, C. (2001) *Parents Plus Families and Adolescents Progamme: A video-based guide to managing conflict and getting on better with older children and teenagers aged 11–16*. Dublin: Parents Plus.

Sharry, J., Madden, B. and Darmody, M. (2001a) *Becoming a Solution-focused Detective: A strengths-based guide to brief therapy*. London: Brief Therapy.

Sharry, J., Madden, B., Darmody, M. and Miller, S.D. (2001b) 'Giving our clients the break: Applications of client-directed outcome-informed clinical work', *Journal of Systemic Therapies*, 20 (3), 68–76.

Shepard, M. (1992) 'Predicting batterer recidivism five years after community intervention', *Journal of Family Violence*, 7 (3), 167–78.

Silver, N. (1999) *Temper Temper East Sussex*: Macdonald Young.

Softas-Nall, B.C. and Francis, P.C. (1998a) 'A solution-focused approach to a family with a suicidal member', *The Family Journal: Counseling and Therapy for Couples and Families*, 6 (3), 227–30.

Softas-Nall, B.C. and Francis, P.C. (1998b) 'A solution-focused approach to suicide assessment and intervention with families', *The Family Journal: Counseling and Therapy for Couples and Families*, 6 (1), 64–6.

Street, E. and Downey, J. (1996) *Brief Therapeutic Consultations*. Chichester: Wiley.

Striker, S. and Kimmel, E. (1979) *The Anti-colouring Book*. London: Scholastic.

Thomas, P. (2000) *My Friends and Me*. London: Hodder.

Turnell, A. and Edwards, S. (1999) *Signs of Safety – A Solution and Safety Oriented Approach to Child Protection Casework*. New York, NY: Norton.

Verkes, R.J. and Cowen, P.J. (2000) 'Pharmacotherapy of suicidal ideation and behaviour', in K. Hawton and K. van Heeringen (eds), *The International Handbook of Suicide and Attempted Suicide*. Chichester: Wiley. pp. 9–29.

Wade, A. (1997) 'Small acts of living: Everyday resistance to violence and other forms of oppression', *Contemporary Family Therapy*, 19 (1), 23–39.

Walsh, F. (1996) 'The concept of family resilience: Crisis and challenge', *Family Process*, 35 (3), 261–81.

Walsh, T. (ed.) (1997) *Solution Focused Child Protection – Towards a Positive Frame for Social Work Practice*. Dublin: University of Dublin.

Watzlawick, P., Weakland, J. and Fisch, R. (1974) *Change: Principles of problem formation and problem resolution*. New York, NY: Norton.

Weakland, J., Fisch, R. and Watzlawick, P. (1974) 'Brief therapy: Focused problem resolution', *Family Process*, 13, 141–68.

Webster-Stratton, C. and Hammond, M. (1997) 'Treating children with early-onset conduct problems: A comparison of child and parent training interventions', *Journal of Consulting and Clinical Psychology*, 65 (1), 93–109.

Webster-Stratton, C., Kolpacoff, M. and Hollinsworth, T. (1988) 'Self administered videotape therapy for two families with conduct disorder: Comparison with two cost-effective treatments and a control group', *Journal of Consulting and Clinical Psychology*, 56 (4), 558–66.

Webster-Stratton, C. and Reid, J. (1999) 'Treating children with early-onset conduct problems: The importance of teacher training'. Paper presented at the American Association of Behavior Therapy, Toronto.

Wheeler, J. (2001) 'Catching butterflies: Solution focused therapy with younger children'. Paper presented at Solutions with Children Conference, Brief Therapy Practice, London: 11 May.

White, M. (1997) 'Narrative therapy'. Seminar, Dublin, 20 June.

White, M. and Epston, D. (1990) *Narrative Means to Therapeutic Ends*. New York, NY: Norton.

Wilson, J. (1998) *Child-focused Practice: A collaborative systemic approach*. London: Karnac.

Wing, L. (1995) *Autism Spectrum Disorders: An Aid to Diagnosis*. London: National Autistic Society.

Winnicott, D.W. (1974) *Playing and Reality*. London: Penguin.

World Health Organisation (1992) *The ICD-10 Classification of Mental and Behavioural Disorders: Clinical Descriptions and Diagnostic Guidelines:* Geneva: World Health Organisation.

Yalom, I.D. (1995) *The Theory and Practice of Group Psychotherapy*, 4th edn. New York, NY: Basic Books.

Yalom, I.D., Houts, S., Zimerberg, S. and Rand, K. (1967) 'Prediction of improvement in group therapy', *Archives of General Psychiatry*, 17 (4), 159–68.

Young, S. (2001) 'Solution focused anti-bullying', in Y. Ajmal and I. Rees (eds), *Solutions in Schools: Creative applications of solution-focused brief thinking with young people and adults*. London: BT Press.

Zeig, J.K. and Munion, W.M. (1999) *Milton H. Erickson*. London: Sage.

Ziefert, H. (1999) *Sara's Potty*. London: Dorling Kingsley.

Index